Spoofing the Modern

Spoofing the Modern

Satire in the Harlem Renaissance

Darryl Dickson-Carr

The University of South Carolina Press

© 2015 University of South Carolina

Published by the University of South Carolina Press
Columbia, South Carolina 29208

www.sc.edu/uscpress

Manufactured in the United States of America

24 23 22 21 20 19 18 17 16 15
10 9 8 7 6 5 4 3 2 1

Library of Congress Cataloging-in-Publication Data
can be found at http://catalog.loc.gov/.

ISBN 978-1-61117-492-2 (cloth)
ISBN 978-1-61117-493-9 (ebook)

For Carol and Maya

Contents

Acknowledgments

This book could not have been completed without the encouragement and criticism of some selfless colleagues and friends, as well as generous funding and support from several different sources. I only hope that my thanks here convey the extent of my gratitude to all parties. Needless to say, I bear full responsibility for all mistakes found herein.

First and foremost, my wife, Carol, took upon herself the arduous task of pushing me in the right direction every time my enthusiasm flagged or my reach seemed to exceed my grasp. Our daughter, Maya, offered her love and understanding as her father disappeared for long hours to work in the office or in local coffee shops.

At Southern Methodist University, I am indebted to the Office of the Dean in Dedman College for granting extended leaves of absence to continue my research and writing and the Department of English for providing research funds for books, travel, computers, and other resources. Kathleen Hugley-Cook of SMU's National Fellowships office helped me obtain—with the dean's endorsement—a Sam Taylor Fellowship from the United Methodist Church's General Board of Higher Education and Ministry.

In the Department of English, Professors Steven Weisenburger, Ezra Greenspan, and Nina Schwartz sought the most generously advantageous resources and helped to protect my time as best they could during their respective tenures as department chair. Professors Schwartz, Dennis Foster, Lisa Siraganian, Dan Moss, Beth Newman, and Rajani Sudan read an early draft of my discussion of Rudolph Fisher and helped shape it into a more readable contribution to the overall project. I am eternally grateful to our Ph.D. program's students, who asked about my progress, applauded the smallest milestones, and taught me more than I could ever imagine.

I began this project while still on the faculty at Florida State University, where funds from the College of Arts and Sciences supported the initial archival research and writing. I would like to thank my former colleagues in the Department of English: Professor Jerrilyn McGregory read early drafts, suggested research aids, and offered unwavering support. Professors Christopher Shinn, Leigh Edwards, Maxine

Montgomery, former English Chair Hunt Hawkins (now at University of South Florida), Professors Marcy North (now at Pennsylvania State University), Barry Faulk, and Chanta M. Haywood (now at Albany State University) also took precious time to read early drafts and offer critical advice. Professor Raymond Fleming in the Department of Modern Languages and Literature continuously inquired about and critiqued my work and served as an indispensable mentor and advisor.

I presented early versions of these chapters at successive conventions of the College Language Association and at Pennsylvania State University's biannual Celebrating African American Literature Conference, among other occasions. In each case I enjoyed a wealth of critical feedback, guidance, and support from peers working in African American literary studies.

Finally, special thanks go to the professional archivists at the Schomburg Center for Research in Black Culture in Harlem, the New York Public Library's Manuscripts and Archives Division, Yale University's Beinecke Rare Books and Manuscripts Library, Brown University's John Hay Library, and the Moorland-Spingarn Center at Howard University.

I

Toward a Revision of the Harlem Renaissance

African America of the "New Negro" Renaissance era—from the 1910s through the 1930s—and Harlem in particular were ready for satire. The period's circumstances primed black communities for the sharp wit and wry comfort of the satirist's perspective like no other in their collective history to date. The horrors of chattel slavery in the United States required the enslaved to use humor and indirection to cope with the unspeakable. Those who gained their freedom had a greater degree of license, however slight, to express their thoughts, often with the aid of abolitionists and through that movement's lens. Activists Frederick Douglass, Harriet Jacobs, David Walker, and Sojourner Truth relied upon parody, irony, and sarcasm to construct their narratives, essays, pamphlets, and addresses against slavery and in favor of women's rights. The myriad of triumphs and setbacks African Americans alternately enjoyed and endured from the beginning of Reconstruction, though, might not have seemed the best material for satire. Between the steady development of black disfranchisement; neo-slavery in the forms of peonage, chain gangs, sharecropping, and tenant farming; and the terrorism of lynching through bloodthirsty mobs and such organizations as the Ku Klux Klan and the Regulators, it seemed that African Americans had scant sources for satire. Whether they did or not, they certainly lacked a critical mass of authors that could have developed the genre.

This is not to say that American writers, broadly speaking, did not attempt satire involving African American characters; quite the contrary. Mark Twain's greatest works—*Adventures of Huckleberry Finn* and *Pudd'nhead Wilson* most prominently among them—challenged the nation's smugness with regard to its opinion of its black denizens, albeit by drawing upon common stereotypes about and images of African Americans that became popular in postbellum America. African Americans figured prominently in the editorial cartoons of Thomas Nast and in Ambrose Bierce's essays, articles, and stories, but often as the objects of ridicule, or as devices allowing the creator to satirize one of the major political parties. While the nation's

1

attitudes toward African Americans came under scrutiny, it was difficult to find signs that they had any positive effect upon the status of African Americans.

The white majority's general attitude toward African Americans reflected beliefs about "race" underscored by science and pseudo-science, with the darker "races" inevitably emerging as childlike, bestial primitives who needed the guidance and dominance of "white" civilization to prevent them from relapsing into the "savagery" that defined Africa and Asia. From Founding Father Thomas Jefferson, to Charles Darwin, Immanuel Kant, and Georg Wilhelm Friedrich Hegel, among many others, intellectual justifications for white supremacy were the norm rather than the exception. As Martin Japtok recounts, these beliefs found expression most prominently in the "Black Codes" that defined white supremacy and black inferiority after the Civil War.[1] Although the U.S. Congress put an end to most of the Black Codes via both the Reconstruction Acts and the Fourteenth Amendment to the Constitution, this short-term support for the freedmen and their descendants did not last beyond the end of Reconstruction. Instead, full support for white supremacy eventually became *de rigueur* in everyday life, from intellectual circles down to the common person. Japtok cites, as but one example, Frederick L. Hoffman's *Race Traits and Tendencies of the American Negro* (1896), which used flimsy "scientific" evidence to determine the inherent "weakness and depravity" of African Americans and the futility of policies of racial uplift.[2]

Published the same year as the *Plessy v. Ferguson* decision, and one year after Booker T. Washington's landmark address at the Cotton States Exposition in Atlanta that conceded African Americans' political rights in favor of industry and segregation, Hoffman's volume was among many signs that convinced such younger black intellectuals as W. E. B. Du Bois, Ida B. Wells-Barnett, Frances E. W. Harper, and William Monroe Trotter that a policy of passive acceptance of white dominance was a policy of failure that would establish a permanent underclass and squelch opportunities for African Americans to speak and thereby to become equal components in the American body politic. Simply to protest the Booker Washington–dominated leadership of the time was to be militant, even radical. Little wonder, then, that satire could hardly be found outside of editorial pages and folk witticisms.

On the rare occasions that African American authors possessing a satirical sensibility and sharp wit found major magazines and publishers willing to print their work, the results were subtle and complex, as seen in Charles Chesnutt's local color stories and gothic protest novels. Chesnutt succeeded in the former primarily via his disarming storyteller, Uncle Julius McAdoo, to undermine common, humiliating literary and cultural stereotypes and to lampoon whites' romantic view of slavery after the peculiar institution's demise. In his novels, especially *The House Behind the Cedars* (1900) and *The Marrow of Tradition* (1901), Chesnutt highlighted the unequal treatment afforded African Americans, especially the "best" of "the race," as embodied in the doctors, teachers, lawyers, and tragic mulattoes that populated his narratives. Withering sarcasm and *litotes* are peppered throughout these novels, but they arguably reside more easily in other genres or modes than satire and wit. In this era, only Pauline Hopkins' novels *Contending Forces: A Romance Illustrative of Negro Life North and South* (1900) and *Of One Blood; Or, the Hidden Self* (serialized in *Colored American* magazine over thirteen months, starting in November 1902) significantly use wit, understatement, irony, and satire as they examine the absurdities of anti-miscegenation laws and scientific racism.

Hopkins's novels create romantic and fantastic visions of African Americans' current conditions and African past, respectively, demonstrating advances of African American communities and black African civilizations rarely found in mainstream publications. As literary achievements they stand as significant landmarks comparing well with the best fictional work of contemporaries Chesnutt, Paul Laurence Dunbar, and Sutton Griggs. Nevertheless, Hopkins's work remains anomalous for the period; not until the New Negro Renaissance did wit, satire, and irony find a prominent place in African American letters. It is telling, perhaps, that Hopkins's pioneering work in creating popular literature at the turn of the century was part of a conscious effort to do precisely what African American intellectuals and artists, including her contemporary W. E. B. Du Bois, would attempt nearly a generation later. As Hazel V. Carby details in her introduction to Hopkins's serialized novels, via the *Colored American* magazine, Hopkins "tried to create the literary and political climate for a black renaissance in Boston two decades before the emergence of . . . the 'Harlem Renaissance,'" as "part of a wider intellectual project that was described . . . as offering 'the colored people of the United States, a medium through which they can demonstrate their ability and tastes, in fiction, poetry and art, as well as in the arena of historical, social and economic literature.'"[3] The reasons for the change in perspective are many, but one factor offers a robust explanation for the more fertile ground that satire encountered in the 1920s: overwhelming hypocrisy in the face of modernity.

If whites in Europe and the Americas imagined themselves the dominant race due to their technological advancements that created colonial empires based upon economic exploitation, World War I placed both advancement and imperialism under question. How could the dominant race justify wholesale murder made possible by technology? Moreover, how could it justify doing so for the sake of colonialism? As W. E. B. Du Bois wrote emphatically and presciently in his scathing postwar collection, *Darkwater: Voices From Within the Veil* (1920),

> Let me say this again and emphasize it and leave no room for mistaken meaning: The World War was primarily the jealous and avaricious struggle for the largest share in exploiting darker races. As such it is and must be but the prelude to the armed and indignant protest of these despised and raped peoples. Today

Japan is hammering on the door of justice. China is raising her half-manacled hands to knock next, India is writhing for the freedom to knock, Egypt is sullenly muttering, the Negroes of South and West Africa, of the West Indies, and of the United States are just awakening to their shameful slavery. Is then, this war the end of wars? Can it be the end, so long as sits enthroned, even in the souls of those who cry peace, the despising and robbing of darker peoples? If Europe hugs this delusion, then this is not the end of world war,—it is but the beginning![4]

Du Bois's hard-hitting assessment of World War I's causes and long-term impact contains within itself a deep irony, one that did not go unnoticed at the time. In July 1918, as the United States became more embroiled in the war, Du Bois published in *Crisis* magazine one of his most infamous editorials, "Close Ranks," which asked African Americans to "forget" for the duration their "special grievances" for the sake of winning a war that could open the same doors of democracy and freedom that he would write of a few years hence in *Darkwater*.[5] Du Bois's pursuit of an Army commission as an intelligence officer during the war only added to the arsenal of scorn that such detractors as A. Philip Randolph, Chandler Owen, George S. Schuyler, and Theophilus Lewis would launch against him for decades to follow. Most famously, Schuyler would lampoon Du Bois in his novel *Black No More* (1931) as Dr. Shakespeare Agamemnon Beard, who "in time of peace was a Pink Socialist" but "bivouacked at the feet of Mars" in time of war.[6]

The apparent disjuncture between Du Bois's professed political principles and his wartime stance highlights a crucial issue facing iconoclastic African American intellectuals and writers in the New Negro Renaissance. Du Bois charged himself, along with other members of the group of elite black professionals he dubbed the "Talented Tenth"—the educated, cultured, and progressive class—to be stewards of African American uplift by fighting unremittingly for civil rights and full exercise of the opportunities that should come to all American citizens, regardless of "race." Inevitably, this corporate appointment resulted in compromise and contradiction, whether through the apparent expediency of Du Bois's wartime editorial or simply because many members of the Talented Tenth possessed few of the qualities Du Bois ascribed to them. Neither education—least of all in Negro colleges based on the Tuskegee Institute model, which favored the industrial or domestic arts largely at the expense of the liberal arts—nor commerce and culture guaranteed an elite capable of uplifting the "race." In the unlikely event that an elite fully dedicated to the task did emerge, what form should such uplift take? If it were purely economic, as Negro colleges had stressed for over a generation, would that leave African Americans impoverished in their intellectual development and ability to defend their rights? If, conversely, the goal of uplift was to transform the black masses into some diluted

Spoofing the Modern

version of their middle-class elite brethren, did that constitute progress or simply the exchange of one limiting ideology for another? Should the masses desire in the first place to become a simulacrum of the elite if such leading members as Du Bois could exchange their activism and pragmatism for expediency?

That African Americans desired both individual and group progress in economic opportunity and civil rights was beyond question, but the leadership class could not always be trusted to bring about such changes out of its own volition. For a full decade, the *Crisis,* officially the organ of the National Association for the Advancement of Colored People's (NAACP), but the de facto, unofficial organ of Du Bois's opinions and ideas, cajoled African Americans, ranging from the Talented Tenth's professionals to struggling sharecroppers, to stay focused on the path to America's promised equality. As David Levering Lewis argues, until the mid-1920s, Du Bois and the *Crisis* held a virtual monopoly in the marketplace of black intellectualism. Only the *Messenger,* founded in late 1917, challenged this status, but it was published intermittently due to harassment from government agents. Not until the National Urban League and editor Charles Spurgeon Johnson founded *Opportunity* in 1923 did another national magazine offer a consistently published alternative to the *Crisis.* Although Du Bois was, for all intents and purposes, the most prominent African American leader after the death of Booker T. Washington in 1915, his occasional misjudgments and gaffes, with "Close Ranks" easily the most controversial example, inspired various rivals and opponents to question his ability to fulfill the ideals espoused in the caustic magazine.

Due to the same energies that produced what we now call the New Negro or Harlem Renaissance, a loosely defined group saw itself as heirs to the radical mantle that Du Bois wore, as a class of intellectuals that considered no one from the elite an aristocrat beyond the reach of the most severe scrutiny and criticism. A central tenet of this class was that the Talented Tenth's goals were too modest and unrealistic, at best, and opportunistic at worst. In *Black No More,* George Schuyler reduces the NAACP and its Talented Tenth officers and members to poor waifs forced to survive on "meager salaries of five thousand dollars a year" (approximately seventy-eight thousand dollars in 2014) to fight "strenuously and tirelessly to obtain for the Negroes the constitutional rights which only a few thousand rich white folk possessed."[7] Although *Black No More* appeared in 1931, well into the Great Depression and past the acme of widespread interest in all things African American, his spoof of the NAACP's bourgeois leadership evokes a commonly held stereotype regarding the organization as a sinecure for the Talented Tenth. Later that year, author Eugene Gordon would suggest sardonically in the leftist journal the *New Masses* that the N in *NAACP* should stand for *Nicest,* rather than "National."[8]

Underscoring the irony within these characterizations was the historical fact that the NAACP was formed in 1909 as a crucial, militant alternative to the Tuskegee

Institute's president Booker T. Washington and his practice of accommodating powerful southern and northern whites. Spread through many allies and lieutenants nationwide, Washington's power and influence were palpably real to black intellectuals attempting to create a new Negro, one who could be included in the United States' modernity in culture, art, economics, and civil rights. Washington's close connections to politicians in Washington, D.C.—especially Presidents Grover Cleveland and Theodore Roosevelt—and innumerable wealthy supporters and trustees, allowed him to create a reserve of cherry-picked black newspaper editors, and plum appointments to foundations and teaching or administrative positions at Negro colleges and universities. As a result, from the 1890s until his death, Washington's public concessions of African Americans' desire for civil rights started and practically ended most debates on the so-called "Negro problem" within and outside African American intellectual circles. Although such contemporaries as Ida B. Wells-Barnett, William Monroe Trotter, and Du Bois objected to the details of Washington's philosophy and to his tactics, Du Bois's *The Souls of Black Folk* (1903) was the text that gave the most eloquent, extended expression of simmering black protest for its time and for much of the twentieth century. When Du Bois, Trotter, and others formed the Niagara movement in 1905 and laid the basis for the NAACP's founding in 1909, their purpose was to open up that debate to a new level of discourse, one that would bring enforcement of the nation's protective laws to African Americans, thereby ending white supremacy.

Without question, from its founding the organization had been the one that virulent racists, North and South, considered most likely to upset the standard racial order, regardless of critics among the African American intelligentsia and masses alike. Between Du Bois's public addresses and scholarly, yet scathing editorials in the *Crisis,* Walter White's passing as a white man to investigate lynchings, and frequent legal action to force local and national government officials to uphold state laws and the U.S. Constitution, the NAACP had profoundly affected the ongoing debate and struggle over African Americans' collective future.

Schuyler and Gordon's pointed remarks nevertheless leave little doubt that dissenting African American voices considered the NAACP and the Talented Tenth in danger of losing their efficacy, whether as forces for civil rights and freedom, or as arbiters of cultural tastes. In the latter area, they seem to suggest, a new class needs to emerge that would not observe or be bound to the niceties of those advocating uplift, that would be radical simply by disrobing icons. As with most imperatives that challenge the status quo, the relationship between the Talented Tenth and its iconoclasts was extremely complicated. James Weldon Johnson, who served as the NAACP's field secretary and, subsequently, as its first African American president, was one of the crucial inspirations for the New Negro Renaissance in literature. Langston Hughes cited Johnson's *The Autobiography of an Ex-Colored Man,* published anonymously in 1912, as one of the works that inspired his generation to begin writing, an influence that only increased when the novel was reprinted in 1927. Du Bois's *The Quest of the Silver Fleece,* published in 1911, also received considerable notice, due in part to the author's broad reputation. Over a decade before Du Bois's arguments for the purpose and function of African American literature in his controversial symposium "Criteria of Negro Art," delivered at the NAACP's Chicago convention in July 1926, and published in the October *Crisis,* Johnson had used his stature as a regular columnist for the *New York Age* as a pulpit calling for achievement in the literary arts. In his December 16, 1915, column, "About Poetry and Poetry Makers," Johnson implores aspiring poets submitting their work to the newspaper to "learn [their] trade, to get the mastery of [their] tools, just the same as an artist or sculptor or a musician," and to become proficient in the nuances of their language. Johnson goes on to recommend several guides to writing better poetry.[9] A little over two years later, Johnson wrote emphatically that "although there is no single recipe to be followed for making a race great, there is a single standard by which the greatness of a race can be measured. The greatness of a race may be measured by the literature it has produced."[10] Finally, in July of 1918, Johnson extols the virtues of reading H. L. Mencken, with whom he had begun a correspondence in 1916, one that would bloom into friendship. Their relationship was based upon many mutually shared tastes, but as Charles Scruggs writes, it was primarily their opinion of literature and the purposes it could serve for a downtrodden people. In his February 21, 1920, column, Johnson drives home the "lesson in Mr. Mencken's method for Negro writers. Take the subject of lynching, for example; when the average Negro writer tackles the subject he loudly and solemnly protests in the name of justice and righteousness. By this method he may reach every one, except the lyncher. As far as this method reaches the lyncher at all, it makes him take himself more seriously. Instead of allowing the lyncher to feel that he is the one to whom appeals for justice should be addressed, he should be made to feel that he is just what he is—a low-browed, under-civilized, degenerate criminal."[11] Johnson's call for a change in the mode African American writers used to create change reveals his own distrust of the tried and true. Despite his public image a decade later as a symbol of a calcified NAACP, Johnson was largely responsible for the organization's enormous growth in the late 1910s.

How should we reconcile these two images? How should we view the caricatures emerging from the pens of the satirists who, whether consciously or not, took to heart Johnson's encomium on Mencken's behalf and began writing satire? The present study seeks, in part, to answer these questions, but not for the simple purpose of either supporting or refuting the claims of the authors under discussion. Rather, I should like continuously to appreciate the rhetorical arcs that alternately brought the piercing ideas and arguments of this subset of New Negroes close to the truths that they wished to discover, yet also carried them away from the polite and precise. If novelist, essayist, short-story author, and occasional poet Wallace Thurman stands as one of the most potent critics of African American literature in his or any other era, his criticism, published or unpublished, also reveals philosophical biases and personal anxieties that open up new dimensions for reading the period.

We should view these individual authors as a class, one simultaneously standing between others while touching them at the periphery. These authors came from backgrounds that ranged from poor to staunchly middle class, yet held in common their iconoclasm in an age in which the fissures within American and African American cultural circles could be probed and struck with less apprehension about the potential effects. As Langston Hughes so defiantly and famously declared, in "The Negro Artist and the Racial Mountain," "We younger Negro artists who create now intend to express our individual dark-skinned selves without fear or shame. If white people are pleased we are glad. If they are not, it doesn't matter. We know we are beautiful. And ugly too. The tom-tom cries and the tom-tom laughs. If colored people are pleased we are glad. If they are not, their displeasure doesn't matter either. We build our temples for tomorrow, strong as we know how and we stand on top of the mountain, free within ourselves."[12] Hughes's satirical peers would perhaps alter his coda to say that they *dynamite* their temples for tomorrow, and stand in the canyons of Manhattan, dodging the lynch mob preparing to flay them alive for their apostasy. We shall track this prey, finding its traces in the lofts of Niggeratti Manor, within a poisoned arrow's shot of Sugar Hill, Morningside Heights, and Villa Lewaro.

New York, New York, Big City of Dreams

If being a New Yorker is indeed a state of mind, then in the ruminations of two African American authors—one a leader of the Harlem Renaissance, the other a leading author today—may be found some of the best definitions of that state. In his autobiography, *Along This Way* (1933), diplomat, civil rights leader, and novelist James Weldon Johnson claims that he "was born to be a New Yorker," as he possessed "a dual sense of home" between the Big Apple and his native Jacksonville, and was "born . . . with a love for cosmopolitanism."[13] "One either is [a New Yorker]," Johnson writes, "or is not," regardless of where he or she was born. The New Yorker, whether native or naturalized, must avoid interfering in his or her neighbor's business, yet embrace all the complexity and diversity of life. The rewards include immeasurable cultural riches.[14] Similarly, novelist Colson Whitehead writes that you become a New Yorker the first time you look at a building with an unfamiliar business or front and say, "That used to be . . ." as you recall what once stood at that spot and how much it meant to you.[15]

Needless to say, I would certainly like to lay claim to the title of New Yorker under either Johnson's or Whitehead's definition, despite never having lived there, and despite having visited for a grand total of a few weeks, give or take a smattering of hours at La Guardia Airport, either waiting for a taxi to shuttle me to the wonders of Manhattan, or for an airplane to return me home. Whitehead is far too generous to people like me, who have read endlessly about New York, dreamed about it, and sampled both its more glorious landmarks and jaded tourist traps out of a desire to taste a fantasy city and to become one of its denizens, knowing all the while that few of us can afford to live those dreams any longer, that the vision is as illusory and fleeting as any sensation.

Yet my love for that vision urges me on to write this book, even if my reader will learn very little about New York itself. I imagine that, in the main, it is the same fantasy that captivated the authors studied here. None of them were native New Yorkers, although many—from those with the greatest physical and literary longevity, to the tragic few who died young—spent the rest of their lives in New York, even in the fabled Harlem that quickly lost the luster it had gained in the 1920s. I also share with my subjects the feeling of the migrant's bewilderment at everything New York has to offer in all its modernity compared to the provinciality of one's native state and town. One of Wallace Thurman's earliest—and best—essays was "Quoth Brigham Young: This is the Place," a sketch of his experiences growing up black in overwhelmingly white, Mormon Utah.[16] In his autobiography, *Black and Conservative* (1966), Syracuse native George S. Schuyler waxes nostalgic about New York in the spring, with the "riot of greenery" in Central Park contrasting with the "order" of Governor's Island, though the latter housed him as he was serving a sentence for desertion from the U.S. Army at the time, a fact he kept hidden from virtually everyone.[17] Zora Neale Hurston's memoir, *Dust Tracks on a Road* (1942), famously recounts how the author arrived in New York City "with a dollar and fifty cents in her purse, 'no jobs, no friends, and a lot of hope.'"[18]

For readers interested in the Harlem Renaissance, this book provides only a sketchy portrait of that amazing community in its physical aspects. Harlem has been and continues to be the object of untold numbers of projections, fantasies, fears, and apprehensions, while also embodying countless desires, joys, and dashed hopes. My knowledge of Harlem is that of the occasional visitor or the scholar studying a subject enthusiastically, albeit frequently from a distance. I will disclose very little information, for example, about vacant businesses and erstwhile landmarks, although I will dwell considerably on established institutions and defunct publications that indelibly and undeniably shaped the community that currently stands and thrives on the same soil. I imagine one aspect of the spirit of George Schuyler reminding me that he, as a good journalist, would let the truth—or something close to it—emerge regarding Harlem and the New Negro Renaissance. I conjure this notion despite the fact that, during the New Negro Renaissance and for the remainder of his career, Schuyler denied vehemently that the very movement with which we most easily identify him was anything more than mere hokum, a fantasy made up for the gull-ible and for the tourists—with scholars forcing order on people who do not want it. His peer, Wallace Thurman, went so far as to ask one of the most provocative questions for his time, one that routinely arises today: how can a movement be called a "renaissance" without an original awakening?[19]

Sincere though they may have been, Schuyler and Thurman's reluctance to accept that a "New Negro" was on the scene in the 1920s, or that they embodied most of what the "New Negro" represented in their desire for modernity, merely extends the iconoclasm they had cultivated over several decades. Schuyler possessed an antipathy towards any movement possessing the slightest odor of religious fanaticism, not least because religions require iconic beliefs and several dogma that adherents must profess. Schuyler and Thurman's resistance ironically places them within the group to which they denied any inherent allegiance or affinity. Most of the young writers of African descent in the 1920s and 1930s may be defined partially by their own antipathy towards a black middle-class that tended to accept only those images and artistic products of African Americans that "uplift" the "race." To widely varying degrees, Schuyler, Wallace Thurman, Langston Hughes, Nella Larsen, Zora Neale Hurston, Dorothy West, and Richard Bruce Nugent, among others, considered the generation embodied in scholar and NAACP activist and *Crisis* editor W. E. B. Du Bois, critic William Stanley Braithwaite, and occasionally Howard University philosophy professor Alain Locke as much an obstacle to freedom of intellectual and artistic expression as the larger white-dominated society.

Of course, not all of these individuals felt precisely the same way towards the older generation, nor did their opinions remain static. Thurman, Hughes, and Hurston alternately praised and vilified Du Bois for his moralistic assessments of literature, while their respective connections to Locke remained fluid and mercurial. In Hurston's case, her actual age made her chronological membership in her peer group questionable.[20] All shared a desire for a modernism in artistic expressions by artists of African descent that allowed them individuality regardless of their comfort with the label of "Negro artist." Each also shared skepticism towards what they perceived as the faddishness and condescension of the New Negro's supporters, which undermined the very idea of a renaissance created and controlled by African Americans. As David Levering Lewis writes, the optimism that Alain Locke expressed regarding the transformative power of art and literature for American racial consciousness and relations in his landmark 1925 essay, "The New Negro," did not win over the younger black generation any more than it did the white readers for whom it was largely intended. The "unique social experiment" of the Negro Renaissance had little hope of succeeding as Locke envisaged it given the general indifference to the arts and letters, much less to those emerging from putatively inferior Negroes.[21] If challenging, "high" literature and art without the additional burden of changing the course of hundreds of years of slavery, peonage, and brutality had difficulty finding acceptance, how much success could the issue of creative minds have in attempting to sway the public beyond circles of progressives, radicals, and Bohemians?

The distance between this stark picture and reality was not as close as the movement's skeptics and satirists often claimed. If Locke and Du Bois felt confident in echoing the New York *Herald Tribune's* original declaration, in May 1925, that a "Negro renaissance" had emerged, it had to do with the fighting spirit of African Americans as they returned from the World War, despite the chaos and murder of the all-too-recent Red Summer of 1919. Despite Locke's arguments to the contrary, the majority of the hundreds of thousands of former sharecroppers seeking a more prosperous life without the twin pestilences of the boll weevil and a ubiquitous Ku Klux Klan had more faith in a future of economic progress found in a North dominated by industry than they did in the rise of a literate class, but each group fed the other.

Schuyler's denials notwithstanding, the "New Negro" or Harlem Renaissance still holds our imaginations, which are stoked and shaped by the institutions that have helped to preserve it: the venerated Schomburg Center for Research in Black Culture, located at 135th Street and the old Lenox Avenue (now Malcolm X Boulevard); the Beinecke Library at Yale University, home of the James Weldon Johnson Collection, and a stunning treasure trove and repository for the papers and manuscripts of many Harlem Renaissance figures; and the Spingarn Collection at Howard University, site of the papers of Alain Locke and many other Harlem Renaissance figures. There are others, of course, and they each hold rich jewels that convince scholars to sacrifice perfectly beautiful spring and summer days in some of the United States' greatest cities and historical sites for the sake of digging through yellowed letters and carbon copies for a scrap of information that would support or refute an elusive thesis.

For the nearly nine decades since the end of 1929, once considered (but no longer) the end of the Renaissance, scholars and historians of this enthralling and complex period in the development of African American culture have argued incessantly over its actual significance and meaning. The arguments typically center on several broad, overarching questions, regardless of the phrasing a particular scholar might use: Was the Harlem Renaissance successful in transforming African American culture? Did it result in literature and other arts that brought African American letters into modernity? Equally important, was the movement's artistic output generally significant in purely aesthetic terms? The answers to these questions run a gamut that is not unusual. Implicit in both the question and its many answers is the notion that African American literature should be responsible, or is always already responsible, for actualizing social and political consciousness within African American communities and individuals. In his "Blueprint for Negro Writing," for example,

Richard Wright makes a barely disguised attack upon the politics that contributed to and emerged from the Harlem Renaissance as "humble novels, poems, and plays, prim and decorous ambassadors who went a-begging to white America. They entered the Court of American Public Opinion dressed in the knee-pants of servility, curtsying to show that the Negro was not inferior, that he was human and that he had a life comparable to that of other people. For the most part these artistic ambassadors were received as though they were French poodles who did clever tricks."[22]

Wright goes on to lambast the alliance between "inferiority-complexed Negro 'geniuses' and burnt-out white Bohemians with money" that allegedly allowed much of the literary production of the Harlem Renaissance to take place. As George Hutchinson has demonstrated,[23] though, Wright's attack paints the movement with a decidedly broad brush, accusing African American artists in general of pandering when only a few at best—most notably Hughes and Hurston—might have been guilty of the charges filed. Nonetheless, Wright's critique is far from a unique instance of a critic looking upon the legacy of the Harlem Renaissance and finding it sorely lacking. To be fair, a retrospective look reveals more than enough instances of the movement falling short of the goals its members aspired to for any critic to declare it a failure. After all, the renaissance did not succeed in creating strong, cohesive literary missions or groups who would follow such missions to their fullest fruition. It consisted of many factions, warring among themselves regarding the future of the Negro and of the form that Negro literature should take. A significant number of the Harlem Renaissance's brightest lights died, fell out of the public eye, wandered in relative obscurity for years thereafter, or generally never reached the height of acclaim and notoriety they enjoyed during the movement.

Although these arguments are persuasive, I have no intention of arguing that the Harlem Renaissance was a failure. In fact, I agree with Houston A. Baker that the standards applied to the Harlem Renaissance in order to measure its degree of success are frequently flawed, since they depend upon an implied comparison between African American authors and their white modernist counterparts.[24] Wright, Nathan Huggins, Alain Locke, W. E. B. Du Bois, and even this book's subjects—especially George S. Schuyler, Wallace Thurman, and Rudolph Fisher—have all either lamented the movement's demise or questioned its very existence. Schuyler, for instance, devastatingly pronounced the Harlem Renaissance "pretty much of a fraud. A lot of people connected with it were phonies, and there weren't many connected with it."[25] Schuyler's logic stems from the assumption that since many writers, such as Claude McKay, did not spend as much time in Harlem as the public thinks they did, it was not really a *Harlem* Renaissance at all. Thurman believed that since most of the African American writers, plastic artists, and painters during the years traditionally attributed to the Harlem Renaissance never reached the artistic heights of their contemporaries Pound, Eliot, Joyce, Fitzgerald, and other artists often classified as "modernist," or of other thinkers and artists they admired, they were not true to their inspirations and therefore to themselves. But as Houston Baker correctly asserts, "Africans and Afro-Americans—through conscious and unconscious designs of various Western "modernisms"—have little in common with Joycean or Eliotic projects. Further, . . . the very histories that are assumed in the chronologies of British, Anglo-American, and Irish modernisms are radically opposed to any adequate and accurate account of the history of Afro-American modernism, especially the *discursive* history of such modernism."[26] The discursive histories Baker writes of, put briefly, are the cultural histories and philosophical orientations that African American modernists do *not* share with their European counterparts, histories that are products of the unique circumstances out of which African American literature has been bred.

Baker and other contemporary scholars of the Harlem Renaissance posit a warning to scholars of the "New Negro" not to make haphazard judgments about the Renaissance based on narrow criteria that fail to take into account the numerous political, intellectual, and social movements that influenced both the Renaissance's leading lights and those overshadowed by history. For this reason, George Hutchinson reminds us that Huggins's and David Levering Lewis's landmark studies "have been framed within limited parameters, with too exclusive a focus upon issues of race, inadequate notions of American modernism, insufficiently particularized narratives of the intellectual and institutional mediations between black and white agents of the renaissance, and curiously narrow conceptions of the larger 'environmental conditions' . . . in which those agents acted."[27] Put in simpler terms, the only honest and fair conclusion that may be made about the Harlem Renaissance is that its achievements were decidedly mixed and ambivalent; if held strictly to the standards contemporaries and subsequent scholars like Wright have used to judge it, it was inarguably—and inevitably—a failure. If viewing the movement as one in which African American artists individually paid too much or too little attention to their white counterparts, again, it certainly appears a failure. But if considered as a movement that opened up discursive and intellectual space for its participants and their literary descendants to experiment with unusual poetic forms, incorporate "classic" and "vernacular" influences, establish lasting dialogues and associations with the intellectual and publishing worlds, and reach those beyond the almost exclusively African American audience of the Black Press,[28] it has to be considered a resounding success. Inarguably, its greatest success was in opening up mainstream publishing houses and a larger portion of the American reading public to the efforts of African American art, literature, and intellectualism, whereas its greatest failure was in not remaining fully conscious of the exploitative elements within the renaissance itself.

Nonetheless, the irony of Richard Wright's critique is that the foundation of his extraordinary career rests solidly upon the work he did during the Harlem

Renaissance and upon his admiration for H. L. Mencken, who equally inspired many of the renaissance's leading lights. Wright's critique itself is lifted from many of the ideas that emerged from some of the renaissance's participants, either during or immediately after the movement's heyday. Very few of Wright's ideas could not be found by searching through the archives of the *Messenger,* the *Crisis, Opportunity, Harlem, Fire!!, Survey Graphic,* the *Nation,* or other influential magazines of the renaissance. The controversies Wright produced through this seminal essay were hardly new and must be read with some degree of irony in retrospect. They were reproduced in the exchanges between Ralph Ellison and Irving Howe and via James Baldwin's eloquent essays in the 1950s, and the Black Arts movement ensured that these same controversies would continue to dominate questions regarding African American literature, which they do.

Spoofing the Modern investigates the people and circumstances within and surrounding the Harlem Renaissance's great debates. Its focus, first and foremost, is on the element of satire that greatly infused the movement, whether within some of its most important periodicals, short stories or novels. My interest in this subject arose after doing extensive work studying the history and content of African American satire from slavery until the present. As I looked at the Harlem Renaissance and the extent to which satirists like Wallace Thurman, George Schuyler, and Rudolph Fisher played in creating the intellectual and creative milieus that enabled some of their peers' best work to see print, it became clear that our knowledge of and curiosity about these figures would be served by attention to their work as both satirists and cultural mediators. Naturally, a few sets of key questions arose:

~ First, which cultural, political, and intellectual forces motivated these authors to create satire? What were the issues at hand? What was at stake in African American literature and culture?

~ Second, how did the period's non-satirical voices and their discourse influence satirical discourse, and vice-versa? Who influenced the principal subjects' satirical discourse? For instance, what sort of effects did Alain Locke's pronouncements and proscriptions for African American art have on Wallace Thurman? Conversely, how did he react? How did Locke react in kind? How far did H. L. Mencken's influence on Schuyler and Thurman extend? Beyond being questions of simple historical fact, this set of questions was meant to gauge satire's overarching influence on all levels of the renaissance's literary life. To what extent, for example, did the satirical mode found most obviously in George Schuyler's columns in *The Messenger* seep into the remainder of the magazine? Did that mode play a significant role *before* Schuyler joined the magazine? I argue that it did, primarily through the magazine's

opposition to certain individuals and institutions, most prominently Marcus
Garvey and his Universal Negro Improvement Association.

~ Finally, I wanted to discover the extent of these satirists' legacy for subsequent generations. What standards did their texts set, either for content or
style? Whom did they influence, and why? Whose works in the decades
since the movement's demise best resemble—or differ from—those of
Schuyler, Thurman, Hughes, Fisher, and company?

From the outset, I have had to draw some temporal boundaries to maintain a
sense of cohesion and unity. I have done this not to claim that we have official moments when the "New Negro" or Harlem Renaissance began or ended; I agree with
Houston Baker that "'[m]ovements' are not made and parceled out in neat chronological packages; there was no 'Harlem Renaissance' . . . until *after* the event."[29] Furthermore, it makes little sense to say for certain that a movement as loosely defined
as the Harlem Renaissance can be restricted to one set of dates. Given that many of
the motivations and ideas that guided the movement originated in the early 1900s,
often as a response to African Americans' grim realities in the late nineteenth century, designating a starting date is at best a difficult task. On the other hand, a few
key events, ranging from the catastrophic (such as World War I) to the seemingly
insignificant (the publication of Langston Hughes's *The Ways of White Folks*) help to
demarcate some boundaries that signify when the idea of the "New Negro," as many
major Harlem Renaissance artists understood it, was in vogue. For that reason, I will
be restricting the majority of this study to the years 1919 to 1940. I have not drawn
these boundaries as a way of arbitrarily including or excluding certain authors, but
rather to argue that a definable movement *did* take place, that we can safely agree
that there were historically and intellectually significant events within it, and these
stand apart from the preceding and following periods. The New Negro Renaissance
was real; it simply refuses to stand still in our imagination.

Creating the Conditions for Satire

If the Harlem Renaissance was a movement devoted to expressing voices that were
kept suppressed by poor access to publishing venues—access often denied by the
ubiquitous and virulent racism that was the norm in early twentieth-century America—it should not be surprising that satiric voices would make themselves heard.
Satire, as a literary genre, has often flourished best when threatened with a world
that would silence both the satirist's voice and the voices of all intellects who would
question the hegemonies of their times.

Hegemonies, though, may take on many different forms. If white racist oppression was the clearest expression of hegemony for African Americans in the early

part of the twentieth century, it was not the only one. The hopes and dreams of the Harlem Renaissance itself could be agonizingly constrictive. Or, more accurately, the ambition with which the African American of the era was charged could overshadow the individual desires of African Americans. The "New Negro" celebrated, supported, and published by such intellectual, political, and social luminaries as Alain Locke, W. E. B. Du Bois, James Weldon Johnson, Jessie Redmon Fauset, and Charles S. Johnson was perhaps equal parts myth and model, constructed to guide black authors and artists towards craftsmanship that would help engender a shift in the ways African Americans participate in American democracy. In addition, the "New Negro" would be the creator of a discrete cultural paradigm that would alter the way the rest of the nation would perceive African Americans. The Harlem Renaissance, as a vehicle for the "New Negro," sought to construct a voluble image that implicitly accepted the importance of full black participation in American institutions while maintaining some degree of cultural difference. Ironically, the goals and standards that the authors of the Harlem Renaissance upheld differed considerably from those of its social leaders. Even though they lived in an era in which vicious racism was commonplace, not every author felt compelled to address "race" problems in his or her poetry and prose. The goal of propagandistic writing had as little appeal to these authors as did critical silence.

Unlike those of most literary flourishings, the Harlem Renaissance's intellectual and artistic leaders were fully conscious of the cultural significance of their entrée into American letters. This consciousness, however, was not solely a product of the historical reality that black writers had been repeatedly excluded from the literary marketplace. Rather, the Harlem writer's awareness was largely the product of an era in which African American communities, particularly Harlem, the South Side of Chicago, and innumerable rural southern towns, were undergoing sharp changes in their cultural makeup and economies. These changes swept African Americans and a gaggle of curious white patrons into a new appreciation of certain embodiments of black life. Given their propensity to engage in shameless gawking, and even more shameless carnal abandon, many African Americans and their white patrons virtually begged the barbs of satire. Numerous writers, most prominently Rudolph Fisher, George S. Schuyler, Theophilus Lewis, Langston Hughes, Zora Neale Hurston, Wallace Thurman, and *Messenger* editors A. Philip Randolph and Chandler Owen, were more than happy to comply with this unspoken request for lampoonery.

While the list of purported buffoons this group targeted is fairly long, a few figures and groups were consistently the most popular recipients of satirical wrath:

~ Marcus Garvey and the Universal Negro Improvement Association (especially after the abysmal failure of the Black Star Line shipping concern and Garvey's subsequent conviction on mail fraud charges);

Spoofing the Modern

- ~ W. E. B. Du Bois;
- ~ James Weldon Johnson;
- ~ Walter White;
- ~ The National Association for the Advancement of Colored People (NAACP) and the National Urban League;
- ~ Alain Locke, in his role as one of the de facto "midwives" of the renaissance;
- ~ Robert Russa Moton of Tuskegee University;
- ~ Dean Kelly Miller of Howard University;
- ~ The Ku Klux Klan and similar white supremacist organizations;
- ~ The U.S. government, especially individual politicians such as Presidents Woodrow Wilson, Calvin Coolidge, Warren G. Harding, and Herbert Hoover, Senator Thomas Watson of Georgia, and Attorney General Harry Daugherty;
- ~ The Marxist/Black Nationalist African Blood Brotherhood;
- ~ The crowds of whites frequenting Harlem.

Finally, the major artists of the Harlem Renaissance themselves and their patrons, usually identified via easily translatable pseudonyms, occasionally found themselves among the satirized. The artists included Countee Cullen, Aaron Douglas, Langston Hughes, Zora Neale Hurston, Rudolph Fisher, Claude McKay, Eric Walrond, Richard Bruce Nugent, Jessie Redmon Fauset, Dorothy West, and Helene Johnson. The two patrons most frequently lampooned were Charlotte Osgood Mason and Carl Van Vechten, the former for her propensity to dictate terms to the artists under her care, the latter for allegedly playing a cloying role in furthering artists' careers.

It might help to define a few terms. The first should be the term "modern" that this book's title suggests our featured authors spoof. In *The African American Roots of Modernism*, James Smethurst argues that notions of the "modern," "modernity," and "modernism" for African Americans meant and manifested itself in ways that differed significantly from their fellow white citizens' experience, yet remained inextricably tied to that parallel reality. "There is an obvious sense," Smethurst writes, "in which the revolutionary democratic experiment that became the United States of America was from the start the first completely modern, capitalist, postfeudal (and even post–early modern) society where . . . no hereditary aristocracy was ever established—even if one could convincingly argue that a semihereditary plutocracy came to exert undue influence and that an already existing racial caste system was further codified and solidified" in the antebellum and postbellum periods alike.[30] Thus, if modernity generally indicates the shift toward republicanism, democracy, and liberalism that succeeded feudalism and tribalism in Europe, then in the United States it describes the state of affairs after the South's de facto feudal economy collapsed after the Civil War with slavery's abolition. American modernity signaled the United States' transformation from a largely agrarian economy into a thoroughly industrialized one, with urban centers in all regions attracting workers seeking higher wages, better working conditions, and a new subjectivity defined by liberalism, democracy, and urbanity, rather than servility. That new subject, at least in the Fourteenth Amendment's vision, would be treated equally before the law, despite any heritage as chattel or indentured servant. The modern subject could make himself anew.

The United States' status as a truly modern state allowed for new possibilities, but given the "existing racial caste system" that defined the republic well before its founding, it appeared unlikely that African Americans could ever fully enjoy democratic freedoms guaranteed by the U.S. Constitution. Yet such enjoyment in all its forms, as "full cultural, economic, and political citizens" despite white supremacist opposition became African Americans' goal after the Civil War, paradoxically gaining greater purchase as legal segregation—Jim Crow—solidified and calcified.[31] Put simply: Jim Crow be damned, African Americans would enjoy full, unfettered citizenship, challenge their invisibility in American social and political life, and become not merely part of the American cultural mainstream, but also its avant-garde, opening the way to democracy's unfulfilled promises.

What, then, were New Negro satirists spoofing? Social, economic, and political progress? The slow but steady decline in lynchings? Growing enlightenment, literacy, and militancy among the black masses? Hardly. Instead, New Negro satirists behaved largely as other satirists do: they criticized, through humor and invective— that is, biting insult—the organizations and individuals seeking black modernity with insufficient humility, intelligence, and perspicacity. This is the satirist's role; to attempt to "keep the knaves honest" or at least "make them stand in fear" that they may be held up to contumely every time they stumble as they step forward.[32] Modernity and arrogance shouldn't go hand in hand—but often do.

That arrogance revolved around the complex roles that folk culture should play in a new black identity. How should the organic, syncretistic materials emerging from the South and black migration to the North find their way into art? How should African Americans' reasons for participating in their own art and culture be revised, and by whom? For whom? By black intellectuals? By the artists themselves? Should this be for the benefit of often indifferent black masses, or for the artists' own creation? Do those black and white creators, intellectuals, and leaders invested in black progress have plans to achieve modernity, or do they have only chimeras and fantasies akin to the Universal Negro Improvement Association's disastrously ill-fated Black Star Line?

To this end, Schuyler, Thurman, Hurston, Fisher, Nugent, and others engage in what Sonnet Retman calls "modernist burlesque, a kind of satire that occupies its subject from the outside in by pushing its most theatrical and technological elements to spectacular excess."[33] Modernist burlesque seeks to "dismantle the authentic aura" surrounding the folk or the masses, to question whether authenticity of any sort resides only in the imagination, thriving in cultural arbiters more concerned with controlling or speaking for the folk and their cultural products rather than allowing them to speak. Modernist burlesque is perhaps akin to *reductio ad absurdum,* the rhetorical technique central to countless satires. Reductio ad absurdum—reduction to the absurd—takes a particular figure or institution's most emblematically lamentable qualities, discards nuances and complexities, and reveals the falsehoods, exaggerations, and puffery at the heart of the satiric target. According to Retman, modernist burlesque "illumine[s] how the clichéd story of American class ascension . . . depends upon impersonation, a performative making of the self" into another, middle-class, white self.[34] As with the self-made man, the New Negro and his renaissance appear to the black satirists to be at many times a facile attempt at literary greatness, hobbled and hampered by overweening ambition—1926's extremely short-lived *Fire!!* magazine serves as but one example—intellectual pretension, and pomp. The renaissance was ever in danger of overselling its significance. As Rudolph Fisher warns in "The Caucasian Storms Harlem," "indifference" and "apathy" are the likely fates for all but a few iconic Negro cultural figures that have attracted white and black interest in Harlem and the New Negro; the rest will be but a "diversion" for whites struck with interminable ennui.[35] Without an organic aesthetic core, African American art will be but a fad.

African American art survived the Jazz Age and any faddishness that peaked in the late 1920s, of course, but the era's satirists doubted it would. To express their skepticism, they engaged in lampoons and parodies, or ironic imitations of individual personages and artistic works, respectively. They created romans à clef such as Thurman's *Infants of the Spring* (1932), Nugent's long-lost *Gentleman Jigger* (composed ca. 1928–1931; published 2008), and Schuyler's *Black No More* (1931). Schuyler and Hurston wrote hilarious specimens of mock encomium, essays that pretend to shower excessive praise upon their subject, but drip with irony and sarcasm. In all cases, irony served as the New Negro satirist's undercurrent, an abiding sense that if African Americans are moving forward into modernity, they die for want of intellectual depth and sincerity. As Thurman writes in *Infants of the Spring,* "[o]ne cannot make movements nor can one plot their course. When the work of a given number of individuals during a given period is looked at in retrospect, then one can identify a movement and evaluate its distinguishing characteristics."[36] Until then, "it is going to be necessary . . . to have another emancipation to deliver the emancipated Negro from a new kind of slavery."[37]

Spoofing the Modern is more than a simple catalogue of satirical discursive practices. In chapter 2, I unearth some of the historical events that brought George Schuyler and his rapier wit to Harlem and gave it its most devastating satirist. In chapter 3, I posit Wallace Thurman as the centerpiece and preeminent critic for the younger generation of New Negroes through his essays and novels, then reveal how his troubled relationships with his peers—notably his friend Richard Bruce Nugent—presaged the movement's decline. In chapter 4, I examine Rudolph Fisher and Zora Neale Hurston's satirical contributions. Although Hurston has become immensely popular over the last thirty years, thanks largely to novelist Alice Walker's campaign to revive Hurston's oeuvre, her role as a satirist has been almost entirely ignored. Fisher remains virtually unknown to all but African American literature scholars, but his *The Walls of Jericho* (1928) stands among the movement's greatest lampoons. Finally, I conclude by reviewing what happened during and after the Harlem Renaissance's fall, and how subsequent generations of African American satirists have either taken cues from the movement or owe it an intellectual debt.

By delving into the historical events that provided fodder for satire, I analyze the impetus behind some of the exaggerations in which each artist eventually indulged. How accurate were George Schuyler's lampoons of Garvey and Du Bois? Did they fully deserve Schuyler's vituperation? At what point did Schuyler and his contemporaries become excessive in their enthusiasm, thereby moving themselves out of the satirical realm and into sheer, virtually humorless invective? How much of Wallace Thurman's indictment of the renaissance's alleged artistic failures rings true? How should these individual authors affect our reading of the movement itself? Should we join them in lamenting a time and a movement that were doomed to failure, or use their criticism to reconsider how they contributed to the movement they disdained and reshaped African American literature?

My goal, then, is to avoid taking these artists at face value by interrogating their critical stance toward the New Negro movement, analyzing their techniques, and determining their relevance to the most dynamic African American literary and intellectual movement to date. In view of recent scholarship, it seems more important than ever to be skeptical of the conventional wisdom regarding the Harlem Renaissance's meaning. George Hutchinson's phenomenal 1995 study, *The Harlem Renaissance in Black and White,* has set a new standard for scholarship in this field, questioning the most popular analyses, especially those driven by an obvious ideological agenda. While I do not claim to be free of my own agendas—my steadfast desire to place African American iconoclasts squarely in the center of scholarly discourse disqualifies me from that distinction—neither do I honor convention when it is not warranted. In this way, *Spoofing the Modern* opens countless possibilities to be found in this most fascinating of cultural flourishes.

2

The Importance of Being Iconoclastic

George S. Schuyler, the Messenger, *and the Black Menckenites*

In July 1923, Howard University professor and Harlem Renaissance midwife Alain Locke wrote author Jean Toomer to solicit submissions for "a volume of race plays or rather plays of Negro Life" that he and a collaborator were organizing. Although Toomer had already garnered some fame for his poetry and short stories, Locke asked whether he "could . . . not give us something more mature. Either in the same vein or a satirical vein. Both are needed—the great lack as I see it is in these two fields of the polite folk-play and the satire."[1] Locke's request is one of the earliest references to satire during the Harlem Renaissance that recognizes the importance this literary form would have for African American literature during the New Negro movement. Ironically, Locke's words echo ideas that journalist and critic H. L. Mencken had shared with NAACP official Walter White nine months earlier, in which he argued (as Charles Scruggs summarizes) that "if [the African American writer] functions as an insider, he will treat . . . 'the drama within the race, so far scarcely touched,'" and "if he functions as an outsider, he will write satire upon the smug, cocksure master race."[2] Perhaps if Locke had been cognizant of his potential and had held slightly different views regarding African American literature, he would have done better to ask George S. Schuyler to fill this particular bill. Toomer was arguably the most talented, influential, and modern author of the renaissance; his *Cane* (1923) remains among the period's most artistically challenging, and betrays Toomer's dogged fascination with African Americans' difficult shift to modernity in the South and North alike. But Toomer had a rather limited feel for satire. *Cane* owes its power more to an understated irony regarding the complexities of race relations than to an openly satirical mode. While Toomer's obvious literary intelligence convinced Locke that he was capable of engaging in satirical projects, this same intelligence could be found in Schuyler, who had a far more prolific albeit less obviously influential literary career than Toomer.

The "Black Mencken"

Although the general public remains unaware of his existence today, George S. Schuyler was for decades the most prominent, prolific, and talented journalist in African America, and a preeminent critic of American and international politics. During the "New Negro" or Harlem Renaissance—a movement Schuyler considered a fraud—his scathing wit earned him a unique sobriquet: "The Black Mencken," in honor of H. L. Mencken's achievements as a tastemaker and satirist. Mencken's tendency to skewer and lampoon American stupidity, particularly in the South, earned him respect in African American circles. As a result, he wielded enormous influence on Jazz Age writers, whether black or white. Like the source of his nickname, Schuyler was well read and respected during his time, but his reputation fell as tastes changed and his career went in different directions, particularly after his death.

Between 1924 and 1964, Schuyler's best-known and most abundant work appeared in the pages of the Pittsburgh *Courier*—second only to the Chicago *Defender* in popularity among African American newspapers—where he served as a reporter and editor until the *Courier's* publisher demoted Schuyler for his continuous criticism of the civil rights movement as a front for international communism and his characterization of Martin Luther King Jr. as a "sable Typhoid Mary" after King won the Nobel Peace Prize in 1964. Schuyler then became a freelance columnist, writing occasionally for the *Courier* for a few more years, but increasingly for William Loeb's right-wing Manchester *Union Leader* and similar publications until his death in 1977 at the age of eighty-two. By that time, Schuyler's archconservative politics—he and his daughter, Philippa Duke Schuyler, wrote and spoke for the ultra-right John Birch Society frequently in the 1960s—were so out of step with the African American mainstream that his decades of meticulously researched, impeccably written, inarguably challenging, and frequently popular journalism and opinion had long disappeared from the public eye. Schuyler's ideological descendants may be found in the black neoconservatives who rose to prominence in the 1980s and 1990s, but as Jeffrey Tucker writes, "the claims of [Thomas] Sowell, [Randall] Kennedy, [Clarence] Thomas, [Shelby] Steele, and others merely echo" Schuyler, "one of the most important, if least recognized, figures in the history of African American letters."[3]

In the early 1990s, Schuyler regained some recognition as these descendants entered the national discourse and such critics as Henry Louis Gates Jr. took another look at Schuyler and black conservatism. After Northwestern University Press reprinted his early novels *Black No More* (1931) and *Black Empire* (serialized in the *Courier* between 1936 and 1938), the public again had access to some of his best work; this access but increased with the Modern Library's more affordable 1999 edition of *Black No More,* and Jeffrey B. Ferguson's *The Sage of Sugar Hill: George S. Schuyler and the Harlem Renaissance* (2005), the first major biography of Schuyler after Michael Peplow's eponymous volume for Twayne's United States Authors series (1980). Most recently, Oscar R. Williams's *George S. Schuyler: Portrait of a Black Conservative* (2007) has taken an extensive critical look at Schuyler's political development to address perhaps the most bewildering question surrounding his career: how did a card-carrying socialist become an archconservative Republican and relentless Red-baiter? More than any other scholar, Williams delves into Schuyler's earliest years in Providence, Rhode Island, and Syracuse, New York, to discover where his wit, sense of irony, and lifelong disdain for mass movements originated.

All of this renewed interest in Schuyler has allowed a rich body of work and a fascinating life to reach a wider audience, certainly one greater than the broad silence granted his achievements immediately after his death. None of it indicates, though, that the literary and scholarly worlds have completely warmed to Schuyler, or that widespread interest is imminent. Those writers Schuyler influenced, such as novelist and satirist Ishmael Reed, enjoy far greater notoriety, as do most of his peers from the New Negro era. In his book on Mencken, Charles Scruggs writes that, when "the subject of Mencken and race is mentioned, the old bugaboo of his racial slurs is dutifully brought up and lamented over, and all discussion stops right there. Furthermore, this obligatory condemnation is rhetorical; it is meant to show the audience that the critic is a good, right-thinking man or woman."[4] Interest in Schuyler has grown in the last twenty years, due in large part to Henry Louis Gates Jr.'s work on Ishmael Reed[5] in the late 1980s and early 1990s. Yet Scruggs's assessment of scholarly interest in Mencken could apply equally to Schuyler, with "his slur of Martin Luther King, Jr.," replacing "racial slurs" as the great offense that can still end discussion of Schuyler before it has begun.

I would like to urge instead a new consideration of Schuyler's sharpest work, namely the satirical jabs of his "Shafts and Darts" column for the *Messenger* between 1923 and 1928. Although I comment briefly upon Schuyler's most notorious work, his novel *Black No More* (1931), as the logical extension of his journalistic efforts, his columns represent the best of his satirical mien and provide the most incisive criticism of the New Negro to be found among his contemporaries. Schuyler's journalism helped push African American politics and literature into modernity through repeated calls for rationalism over superstition, blind adherence to tradition, and unflinching group loyalty. To that end, Schuyler established himself as the iconoclast par excellence in African American letters. As Ishmael Reed writes, "John Henrik Clarke perhaps best explained Schuyler's life when he observed: 'I used to tell people that George got up in the morning, waited to see which way the world was turning, then struck out in the opposite direction. He was a rebel who enjoyed playing that role.'"[6]

Schuyler: The Lost Cause Célèbre

In 2002, Duke University Press published *Gay Rebel of the Harlem Renaissance: Selections from the Work of Richard Bruce Nugent,* a collection of the writings and art by one of Schuyler's contemporaries. The following year, Rutgers University Press released *The Collected Writings of Wallace Thurman,* the first comprehensive edition of Thurman's work, including both published articles and book excerpts, and unpublished materials previously available only in university archives. These two volumes represent some of the finest and most provocative work to emerge from the movement, yet an overwhelming proportion of Schuyler's earliest and most incisive work remains generally out of easy reach of the general public. The reprinted editions of Schuyler's novels and novellas, Jeffrey Ferguson's 2005 biography, George Hutchinson's *The Harlem Renaissance in Black and White* (1995), minimal excerpts in Harlem Renaissance retrospectives and anthologies, and a small body of fairly recent articles and essays comprise the means through which readers interested in Schuyler's work may find it. Direct access to the bulk of Schuyler's editorial and satirical columns may be had only by sifting through microfilm archives of the magazines and newspapers for which he wrote in the 1920s and 1930s, significantly more daunting than the extant readers and anthologies that feature his contemporaries.

The reasons for a relative lack of interest in Schuyler follow Scruggs's outlines. Schuyler's positions on most political issues after World War II, including those concerning African Americans, departed radically from mainstream opinion, as his comments about Martin Luther King Jr. and the civil rights movement indicate. Although Schuyler always wrote clearly and eloquently, his views on civil rights came uncomfortably close to echoing white southerners who opposed the movement. Ultimately, this cost Schuyler his position at the Pittsburgh *Courier*; publisher Robert L. Vann refused to print his remarks about King.[7] This led Schuyler toward opportunities at conservative publications such as the Manchester *Union-Leader* and the John Birch Society's *American Opinion,* but little in the cultural or political mainstream.

Schuyler's autobiography *Black and Conservative* (1966) nearly says everything necessary in its title and date. It posits Schuyler as—quite obviously—black with a lifelong interest in African American history and culture, yet also staunchly conservative in observing peoples of the African Diaspora and American politics, despite his youthful flirtation with socialism, and with little respect for the popular status quo. When published, *Black and Conservative* characteristically threw down a gauntlet before the civil rights movement's left-leaning rhetoric and populism. The era's emerging Black Power militants and radicals served as perfect ammunition for Schuyler's arguments that 1960s black activism was a communist plot.

To be fair, throughout his career Schuyler consistently exhibited some distrust of mass movements of any sort, whether they involved political ideologies, religious orthodoxies, or cultural trends. Yet he also enjoyed the camaraderie and activities of A. Philip Randolph and Chandler Owen's Friends of Negro Freedom, gave numerous addresses at socialist gatherings, worked for the NAACP and its journal, the *Crisis,* and supported community-based African American business organizations in Harlem and elsewhere, particularly the Young Negroes Co-operative League.[8] Like Mencken, who characterized democracy as "mobbocracy," Schuyler would later consider virtually all mass movements collectivistic enterprises that feared and demeaned individual merit, sound intellect, or realism, in line with John Birch Society dogma. But as Jeffrey Ferguson argues, "in the 1920s Schuyler believed in the possibilities of collectivism and regarded it as an answer to social problems."[9] Naturally, this rather severe form of conservatism guaranteed that Schuyler would see the civil rights movement's nonviolent direct action as "part of the Red techniques of agitation, infiltration, and subversion" led by "professional collectivist agitators."[10] Schuyler feared that "this increasing racial animosity, exacerbated by the Communist-influenced policies of Negro racial agitation, might lead to actual civil war which would certainly lead to genocide" in view of the United States' treatment of Japanese citizens during World War II and its general treatment of American Indians.[11] Those who took the lessons of Schuyler's late, erstwhile debating opponent Malcolm X to heart after his assassination and consequently found the appeal of black nationalism more compelling could only read the title as Schuyler's final and irrevocable stamp on his opinions. The contents bore out this promise: Schuyler would brook no allegiance to any part of the "insanity" of the Marxist/communist-inspired civil rights movement, choosing instead to support thrift, hard work, and individual achievement within the race.[12]

Many answers about Schuyler's life remain missing from the narrative, in fact, especially about Schuyler's innermost thoughts and motivations. In their place, we find a thrifty, driven, creative journalist and chronicler with a relatively flamboyant youth, one that merely happened to include a membership in the Socialist Party among his juvenilia. In this sense, *Black and Conservative* has more in common at points with Hurston's *Dust Tracks on a Road,* which conceals as much as it reveals about Zora Neale Hurston's inner life. Both authors either exaggerate, play down, or delete crucial details of their younger days that would interfere with their respective portraits of the artist as a young (wo)man, details that later scholarship has filled in. Valerie Boyd points out, for example, that while the first part of *Dust Tracks on a Road* is "devoted to an exuberant description of [Hurston's] uphill climb" from the hardships of her youth, the last part comprises opinions about diverse subjects. Hurston, Boyd continues, "does not tell many (if any) out-and-out lies about her life," but "through omission . . . she presents a questionable and carefully constructed version of the truth," with few mentions of the racism she encountered, only a brief mention of her now-celebrated Harlem Renaissance years, and no mention whatsoever of her second marriage.[13] With a few alterations, Boyd's assessment of Hurston's autobiography fits Schuyler's as well. Schuyler deletes at least one crucial detail of his youth and ignores much of his later home life and its conflicts, which his more recent biographers have discovered.[14]

Of course, omissions of the sort found in Schuyler and Hurston's autobiographies are hardly unusual, but Schuyler's choices, like Hurston's, warrant some attention due to his career's strange arc. Again, how could a former socialist become a staunch anticommunist, proponent of and writer for the John Birch Society, and defender of Senator Joseph McCarthy? Public conversions from the left to the hard right (and vice-versa) may be found with little effort. A similar question might be asked of a more recent figure such as David Horowitz, who worked with the radical Black Panther Party in the 1970s, yet eventually became a hard-line neoconservative.[15]

Unlike with many other such converts, though, it is difficult to point to a specific event that indicated a political shift. The roots of Schuyler's anticommunist diatribes and activism stand exposed within his gleeful denunciations of the Harlem Renaissance as so much "Negro-Art Hokum"; the black church, particularly as represented by its clergy; Marcus Garvey and his lieutenants within the Universal Negro Improvement Association; the NAACP; and other favorite targets of his columns in the 1920s and 1930s. For Schuyler, each of these individuals and institutions suffered from the malady of collectivism, which converted the victim into a member of at least one Menckenian "mobbocracy" that softens the brain, liquidates the spine, and transforms the afflicted into irrational dupes who would gladly surrender their independent thought to any dubious social cause. Echoes of this general thesis resound in every decade since Schuyler found regular employment as a journalist and editor, and he routinely received—and apparently delighted in—condemnation for his iconoclasm.

If his remarks regarding Martin Luther King Jr. seem particularly outrageous now, then we also have to concede that, unlike most of the earlier recipients of Schuyler's barbs, King was popular, albeit embattled, for most of his career as a human rights leader and activist, and remains an icon in American history today. Marcus Garvey commanded during his glory years the sort of following that King enjoyed, and is celebrated as a hero of his native Jamaica and other Caribbean nations, as well as parts of Africa. Garvey, however, was far more controversial, and openly hostile to the mainstream civil rights leadership of his time; King by contrast was *part of* the civil rights establishment, and presented a program that eschewed the black nationalism of his own time, yet excoriated the segregation of its time in terms that appealed to a wider swath of the public. Schuyler, of course, would have none of this, as popularity of a new idea, leader, or organization only signaled that the masses had been flim-flammed once again.

Schuyler's deep skepticism and rationalism provided the impetus for his views regarding mass movements, each of which appeared to require a strong appeal to emotionalism, using half-truths and either fabricated or nonexistent facts. He found Christian revivals and camp-meetings as distasteful and flabbergasting as street-corner rallies, parades, and various schemes to interest African Americans in a new form of salvation. On the surface, this antipathy does not fully explain Schuyler's early interest in socialism and frequent work for the Socialist Party's program. In *Black and Conservative*, Schuyler plays down or dismisses this interest as a mere intellectual curiosity made more torturous by the turgid prose of Marx and Engels, to say nothing of tracts issued by more contemporary avowed socialists. As Jeffrey Ferguson argues, Schuyler's later assessment of his youthful days simply does not ring true. To have an interest in socialism during and after World War I, especially if one despised its literature, was not only counterintuitive but a likely avenue to harassment and a prison sentence at hard labor. The U.S. Department of Justice actively and aggressively investigated and prosecuted parties or individuals who professed beliefs or membership in any group considered seditious.

Moreover, Schuyler's philosophical perspective jibed with his personal demeanor. His last close associate, William Loeb of the Manchester *Union Leader*, remarked that, at his daughter Philippa's funeral, Schuyler was a "'composed man. Whatever he felt inside he knew that a gentleman doesn't bare [his feelings] to the rest of the world.'"[16] None of this is to suggest that Schuyler lacked feeling, emotion, or passion. Schuyler's friends consistently found him a warm, affable, and courtly gentleman who delighted in good drink, good food, and even better conversation. Yet his propensity for iconoclasm in service of a rational, ordered view of the world ultimately moved him from the distinction he enjoyed as a prominent and accomplished journalist, and arguably one of the greatest African American journalists ever, to obscurity. Schuyler's earliest work for the *Messenger*, the Pittsburgh *Courier*, and Mencken's *American Mercury* magazine vividly underscores his power as a writer and critic, and remains, arguably, his best and most exciting contribution to African American letters.

Yet even this work provides evidence of Schuyler's idiosyncratic position among his contemporaries. Schuyler stressed in accounts of his years in the New Negro movement that his early essays in *American Mercury*, for example, were "regarded as something" by people he met in later years, that they "[couldn't] help but influence the minds of enlightened and liberal people," and were "contributory factor[s] to the development of the Negro renaissance or writing group."[17] Schuyler did not perceive this relationship as one of mutual influence. He "never associated much" with the other New Negroes, as he "felt that a lot of the things that they went for and believed in were not healthy, and they were not representative, and I could learn just as much going to a bar in Harlem as I could going to a wine joint in [Greenwich] Village, probably more."[18] Schuyler's distinction between Harlem and Greenwich Village underscores his difference with his peers, who were part of a "sort of racket" that white publishers and patrons "were making out of Negro art," and were therefore "creating something segregated and different" that subsumed the fact of their American identities in favor of a distinct "Negro" culture.[19] Schuyler instead spent much of his literary and intellectual career undermining these stated differences.

From 1924 until 1928, excepting a few months in which he traveled the South soliciting subscriptions on behalf of the Pittsburgh *Courier*, Schuyler worked as an editor at the *Messenger*, first as the de facto managing editor, then later with a full credit in the masthead. The *Messenger* contained a heady, fiery mix of economic, social, and political analysis from an unapologetically socialist perspective. Although the magazine's early issues were partially underwritten by the Socialist Party of the United States, the magazine's cofounders, A. (Asa) Philip Randolph and Chandler Owen were ultimately responsible for its tone and approach. They sought to tear down the icons of the American and African American political scenes. In George Schuyler they found a sympathetic intellectual, a shrewd—if overworked—editor, and a mind that helped mold the magazine's iconoclasm into crisp, merciless satire. Together they shaped the *Messenger* into more than a vehicle for socialism; the magazine's refusal to accept the hegemony of bourgeois culture and capitalism made it a crucial alternative African American challenge to the program of the National Association for the Advancement of Colored People, its organ, the *Crisis*, and particularly its editor, W. E. B. Du Bois.

Schuyler's most celebrated contribution to the *Messenger* was his regular column, "Shafts and Darts" (later subtitled "A Page of Calumny and Satire"), which debuted in February 1923. Schuyler coauthored the column's earliest installments with *Messenger* drama critic and occasional publisher Theophilus Lewis.[20] "Shafts and Darts" sprang organically from both Schuyler's mind and from the *Messenger*. Both the magazine and its resident satirist were instrumental in grinding into dust the reputations of such "race leaders" as Du Bois, Marcus Garvey, James Weldon Johnson, Robert Russa Moton of the Tuskegee Institute, Dean Kelly Miller of Howard University, Mississippi's race-baiting Senator Bilbo, and Cyril V. Briggs's stridently Marxist African Blood Brotherhood. Schuyler presaged his later Red-baiting by reserving special scorn for the last group. Some three decades hence he would call Joseph McCarthy a "great American," and once wrote, regarding the "witch hunt" for communists in the 1940s and 1950s, "If these Communist witches want society to stop hunting them, they have only to stop giving society cause to fear them."[21] Schuyler's wrath for the African Blood Brotherhood, however, had just as much to do with ideology and later ties to the Communist International as it did to the brotherhood's ruling Sanhedrin of *five*, which Schuyler liked to pretend was the entire membership. Schuyler excoriated individuals and their supporting organizations with impunity, often for pretending to know anything at all about rational, hard-nosed leadership. Schuyler levied very similar accusations towards the black literary scene in Harlem and elsewhere, arguing that it was largely the invention of intellectuals, most of whom knew nothing about African American culture and history; even fewer actually lived in Harlem!

The Messenger *and Radical Iconoclasm in Harlem*

When a twenty-five-year-old radical named A. Philip Randolph met Columbia University student Chandler Owen in early 1915 at one of the parties thrown by cosmetics entrepreneur Madame C. J. Walker, the groundwork was laid for the *Messenger,* one of the most significant and groundbreaking magazines in American history. Both Chandler and Own were interested in economics, particularly the economic status of African Americans. Randolph was inarguably more radical than Owen, who was interested in his personal economic situation at least as much as that of other blacks, while his friend was a devotee of Eugene Debs and Karl Marx.[22] Nevertheless both were inveterate iconoclasts who were likely to read and appreciate anything that questioned the social and economic state of the world. By the end of 1916 both had joined the Socialist Party and taken a cue from Hubert H. Harrison, the celebrated local black socialist and Black Nationalist, by speaking on Harlem street corners to espouse their radical economic and social views and get the feedback that corner soapbox speakers in Harlem generally enjoyed: frank, blunt, and immediate.[23] Over the next year of working the crowds and attending Socialist Party meetings, Randolph and Owen became seasoned speakers and organizers, "the most notorious street-corner radicals in Harlem," more audacious than Harrison himself.[24] They also reorganized the Independent Political Council, which Randolph had founded in 1912 as a discussion group around a radical, quasi-socialist program. Randolph and Owen's plan was to educate the populace by distributing literature and continuing their schedule of public lectures "on the vital issues affecting the colored people's economic and political destiny," among other matters, but their goals "to examine, expose and condemn cunning and malicious political marplots" and "to criticize and denounce selfish and self-styled leaders" both let their iconoclasm shine through and best presaged the founding principles of the *Messenger.*[25]

In early 1917, Randolph and Owen began publishing the *Hotel Messenger* magazine at the behest of William White, president of the Headwaiters and Sidewaiters Society of Greater New York. This arrangement gave the two young men a new office space for their radical activities, an equally advantageous printed outlet for advocacy, and rapid connections to such major players in Harlem's political world as

Hubert Harrison, W. A. Domingo, and Cyril V. Briggs. They also found themselves in a bind eight months later, when they exposed a kickback racket among their readership.[26] White fired Randolph and Owen, who immediately set up an office next door and, with the financial assistance of Randolph's wife, Lucille, founded the *Messenger: A Journal of Scientific Radicalism* in November 1917 as an outlet for unabashed socialism and trade unionism. That November 1917 debut, of course, coincided with the United States' involvement in World War I, when anti-sedition laws suppressed most dissent in the press and rumors of German subversion of the war effort via propaganda aimed at African Americans abounded. It was, perhaps, the least auspicious time to begin a magazine that not only called for a socialist program, but also openly and vociferously opposed the war effort. In that regard, Owen and Randolph spoke and wrote for millions of African Americans who gave material support to the war in hopes that it would help bring an end to Jim Crow but also quietly opposed it in principle. Thus the mavericks would blast President Wilson in January 1918, arguing that "Lynching, Jim Crow, segregation, discrimination in the armed forces and out, disfranchisement of millions of black souls in the South—all these things make your cry of making the world safe for democracy a sham, a mockery, a rape on decency and a travesty on common justice."[27]

No surprise, then, that the Department of Justice began monitoring Randolph and Owen and arrested them publicly at a rally in Cleveland, charging them with treason. The charges were later dismissed; the judge in the case could scarcely believe, as Theodore Kornweibel writes, that "the two twenty-nine-year-old 'boys' could possess the knowledge and intelligence to write the inflammatory editorials presented as evidence by the prosecutors," thinking instead that they were mere fronts for white agitators.[28] As Randolph later recounted the incident, the judge asked the pair what they knew about socialism, whereupon they professed their study of Marx and their hopes for socialization of private property, even though their government opposed them. The judge threatened to jail both of them, but dismissed the charges and told Randolph and Owen to "get out of town" immediately. After leaving the courthouse, they promptly disobeyed and sought out another rally to continue their campaign, although frightened activists initially shunned the defiant journalists.[29] Nevertheless, Randolph was ordered to report for induction into the Army (although he requested and received a deferment), and the New York *Age* declared him "the most dangerous Negro in America";[30] Harlemites later nicknamed Randolph and Owen "Lenin and Trotsky."[31] Operating within the broad boundaries it enjoyed under the decidedly jingoistic tenor of the war years, the U.S. Post Office under Postmaster General Albert Burleson read such sentiments as sedition and therefore unworthy of First Amendment protection. In August 1918 the Post Office yanked the magazine's second-class mailing permit and did not return it for three years after Owen and Randolph were arrested for sedition.[32] This caused the expenses for the magazine to rise precipitously, leading in turn to an irregular publishing schedule.

Despite this setback, the *Messenger* continued to expose the fallacies of capitalism, racist political figures, segregation, Black Nationalists, mainstream African American leaders, lynchings, and the various outrages being perpetrated in all parts of the country against African Americans, especially in New York City and the South. It took special pride in printing materials that other prominent African American–run magazines—in particular, the NAACP's *Crisis*—would not touch out of fear of government persecution, or at least not until other magazines took the initial risk. The *Messenger* was among the first magazines to publish Claude McKay's militant "If We Must Die," in 1919; that same year, it proudly printed Archibald Grimké's poem "Her Thirteen Black Soldiers," which protested the murders of returning black soldiers in uniform, after the *Crisis*'s W. E. B. Du Bois rejected it in the face of Justice Department threats. The *Messenger*'s editors, true to form, blasted Du Bois for failing to see the soundness of the poem's logic, and for succumbing to official intimidation tactics.[33]

Logic in the service of science, after all, formed the heart of the magazine's political and editorial credo. True to the magazine's original subtitle, the *scientific* character of the editors' socialism focused upon their perception that America teetered between fundamentalism, capitalist economic exploitation, and racism on the one hand, and modernism, science, and socioeconomic freedom on the other. Socialism provided the means to organize the African American populace—particularly in the South—into a modern economic force that would slough off the influence of the ruling class once it set aside the prejudice and superstition in established black institutions, including the Black Church and the normal/industrial-school model that flourished under the leadership of Booker T. Washington. In the wake of Washington's death in 1915—despite the gradualism of his successor, Robert Russa Moton—Randolph and Owen argued that black workers could create wealth and institutions that would effectively destroy segregation and peonage.

Over the magazine's eleven-year run, Randolph and Owen managed to attract to their editorial staff—and break with—a wide variety of black progressives and radicals, including George Frazier Miller, William Colson, Ernest Rice McKinney, Abram L. Harris, J. A. Rogers, Robert Bagnall, William Pickens, Wallace Thurman, and, of course, Schuyler and drama critic Theophilus Lewis. Due to endorsements from various radical or socialistic organizations, such as New York's Rand School of Social Science and the Socialist Party, white radicals, including Eugene Debs and Morris Hilquit,[34] either contributed to the magazine or received praise and support in its pages. Some of the magazine's readers who felt threatened by its radicalism would denounce it as "Bolshevist," without understanding the distinction between Bolsheviks and socialists.[35] Later, and more troubling, Marcus Garvey and his cohort would use the existence of the magazine's white contributors, its spotty publishing record due to the Post Office's interference, and Randolph and Owen's own phenotypical characteristics—their lighter color—as evidence that African Americans should not trust the *Messenger*'s editors.[36]

The *Messenger*'s editorial position during its early years in defense of socialism and African American workers was inarguably a reflection of its time. Not only was the labor struggle capturing the attention of the American public, but the nation was also experiencing what could be euphemistically called a period of racial revisionism. The body politic was once again considering the so-called "Negro question" in its deliberations over its fate as a nation, and the results were mixed, steering precariously to the negative. More specifically, post–World War I America saw the resurgence, enormous growth, and horrific influence of the Ku Klux Klan, as well as the deadly "Red Summer" of 1919, consisting of over twenty riots against African Americans, and an equally chilling series of lynchings: seventy-six, the worst year of the 1910s, and one of the worst in the twentieth century. Out of fear that African Americans would gain social equality after their impressive performance in the war, whites nationwide collectively answered black demands for equal treatment with a resounding "no." Although the South was typically the most conspicuous voice in this cruel chorus, resistance to blacks seeking jobs and civil rights could be found everywhere. The *Messenger*'s response was to transform racial injustice into a primary satirical target. The editors' original purpose of advocating and spreading socialism among African Americans, however, eventually diffused as numerous distractions—such as the "Garvey Must Go" campaign of 1922 that Owen largely spearheaded—and an increasingly improbable financial status made editorial consistency virtually out of the question by the early 1920s, when Schuyler joined the masthead. Instead, the magazine gradually cooled its political stance, reformatting the magazine to include news on sports, bourgeois society, and other areas normally the province of mainstream black magazines.

The *Messenger*'s essential rhetorical stance of iconoclasm, however, remained a constant, even as its focus shifted from hard socialism to advocacy of Pullman porters in the mid-1920s. George Schuyler's own affinity for iconoclasm and satire made his tenure at the magazine virtually inevitable, regardless of when he joined, but it needed someone with his background by 1923, when the fervor and violence of the postwar years had receded somewhat. Whereas 1922 saw an unemployment rate of 6.7 percent and fifty-one lynchings of African Americans, in 1923 the jobless rate had fallen to a prosperous 2.4 percent, accompanied by fewer lynchings of blacks—twenty-nine for the year—even as the Congress killed the Dyer Anti-Lynching bill.[37] Conditions were far from ideal for African Americans, but compared to the years immediately following the war, they offered some hope that the deadly days of the Old Negro were passing. This matched the situation of the *Messenger*'s most celebrated contributor as he made his way to its offices that year.

32   *Spoofing the Modern*

Enter the Dragon and Épater le Bourgeois: Schuyler Arrives

When George Schuyler arrived in Harlem in 1919, his circumstances gave scant indication of the role he would play in shaping the literary and critical tastes of the renaissance that was underway. Although he concealed the fact throughout his adult life, revealing it to only his closest confidants, Schuyler ended up in New York as a result of a prison sentence for desertion from the U.S. Army, after a Greek immigrant refused to give the young, black first lieutenant a shoe shine. This incident followed on the heels of the Army's broader refusal towards its African American troops to fight on the front lines of World War I. As an experienced drill sergeant, Schuyler saw how the limited and underfunded training for black officers at the Fort Des Moines facility—the first of its kind in the Army's history—was designed to ensure that the Army would remain segregated and decidedly unequal in its treatment of black soldiers. After nearly six years of service in or amongst black and white soldiers, many of whom lacked his education and skill, and being unable to get basic service and respect as an officer, Schuyler's decision to desert—particularly dangerous during wartime—was less foolhardy than it might seem.

Yet during his first stint in the U.S. Army, from the spring of 1912 to July 1915, Schuyler racked up an impressive service record while posted in Fort Lawton, Washington (near Seattle), and Honolulu. In particular, starting from his January 1913 billeting in Honolulu's Schofield Barracks, Schuyler developed into an audacious leader among the enlisted men, many of whom had less education than the Syracuse native, and looked to him to resolve conflicts, whether between black soldiers or across racial lines. From the moment of his arrival, Schuyler witnessed firsthand the most common effect of racism, one all too familiar to his southern compatriots: fear of black sexuality. When Schuyler and his peers visited Honolulu's prostitution district, they discovered that white soldiers had spread anti-black propaganda in the area, which also affected how the soldiers were treated in their daily commerce with the island's denizens.[38] Although the effects of this propaganda lessened over time, as more black soldiers arrived at the barracks and wanted to spend their pay in pursuit of sex and drink, they never completely dissipated. The tensions along racial and sexual lines came to their apex in 1915, when a riot ensued after new white prostitutes refused black soldiers, and the soldiers responded with violence, leading in turn to a crackdown by white military police and other white regiments. In his autobiography, Schuyler notes sarcastically that the abolition of the Iwilei brothel district via the "reformistic" efforts of the island's "forces of goodness and purity"—its missionaries—led to dramatic increases in "homosexuality" amongst the soldiers, as well as more drunk and disorderly behavior.[39]

Although Schuyler's focus upon the sexual proclivities of his fellow soldiers may appear to reflect little more than his more personal interests, it also offers a fairly revealing glimpse of the issues that would shape his political and literary interests for years to come. As Schuyler began to model himself after H. L. Mencken in the 1920s, he adopted Mencken's distaste for the slightest whiff of "Puritanism," in all of its forms. Mencken's public and private views of African Americans often resided in condescension and derision but were matched if not exceeded by his disgust towards Puritanism as a particularly repugnant form of American exceptionalism. Puritanism manifested itself as the fundamentalism that dominated the South and threatened to overtake the nation via such entities as the Ku Klux Klan, the Justice Department, and the impositions of the Volstead Act. Each opposed and impeded any form of modernity or liberalism, especially if African Americans seemed to crave and embrace modernity more readily than their white neighbors. Mencken, for example, admired Dean Kelly Miller of Howard University for his arguments in favor of full protection of African American suffrage and civil rights during and after the war.[40] Later in life, Mencken noted in his personal diary that Schuyler "is unquestionably the most competent Negro journalist ever heard of. Unlike nearly all the rest, he has no itch for public office, and is completely devoid of the usual cant."[41]

While Mencken's evaluation of Schuyler's ambitions could be applied to any period of his life, at this early stage Schuyler found the Army's decision to close the "regulated" Iwilei district to be yet another example of an efficient institution with a rational purpose destroyed by do-gooder spoilsports enthralled by irrational religious fervor, who could not perceive the glories of human sensuality. The result, typically, was chaos and disorder: homosexuality, excessive drunkenness, crime and venereal epidemics ("no police protection and no military clinic to protect the uniformed patrons from robbery and disease").[42] Schuyler's indifference to the situation of the women involved, to say nothing of his implicit homophobia, might give us pause today, but in the context of *Black and Conservative,* his later writings, and his admiration for Mencken, these concerns would have no place. Regulated, ordered satisfaction of pleasure for heterosexual males trumps putatively Christian moralism and sexualities routinely considered deviant at the time. In many respects, this stance both led to and resembles Schuyler's later denunciation of white racists' opposition to sexual liaisons between black men and white women as hypocritical, given the degree to which white males sexually exploited women of color, especially black women, in clandestine ways. In "Black Supremacy in Love," Schuyler writes that "no one more than casually acquainted with American life after dark can doubt that [white males endorse unions between themselves and black women]. From Canada to the Gulf the setting of the sun is the signal for the rush to the Black Belt and especially below the well known line of Messrs. Mason and Dixon," where, ironically, "the gendarmes periodically descend upon some Black Belt honky tonk and with great display of force and fierce fervor scatter or jail its customers and padlock its doors," invariably because "the joint has become a rendezvous for white women and black men."[43]

34   *Spoofing the Modern*

Schuyler's apparent preoccupation with the question of miscegenation and sexuality had both intellectual and personal roots. First, Schuyler understood, as many other African Americans did, that regulation and control of black male sexuality was a major cornerstone of white supremacy. As Ida B. Wells-Barnett had indicated years earlier, one of the excuses for lynching was to save white women from "rape" by black men. The truth of the matter was that "there are many white women in the South who would marry colored men if such an act would not place them at once beyond the pale of society and within the clutches of the law."[44] Wells-Barnett goes on to describe a grisly lynching in which the lynchers dragged the black victim accused of rape from his jail cell, while leaving inviolate a white prisoner who had raped an eight-year-old black girl.[45] Few African Americans in either Wells-Barnett's or Schuyler's time were under the illusion that the sexual divide established by white supremacy was intended never to be crossed. The frequency of miscegenation before, during, and after chattel slavery put the lie to that.

Second, Schuyler's later personal investment in this issue can be neither ignored nor denied. When he married the white Texan heiress Josephine Cogdell on January 6, 1928, in New York, it meant the severance of her ties to her family, and a lifetime of skeptical if not hostile stares and treatment from much of the world.[46] It was certainly not a legal status that Schuyler would have been able to discuss openly when he traveled in the South on behalf of the Pittsburgh *Courier* several years earlier from November 1925 to July 1926. None of this is to suggest that Schuyler's interest in miscegenation was the product of ardent desire for white women; no evidence of this exists. Neither does it mean that Schuyler stood continuously on the defense regarding his marital status. Instead, Schuyler wished to debunk extant myths, both social and pseudoscientific, regarding miscegenation. The crux of *Black No More's* plot turns upon the discovery that few "pure" blacks or whites exist in the United States, given the voluntary liaisons that occurred during the period in which indentured servants of both European and African origins mixed in their working and living quarters, to say nothing of involuntary and voluntary encounters during chattel slavery. The fear of miscegenation remained then, as now, one of the last bulwarks of "racial" division and white supremacy, and the one that evinces the most irrational responses. For the young Schuyler in the army, the issue was inescapable.

When his first enlistment ended, Schuyler re-enlisted for four years in November 1915 and returned to Hawai'i, where he soon earned an appointment to corporal in a different company. In 1916, Schuyler began contributing satirical pieces to the *Service*, a weekly magazine edited by civilians for the military, as well as columns for the Honolulu *Commercial Advertiser*. Schuyler also edited and published a company bulletin entitled the *Daily Dope*, containing news and more of the editor's trademark acerbic wit. Most of this material is lost, but we may safely assume that, like so many other military-oriented newsletters, the content focused upon the foolishness of the rank-and-file, with occasional jabs at perennially aloof officers. By the time he was finally discharged due to his desertion, Schuyler was certainly no stranger to iconoclastic journalism.

Schuyler and the Messenger

Schuyler's work at the *Messenger* may have had humble beginnings—his duties initially included substantial work of the clerical and janitorial variety—but he soon became a vital force on its editorial staff. A mere two months after the publication of his first essay, "Politics and the Negro," in April 1923, he was listed on the magazine's masthead as one of its contributing editors after Owen began to question the efficacy of the Socialist Party in the wake of a personal crisis.[47] In Owen's absence, Randolph relied more heavily upon Schuyler to manage the magazine's affairs and act as a cynical intellectual foil in much the same way Owen did prior to his personal troubles. Schuyler, deep-set cynic that he was, was more than happy to fulfill this role, despite the ludicrously low pay—ten dollars a week, or sixty per week in today's dollars—that Randolph offered him.

Schuyler's motivation for editing the magazine, however, was greater than the paltry monetary reward; he had an opportunity to use his "attractive writing style," in Randolph's words, to "[make] fun of everything—including socialism," thereby fulfilling his greatest calling. Moreover, Schuyler thrilled to have a cadre of intellectual peers in the form of Randolph's Friends of Negro Freedom organization, founded in May 1920, which, albeit ostensibly a political organization, was primarily a weekly bull session for Randolph and his friends. The attendees included Owen, Socialist Frank Crosswaith, progressive Robert Bagnall, NAACP official William Pickens, historian J. A. Rogers, Theophilus Lewis, and Schuyler. Although the organization would later be one of the many forces opposing the cult of personality that sprang up around Marcus Garvey and the UNIA (Universal Negro Improvement Association), it did little more at first than sponsor local lectures in Harlem and provide Harlem's stronger intellects an opportunity to gather and hash out the world's problems.[48] The intense parley that was invariably part of these gatherings supplied much of the material that Schuyler would later use for his columns in the *Messenger.*

Schuyler's career as a Socialist was a rather brief and comparatively passive one, so short that one wonders if he had any sincere investment in socialist ideals at all. From his early writings, though, we may easily argue that Schuyler's temporary subscription to socialism was but one of many opportunities he perceived to engage in intellectual debate with those individuals he considered his intellectual equals, and to emulate H. L. Mencken's own critique of American culture. By his own accounts, Schuyler's dedication to the Socialist Party had less to do with ideological affinity than with his need to avoid intellectual boredom.

On the surface, Schuyler's association with Randolph and Owen alone in any form would seem to indicate that their political views were highly similar. With their irreverent magazine and political activism, the two young Socialists had managed to run afoul of the U.S. Justice Department, risk prison sentences, and become regarded as two of the most dangerous Negroes in America. It would seem logical to assume, therefore, that as a regular contributor to and managing editor of the *Messenger* from 1923 until the magazine's folding in 1928, Schuyler was a dyed-in-the-wool radical.

The truth, predictably, was far more complex. In his autobiography, Schuyler indicates that any flirtation he might have had with the Socialist Party was at best brief and superficial compared to that of other *Messenger* staffers. His employment was far less an opportunity to advocate socialism than to gain invaluable experience as a journalist and editor. "The *Messenger* was a good place for a tireless, versatile young fellow to get plenty of activity and exercise. I swept and mopped the office when necessary, was first to arrive and last to leave, opened the mail and answered much of it, read manuscripts and proofs, corrected copy. . . . In between these chores I would take Randolph's dictation directly on the typewriter. Many a time we would stop and laugh over some Socialist cliché or dubious generalization, and at such times I realized Randolph was wiser than I had imagined."[49]

Moreover, Schuyler avers that Chandler Owen was even less dedicated to socialism than was co-publisher Randolph: "He had already seen through and rejected the Socialist bilge, and was jeering at the Bolshevist twaddle at a time when most intellectuals were speaking of the 'Soviet experiment' with reverence. Incongruously his conversation contradicted or disputed everything for which the *Messenger* professed to stand. He dubbed the Socialists as frauds who actually cared little more for Negroes than did the then-flourishing Ku Klux Klan."[50] According to Schuyler, Owen's strange disputation of his own magazine's editorial stance stemmed from personal observations of and encounters with hypocritical Marxists and Socialists who refused to back their own party lines.

In the early days of their affiliation, though, Schuyler, Randolph, and Owen downplayed such problems in favor of the promising ideals socialism offered. Schuyler's affiliation with the *Messenger*'s editors was less a precise collusion of political views than a basic ideological agreement regarding the plight of African Americans, the importance of some type of collective uplift, and a vehicle that would, at the very least, get African Americans to become more scientific and rational regarding their situation. All three men agreed that African Americans were living in a nation with a deeply entrenched racial caste system begun and perpetuated for the sake of the exploitation of black labor and bodies. Each believed that racism, no matter who practiced or supported it, was a pernicious part of American society and could be abated, if not destroyed, by being carefully and systematically exposed as an intellectual and social fraud. If each man held some reservations about socialism, their consensus was that racism undergirded by American capitalism remained the greater fraud. Socialism was, at the very least, one means to the end of eradicating racist laws and practices in the nation. In short, despite their differences, all three men were progressives on racial questions, even if they were decidedly conservative on other issues.

Perhaps most important was the common rhetorical expression these men chose for their beliefs. Journalism was Schuyler's calling and career, and he was among the best at it in the country, and certainly one of the greatest African American journalists ever. Over a forty-year career at the Pittsburgh *Courier*, Schuyler documented the political, cultural, and social lives of African Americans throughout the country with the ideal of journalistic objectivity squarely in mind. He made many trips to the South on behalf of the *Courier* in the 1920s and 1930s, both to solicit subscriptions and to investigate the conditions in which African Americans lived in the region whence the New Negro had ultimately sprung. Those conditions, in turn, provided Schuyler with ample material for his satirical barbs and slowly transformed his writing from bon mots, quips, and false news items to parodic short plays and stories that provided the fodder for his satirical and fantastic novels.

In July 1923, three months after Schuyler first appeared on the *Messenger's* masthead, "Shafts and Darts" made its first appearance. The column began and ended with Schuyler as sole author, but most of its strongest material appeared after Schuyler's friend and regular *Messenger* drama critic Theophilus Lewis joined the fray. The oft-quoted raison d'être for the column, published seven months after the column's first appearance and upon the first occasion of Lewis's collaboration, remains a precise representation of both the column's critical stance and of Schuyler's outlook as an intellectual:

> [Our] intention is . . . to slur, lampoon, damn and occasionally praise anybody or anything in the known universe, not excepting the President of the immortals. . . . Furthermore [we] make no effort to conceal the fact that [our] dominant motive is a malicious one and that our paragraphs of praise shall be few and far between, while [we] go to greater lengths to discover and expose the imbecilities, knavery and pathological virtues of [our] fellowman. . . . If any considerable body of Americans were intelligent in the human sense, or even civilized, . . . their manly and dignified behavior would be copied. . . . It pains this pair of misanthropes even to think of such a state of affairs, and they fervently hope their excursions into morbid humor will not be confused with the crusade of benevolent killjoys to change America."[51]

Spoofing the Modern

Schuyler and Lewis echo here the tenor of Mencken at his most caustic. As Scruggs writes, for both Mencken and Schuyler "the world was made up of knaves, fools, and a few honest men. The fools comprised the bulk of mankind, and the knaves and the honest men were constantly at war over their souls. Usually the knaves prevailed, but the honest men never quite gave up, never quite despaired altogether."[52] If the *Messenger* was not always successful in its mission of convincing the black masses of their need for socialism, "Shafts and Darts" was inarguably successful at delivering its promised misanthropy, undiluted cynicism, and frequently brilliant satire to its audience. It is perhaps for this reason that Langston Hughes judged Schuyler's columns to be "the most interesting things in the magazine."[53] Positing themselves as the "honest men" of Scruggs's assessment, Schuyler and Lewis replenished the stream of cynicism that had been reduced to a slow trickle as Randolph and Owen became distracted by other affairs and as the magazine had attempted, with limited success, to broaden its readership.

By the time "Shafts and Darts" entered the *Messenger's* regular lineup, the magazine had already shifted noticeably to the center from its original far-left position. Although still an organ of racial and economic uplift for African Americans, it lost much of its original socialist firebrand journalistic stance in favor of rhetoric that generally would not have raised an eyebrow if it had been published in the NAACP's *Crisis* or the Urban League's *Opportunity*. This does not mean that the magazine had become conservative; Randolph and his contributing editors consistently blasted individuals and organizations that discriminated against African Americans, and, as the eventual organ of the Brotherhood of Sleeping Car Porters, the *Messenger* was by definition a pro-labor publication. But the magazine was no longer in danger of bringing the burden of sedition charges upon the editors' heads. Its only major burden was finding sufficient sponsors to finance issues every month.

"Shafts and Darts": Finding the Targets

By July 1923, George Schuyler must have felt as if he had found his proper niche at the *Messenger*. The extreme disorganization he found when he first arrived at the magazine's offices had been corrected largely through his strong discipline.[54] Its finances—never stable—were at least manageable, and the editorial stance had by now shifted slightly away from the austere socialism of the earliest years. This brought in a readership that went beyond radical circles. Schuyler quickly resolved to extend the journal's content beyond the "solemn and serious" fare found in most African American publications. "Shaft and Darts" was indeed as iconoclastic as Schuyler and Lewis advertised it to be. The most popular targets were groups and individuals who represented the worst of American racism, such as President Wilson, the Ku Klux Klan, and Senator Bilbo. Even fellow leftists who agreed with some of the magazine's positions were not spared. Schuyler took special glee in mocking the political irrelevancy of the African Blood Brotherhood, a Marxist, sometimes anti-Garvey cadre whose members included respected poet Claude McKay and former *Messenger* contributing editor Cyril V. Briggs. At its height, the ABB had some seven thousand dues-paying members, but since those dues—25 cents or whatever members could afford—were paid on the honor system, its finances were never stable. By the third month, the opening feature of each column was the "Monthly Award," which first consisted of an "elegantly embossed and beautifully lacquered dill pickle" to be given to the individual most responsible for the "mirth of the nation" in the news. This later became a "beautiful cutglass thunder-mug." Recipients of the Monthly Award, if African American leaders, had either to display their obsequiousness and accommodation of racism, or to reveal their lack of insight. Regular recipients in the first category were Du Bois, Alain Locke, Kelly Miller, Moton, and radical Ben Davis; in the second, the ABB, Garvey, and the UNIA.

Garvey was by far the favorite target of Schuyler and Lewis's ire, especially during the precipitous fall from grace resulting from Garvey's federal trial for mail fraud. The calumny was merciless; Garvey was dubbed "Emperor Marcus du Sable," "Emperor Marcus the First," "The African Potentate," "Provisional President of Africa," and many other dubious honorifics. To be fair, at least a few of the titles Schuyler bestowed upon Garvey were simply titles that the UNIA leader had already given to himself. Schuyler therefore had little trouble touting Garvey as an arrogant fool; all he needed was Garvey's very public image and pretensions as the future leader of a re-colonized "Africa for the Africans" who somehow managed to alienate many of his purported followers. Moreover, compared to earlier diatribes printed in the *Messenger* and elsewhere, some of Schuyler's columns appear almost tame. The most infamous of the former would be Reverend Robert Bagnall's infamous assessment of Garvey as a

Jamaican Negro of unmixed stock, squat, stocky, fat, and sleek, with protruding jaws, and heavy jowls, small bright pig-like eyes and rather bull-dog-like face. Boastful, egotistic, tyrannical, intolerant, cunning shifty, smooth and suave, avaricious; . . . as adept as a cuttle-fish in beclouding an issue he cannot meet, prolix in the *n*th degree in devising new schemes to gain the money of poor ignorant Negroes; gifted at self-advertisement, without shame in self-laudation, promising ever, but never fulfilling, without regard for veracity, a lover of pomp and tawdry finery and garish display, a bully with his own folk but servile in the presence of the Klan, a sheer opportunist and demagogic charlatan.[55]

Bagnall's invective—of which Schuyler borrowed freely in subsequent "Shafts and Darts" columns—is particularly vicious for the time, but hardly unique in the pages of the *Messenger,* whose editors had been waging an open war of words against Garvey and the UNIA for nearly a year. The "Garvey Must Go" campaign started after Garvey admitted that he had conferred with the Ku Klux Klan's kleagle, Edward Young Clarke, in 1922 and argued in subsequent columns, like Clarke, that since African Americans were living in a white man's country, where whites made the rules, they had little cause to complain about how they were treated. Far better, Garvey asserted, for people of the African Diaspora to have their own nation, where they were responsible for all, and therefore not required to petition for equal treatment. "Prejudice of the white race against the black race," Garvey wrote, "is not so much because of color as of condition; because as a race, to them, we have accomplished nothing; we have built no nation, no government; because we are dependent for our economic and political existence."[56]

Garvey's rather startling break with the essential position of the NAACP and other uplift organizations persuaded the *Messenger's* editors and their associates, including Bagnall, that Garvey's influence and popular leadership made him a significant menace to the struggle for civil rights. The foci of the Friends of Negro Freedom's activities became Garvey's condemnation, isolation, and deportation; their campaign slogan was "Garvey Must Go!" With the conspicuous leadership of Chandler Owen and the *Messenger* as a major vehicle, the push to send Garvey back to Jamaica evolved into a significant conflict within the ranks of African American intellectuals that the black woman or man on the street could see played out in the *Messenger* and Garvey's *Negro World.* The conflict extended all the way to the U.S. Justice Department, which received a letter from Owen and his cohort calling for Garvey's arrest and trial on various charges, as well as his deportation as an undesirable alien.

Theodore Kornweibel illustrates that, in many ways, the viciousness of the attacks upon Garvey served poorly to improve the discourse amongst black intellectuals. In fact, it either created or deepened intragroup rifts that remain sore points within African American intellectual and social circles until the present. First, the conflict represented an ideological dispute regarding the desirability of assimilation both for African Americans vis-à-vis the white majority in the United States, and for other peoples of the African Diaspora, particularly in the Caribbean. Second, the dispute highlighted real differences and demeaning stereotypes that stood between American blacks and blacks from Caribbean nations. Finally, the conflict relied upon color-caste prejudices and class differences among these same peoples, with Garvey as the primary exemplar of the "unmixed Negro," and such "mulattos" as Owen, Du Bois, and James Weldon Johnson lambasted for their lack of biological purity and race loyalty.

All of these rifts pushed the fight between the Friends of Negro Freedom and the UNIA to go beyond the virulent rhetoric that defined it and into physical violence as UNIA members frequently disrupted FNF meetings.[57] In September 1922 a package from New Orleans arrived at *Messenger* offices containing a white man's severed hand, accompanied by a note warning Randolph that the author wanted to "see [Randolph's] name in your nigger improvement association as a member, paid up too, in about a week from now," or his hand would be sent to someone else.[58] This horrific parcel was followed a week later by a note signed by "KKK," informing Randolph and Owen "we don't want niggers like you here."[59] To this day, definite proof of the sender's identity has yet to emerge, although some evidence points to UNIA lieutenants posing as the Klan for the sake of intimidating the editors. In any event, Randolph published both of these incidents in the *Messenger,* accompanied by editorials emphasizing that the "Klan had come to the rescue of its Negro leader, Marcus Garvey."[60] The intensity of the anti-Garvey campaign soon revealed how the opposition to Garvey had as much to do with his heritage and color as with his politics. Bagnall's infamous assessment was hardly worse than Chandler Owen's relentless linking of the terms "West Indian" and "Negro" to "ignorant" and "savage," thus playing into the hands of both white racists and anti-West Indian or color-struck African Americans, who could see little common ground with blacks from the Caribbean. When Owen, Bagnall, William Pickens, and several others sent Attorney General Harry M. Daugherty a letter asking for Garvey to be deported as an undesirable alien, they committed themselves to a course of action that went against everything the *Messenger* supported as a putatively Socialist organ. As Kornweibel highlights, the irony of the magazine seeking Garvey's expulsion just two years after finally being freed from the political persecutions of the Justice Department and the U.S. Post Office is inescapable.[61]

In the short term, the campaign caused the *Messenger's* W. A. Domingo, a Jamaican immigrant and stalwart critic of Garvey, to challenge Owen's position on the Garvey question, then quit the magazine. The unintended and more deleterious long-term legacy of the conflict was that Black Nationalists who arose in Garvey's wake were able to use the class and color facets of the dispute to their advantage for many years to come. Garvey and his lieutenants argued, with substantial evidence to support their position, that many of the mainstream African American leaders either hated those of the lower classes, or their own black selves. Even more troubling, the nativist sentiments the anti-Garveyites expressed sounded little better than the anti-immigrant, anti-radical "100% Americanism" platform of the hated Ku Klux Klan. If Garvey was guilty of rubbing shoulders with the Klan and southern whites, then his black opponents unconsciously found themselves rubbing ideological shoulders with the very enemy they condemned Garvey for accommodating, the same enemy that would cheer at the moment of their extirpation.

Schuyler and Garvey

Although the anti-Garvey campaign in the *Messenger's* editorial pages lasted less than eighteen months between July 1922 and the end of 1923, Schuyler the satirist dined out for many years on the African potentate's demise. After Garvey's arrest, Schuyler drily noted in his October 1923 column that "Garvey's 2,000,000 (sic) members were mighty slow getting that $25,000 [bail] together. One Negro paper announced 'Garvey Not to Jump Bail,' as if you could run that guy away from this gravy-train! It is to laugh!"[62] In the wake of the "Garvey Must Go" campaign, Garvey's meeting with the Ku Klux Klan, and the decidedly ill fate of the UNIA's Black Star Line—comprising four old ships, freighters and yachts, none particularly seaworthy and all purchased by the UNIA for well above their actual value,—Schuyler had enough fodder against Garvey to last him years, well beyond Garvey's conviction and imprisonment in 1924 and deportation in 1927. For Schuyler, Garvey was not only a fool, but yet another charlatan who secretly admired the same oppressor against whom he inveighed and possessed a phantom following. Garvey did command a substantial following among African Americans and in the Caribbean, albeit never as great as he claimed.

Schuyler never intended his calumny to acknowledge the positive influence that Garvey has wielded over time by encouraging African Americans to take control of their own identities, economies, and histories via the sort of black nationalism that Schuyler sometimes favored. Rather, Schuyler found Garvey the same as any other leader in that his leadership had at least as much to do with rhetoric, ambition, a swaggering image, and the gullibility of the masses as it did with visionary ideas. The height of Schuyler's personal crusade against Garvey may be found not in "Shafts and Darts," ironically, but rather in July 1924's separate "A Tribute to Caesar" column, a perfect example of what Leon Guilhamet calls "demonstrative satire," a mock oration extolling the dubious virtues of the subject.[63] Schuyler berates Garvey's critics for failing to recognize his leadership abilities, in particular his propensity to lead his followers away from their money and good sense and towards the arms of the Ku Klux Klan.[64] In Schuyler's hands, Garvey's decidedly ill-fated Black Star Line of cargo ships and yachts becomes the stuff of legend, since no other crew before it managed "to quaff $350,000 worth of liquor" and "signal the historic message 'Save Us. We Are Drinking.'"[65] Schuyler saves special relish for the routine denunciation of racism by white oppressors in the UNIA's *Negro World*, while "the hair straightening and skin-whitening ads can hold their own with those in any Negro weekly" and the publication "is printed . . . by a friendly white printer" when "the New York *Age* press (Negro) [is] one block west."[66]

Garvey's sins in Schuyler's eyes are many, but none are more severe than the vast difference between the would-be potentate's visionary rhetoric calling for a new, modern age for the African Diaspora and his rather pedestrian—albeit spectacularly public—flaws. Garvey becomes no better than the typical demagogue or opportunistic politician. In the "Shafts and Darts" column of August 1924, Schuyler and Lewis transmogrify him into their candidate for U.S. president, Mr. Amos Hokum, whose wisdom in gauging "the strength of Klan sentiment months before the Republicans and Democrats took a tumble" and realizing "that the Klan spirit is virtually indistinguishable from the Spirit of the U.S.A." makes him the most viable for the position.[67] The populist appeal of both Garvey and the mythical Hokum reveals that populism has little to do with the slow, complex workings of democracy; it is but a manifestation of the "boobocracy" that rejects the rational for the expedient.

The timing of Schuyler and Lewis's attacks upon Garvey at this point warrant some attention, inasmuch as each missive seems designed to maintain the momentum of the "Garvey Must Go!" campaign long after the Friends of Negro Freedom had ceased having any influence in the matter at all. By mid-1924, Garvey had long been convicted of mail fraud due to his solicitation of investors in the Black Star Line, and was free on bail as his appeals made their way through the courts. Both during and after the original trial, such Garvey critics as W. E. B. Du Bois took great pains to highlight Garvey's actions as his own attorney, often reducing them to "monkey-shines" that underscored the accuracy of his opponents' allegations against him. In his most heated editorial against the leader, Du Bois wrote that "no Negro in America ever had a fairer and more patient trial than Marcus Garvey," who "convicted himself by his own admissions, his swaggering monkey-shines in the court room with monocle and long tailed coat and his insults to the judge and prosecuting attorney."[68] Up to this point, Du Bois's public critique of Garvey in print had been pointedly critical, but retained the air of objectivity. His January 1921 column, "Marcus Garvey," concludes that Garvey "is a sincere, hard-working idealist; he is also a stubborn, domineering leader of the mass; he has worthy industrial and commercial schemes but he is an inexperienced business man. His dreams of Negro industry, commerce and the ultimate freedom of Africa are feasible; but his methods are bombastic, wasteful, illogical and ineffective and almost illegal." "If," Du Bois continues, "he learns by experience, attracts strong and capable friends . . . instead of making needless enemies; if he gives up secrecy and suspicion and substitutes open and frank reports . . . he may yet in time succeed in at least starting some of his schemes toward accomplishment."[69] A year and a half later, Du Bois devoted an extremely detailed editorial to the Black Star Line and Garvey's defense of it in his trial, illustrating in intricate detail that Garvey's pursuit and execution of a role in the shipping business was, at best, incompetent and irresponsible and, in the words of presiding judge Panken, predicated upon the "'gullibility'" of Garvey's followers. Du Bois quotes one such formerly loyal follower as proof that the tide of skepticism was turning against Garvey.[70] Du Bois takes equal pains in all of these columns to deny what many contemporary observers as well as subsequent scholars understood: professional envy on the part of mainstream leaders. "American Negro leaders are not jealous of Garvey," Du Bois insists, "they are not envious of his success;

they are simply afraid of his failure, for his failure would be theirs."[71] Not envy but fear of embarrassment for the "race" in the eyes of whites drives his opponents.

As Kornweibel and Anderson have shown, though, some degree of jealousy had to affect why, when, and how Garvey's opponents attacked him. Anderson quotes Randolph allowing that "all of us had to admit . . . that [Garvey] was an organizational genius. He organized more Negroes than any other single Negro in the history of this country. His impact upon black pride and consciousness—though not always with the best result—was tremendous."[72] The extent of Garvey's organizational skills represented everything that other leaders, Randolph, Owen, and Du Bois notwithstanding, would have gladly enjoyed, had they the pulse of the African American masses to the extent Garvey did, or if they possessed his charisma. Garvey possessed one crucial trait that separated him from his rivals: largely independent financial support. Whatever may be said about the failure of Garvey's business enterprises and other organizations, their funding came overwhelmingly from blacks in the United States and the Caribbean. To one extent or another, Randolph, Owen, Bagnall, Du Bois, and many others relied upon support from whites, and therefore had to compromise with people who might not always have African Americans' best interests at heart.[73] As Kornweibel and other critics have shown, though, Garvey failed to realize how his ideological hero, Booker T. Washington, fit this same description even as he condemned his rivals for accepting white people's dollars.[74]

Behind the veil of rationalism, Schuyler could and did deny accusations of professional envy; after all, Schuyler had few if any designs upon leadership, and when he first arrived as a civilian in New York, he did stay for a brief period at the Phillis Wheatley Hotel on 135th Street (which the UNIA operated), attended UNIA meetings, and read *Negro World*, the organization's newspaper.[75] This made Schuyler somewhat more authoritative in his views of the actual worth of UNIA enterprises. Neither his nor the *Messenger's* judgment was kind. In his scathing "Reply to Marcus Garvey," Randolph dismissed the UNIA's operations by spitting, "these two-by-four, dirty, dingy, mismanaged dumps, misnamed enterprises are a liability instead of an asset. They are a disgrace instead of a credit. They are rat holes in which to dump money. Nobody but an idiot would mention them as an achievement."[76] In "A Tribute to Caesar," Schuyler writes,

It is Marcus Garvey's success as an industrial magnate that grips the imagination. Think of the nation-wide chain of grocery stores, tailor shops and factories that spring into being at his Aladdin touch! What other Negro can point to such an achievement? Without the racial solidarity that Mr. Garvey preached to his followers, the entire 2,000,000 might have traded elsewhere and allowed these magnificent businesses to fail. But they stuck loyally to him and now nearly all the white merchants have withdrawn from Harlem and left Mr. Garvey's enterprises in possession of the field. I know personally of only about 4,000 white businesses in the Negro community.[77]

Garvey was an organizer par excellence, but the economic impact of his movement could never be classified an unqualified success. If it was difficult for the *Messenger*/Friends of Negro Freedom crowd to convince African Americans to organize, they at least enjoyed watching Garvey misapply the lessons in industry and self-reliance he took from Booker T. Washington. Whereas Washington conceded power to southern whites to obtain and preserve his own place of eminence among black leaders, Garvey never obtained the power his predecessor enjoyed. Whether the UNIA's businesses were as filthy and decrepit as Randolph and Schuyler described them is practically irrelevant; for Schuyler, the fact that all the financial power at the African potentate's command did not result in an *independent* black community in Harlem—which was still a relatively small enclave in 1924, compared to its present boundaries—not only cast serious doubt upon his program of racial uplift, but also highlighted the extent to which it was predicated upon irrationality. A major challenge of any nationalist movement, black or otherwise, is to convince potential followers that they constitute a nation, and should patronize only those businesses run by members of the defined nation. They should do so despite any extra expense or inconvenience required, which goes against basic economic principles. Making this case is a challenge that the UNIA failed in the short term. It pointed to a modernity of its own, in which people of African descent would throw off the shackles of psychological imprisonment and colonialism, but it eschewed the logic that ideally should accompany modernity.

Schuyler, like Mencken, simultaneously championed modernity while feigning blindness to the potential of African American leaders and institutions to reshape the face of African American culture and to give it a narrative. Despite portraying these leaders as a collection of mountebanks and charlatans, Schuyler also owed them a number of great intellectual debts, many of which are revealed in his columns. In the item "The Klan versus the Negro" within his January 1927 "Shafts and Darts," for example, Schuyler echoes Alain Locke's argument in "The New Negro" that African Americans "have touched too closely" their white counterparts "at the unfavorable level and too lightly at the favorable levels" and are, in fact, "radical on race matters, conservative on others," and therefore more in league with their white counterparts than a first glance reveals.[78] As Schuyler puts it, "on Catholicism, the average Negro being a raging Protestant, is in agreement with the Klansman. Few are in the Catholic church and most of them interviewed express fear of Papal domination. They insist on being booted by their own native Protestant white folks."[79] The comparison, of course, is unflattering, but Schuyler's project highlights the degree

Spoofing the Modern

to which African Americans and whites alike resist most strains of modernity, to the detriment of "social progress," which Schuyler declares in the same column to be as much a fraud as a personal God and the sanctity of the U.S. Constitution.[80] Such recent critics as W. Lawrence Hogue have argued that the Enlightenment ideal of human progress has served the interests of racists more than those of African Americans, inasmuch as it has historically allowed those who would delimit black progress to cite the alleged inability of African Americans to progress on their own to maintain the status quo.

In contrast, though, Schuyler argues ironically for a sort of intellectual elitism that both resounds with Du Bois's championing of the Talented Tenth, the "better men" of the race who shall save it, and presages the writings of Ayn Rand, who later became one of Schuyler's acquaintances in the anticommunist ranks of the 1940s and 1950s. In the same January 1927 column, Schuyler decries public education as a means to transform illiterate independent thinkers into intellectual snobs and camp followers: "Better to go back to illiteracy, in which sad state one's opinions are at least one's own rather than those of libidinous clergymen, neurotic philosophers and reptile editors. . . . Popular education is a waste of time and money and helps no one but the yokel fleecers."[81] Modernity cannot be found in an institution, a movement, or a consensus; it must come from a decentered attack upon orthodoxies, akin in some ways to Hogue's polycentric ideal, in which the intellectual trends of the moment remain subject to continuous scrutiny.[82] The link between Schuyler and Du Bois, whom the former continually lampooned, may also be found in the latter's pragmatic view of human progress in the 1920s, which deferred any dogmatic adherence to ideology.[83]

Schuyler argued that the only consistent ideology dominating American life was white supremacy, as it dominated all forms of economic, social, and sexual interactions. Americans, black and white, will generally resist modernity in all its forms precisely because it undermines white supremacy. In the rare instance in which each "race" makes a half-hearted attempt to achieve "uplift," it is only in the most superficial forms, and only for the sake of reifying white supremacy. In his unpublished manuscript "How to Be Happy, though Colored," Schuyler includes a chapter ("Our Comic Contribution") noting that in the major Western democracies—the United States, Britain, and France—people of African descent have great value to all whites, especially the poor and uneducated, precisely because they have always occupied a position of inferiority highlighted by their comedic skills. "How different this country would be," Schuyler opines, in mock wistfulness, "without the happy Negro. The Smiling Sambo stereotype is part and parcel of our national heritage. Deprived of this eternal comic character with his oft-depicted sausage lips, rolling orbs, shuffling gait, whining speech, tonsil-revealing laughter, genial incompetence, comical ignorance, petty-criminal propensities, and general indifference to everything worth while, America might quickly become a very different place. . . . His seemingly perpetual degradation has buoyed up the moronic millions vaguely conscious of their inferiority and fearful of the future."[84] A future in which African Americans transformed by "growing literacy, popular miseducation and the sinister influence of the democratic dogma" would begin "openly expressing anger over certain hallowed American customs like lynching, disfranchisement, segregation and color discrimination." Schuyler continues by berating any fellow African Americans who might commit the unpardonable sin of refusing to serve as "national jesters, omnipresent for purposes of invidious comparison," as this might upset the delicate balance of white supremacy.[85]

In few instances is Schuyler's affinity to Mencken more apparent. Charles Scruggs examines Mencken's attitude toward post–World War I America, in which "the old American virtues had disappeared: 'Free discussion, general tolerance, and a fair fight,'" to be replaced by "'government by usurpation and tyranny, a complete collapse of national decency . . . the bitter and senseless persecutions of minorities, Know-Nothingism, Ku Kluxism, terrorism and espionage,'" supporting a system of barbarism and lynching that despises anything evoking either beauty or liberalism.[86] To be sublime, or to engage in activities that require subtle, careful thinking, violates a creed that keeps Americans mired in parochialism, and therefore easily swayed by leaders barely more informed than they. Little wonder, then, that Schuyler gleefully lampooned William J. Simmons, founder of the modern Ku Klux Klan, in *Black No More* as Imperial Grand Wizard Rev. Henry Givens of the Knights of Nordica. When Givens encounters black protagonist Max Disher, who is passing as white Matthew Fisher and posing as an anthropologist supporting white supremacy, he ruminates 'Anthropology. Better git that word straight 'fore I go talkin' too much about it. . . . Humn! Humn! . . . That boy must know a hull lot.' He read over the definition of the word twice without understanding it, and then cutting off a large chew of tobacco from his plug, he leaned back in his swivel chair to rest after the unaccustomed mental exertion."[87]

Similar to Mencken's notorious 1920 essay, "The Sahara of the Bozart," Schuyler's portrayal of the white South is a picture, in Mencken's words, that

gives one the creeps. It is as if the Civil War stamped out every last bearer of the torch, and left only a mob of peasants on the field. One thinks of Asia Minor, resigned to Armenians, Greeks, and wild swine, of Poland abandoned to the Poles. In all the gargantuan paradise of the fourth-rate there is not a single picture gallery worth going into, or a single orchestra capable of playing the nine symphonies of Beethoven, or a single opera-house, or a single theater devoted to decent plays, or single public monument that is worth looking at, or a single workshop devoted to the making of beautiful things. . . . There is not even a

Spoofing the Modern

bad [critic] between the Potomac mud-flats and the Gulf. Nor a historian. Nor a philosopher. Nor a theologian. Nor a scientist. In all these fields the South is an awe-inspiring blank—a brother to Portugal, Serbia and Albania.[88]

Mencken's vilifying assessment of the South rests upon several factors, not the least of which is his low opinion of entire European nations and ethnicities, which he in turn bases upon common contemporary prejudices (hence the essay's inclusion in the second volume of Mencken's *Prejudices*) of their peoples, per eugenic categories. In other parts of the essay, Mencken acknowledges the rich, folk-based cultures emerging among black southerners, but fails to mention such intellectuals as W. E. B. Du Bois—formerly affiliated with Atlanta University, where he garnered great renown for his researches—and other black educators. In his defense, in 1920 Mencken barely knew any African American intellectuals, directly or indirectly. The essay, of course, cannot be read as a fair or balanced assessment of the region; it is filled with absolutist satiric invective intended not only to excoriate the South, but also to inspire a "revival of Southern letters," which Mencken later argued it aided.[89]

Schuyler's own view of the South in his *Messenger* columns evolved from his reading of Mencken, his own travels through the region in 1925–26, and the folk-centered, anthropological view of Zora Neale Hurston, whom Schuyler admired as "one of the soundest writers" of the period, who "was earthy and a product of the earth; she wrote about what she knew, and if it didn't always present the Negro as a . . . tailored gentleman or a Paris-gowned lady . . . she wasn't ashamed of it."[90] Mencken took a more generalized, abstract view of the region, placing its history in the context of the foundational myths of the nation. Mencken blasted Virginia as a fallen nation of sorts, precisely because he "loved it," and bemoaned the temporal and intellectual distance between its colonial days and his present, in which it could lead no nation to greatness.[91] Where Mencken found both Virginia and the South full of bellicose, uncultured savages, Schuyler and Hurston saw it as a collection of states, regions, communities, and individuals that resisted broad portraits. Hurston's celebrated portrayals of her cherished hometown, Eatonville, Florida, underscore her desire to show through an all-black community the diversity of African American lives and experiences. For "The Eatonville Anthology," serialized in the *Messenger* from September through November 1926, Hurston drew from childhood memories of her native town to show that its citizens contained most aspects of humanity, from the depraved to the heroic, and every stage between. For Schuyler, Hurston's writing stood against the "racket" that his peers "were making out of Negro art[,] that they were going to create something segregated and different, even though they were products of this culture. That seemed to me to be ridiculous. Many of the things that they were branding and stamping into Negro work—the Negro—they were just American, and happened to be the expression of people who suffered restrictions and discrimination and all."[92] Hurston, on the other hand, was "one of the soundest" writers of the movement for seeing African Americans as "just American," and "for that reason she wasn't too popular among these others."[93] Besides her iconoclasm, Schuyler found in Hurston a sincere appreciation for the vagaries of black southern life, which he may have found useful as he collected during his travels below the Mason-Dixon Line.

Schuyler and Hurston's shared view finds one of its most caustic and (in)famous expressions in Schuyler's 1926 *Nation* essay, "The Negro-Art Hokum," which declares "Negro" art a fantasy generated by simpletons unwittingly buying into the same racialist thinking as the Ku Klux Klan.[94] Schuyler argues that African Americans are "lampblacked Anglo-Saxons," raised in the same nation, educated in the same school systems, worshipping the same and exposed to the same culture as their white counterparts. This leads educated African Americans to read the same books, write in the same language, and as a consequence, absorb the same philosophies and prejudices as their fellow citizens. Such musical expressions of African American folklife as sorrow songs, Negro spirituals, the blues, and jazz are "foreign to Northern Negroes, West Indian Negroes and African Negroes," as they are produced by African Americans of a certain region—the South—and only those of the lower classes.[95] Schuyler contends that the blues are similar to other musical forms produced among the peasantry of other nations; they are not so unique as black intellectuals and artists such as James Weldon Johnson, W. E. B. Du Bois, and Alain Locke would have their audiences—with the white members of those audiences named explicitly—believe.

Schuyler clearly intends to dismiss the prevailing order of the New Negro movement, but not for its own sake. The "Monthly Award" that Schuyler delighted in presenting in his "Shafts and Darts" columns went most often to the aforementioned leaders primarily for any instance in which they seemed to be accommodating the prejudices of whites. In Schuyler's view, going "hat in hand" to whites often meant rubbing shoulders with the Klan, like Marcus Garvey; conceding the futility of voting (like Rev. Charles Plummer of Lower Institute and Industrial School, South Carolina);[96] or accepting segregation (whether Garvey or John L. Webb, supreme custodian of the Woodmen of Union, May 1926).[97] In a broader sense, Schuyler found *any* acceptance of common beliefs about the inherent difference of African Americans, arguments that they are more or less capable, or that they have a greater or lesser affinity for any type of art or expression to be one more step towards being a "descendant of the renowned Uncle Tom."[98]

Schuyler appeared to apply this argument inconsistently. Beginning in February 1926, he incorporated the feature "Aframerican Fables" within "Shafts and Darts," consisting of fantasies in which African Americans would behave rationally, instead of according to cultural traditions and stereotypes. In the March 1926 column,

Schuyler imagines a lecture by a Negro leader in a hall "nearly filled with people," which the dreamer believes has to be a blues concert or revue, but discovers is instead "an educational meeting" that has attracted a large crowd. The host "concludes a simple introduction inside of five minutes," and the "audience is all attention. No one is trying to hold a conversation with a friend four rows away." The lecturer himself discusses his subject without referring to "God, Jesus Christ, Abraham Lincoln, Theodore Roosevelt, the Negro's patriotism and devotion to the United States, or his great progress since emancipation."[99] In short, the lecture proceeds without any trace of hokum or balderdash, specifically the platitudes that degrade African Americans simply by insulting their intelligence and pandering to their insecurities and fears. Although Schuyler berates his black audience for failing to give its due to rational leaders, it is the leaders themselves that have helped maintain a cycle of obsequiousness that obviates any possibility of progress.

Throughout his work for the *Messenger,* this fundamental argument undergirds Schuyler's art. The icons that he and the editors lampoon deserve derision precisely because each has at some point relinquished any hold upon a rational approach to African Americans' problems. Rather than remain bold and independent, they have conceded ground to the forces of Mencken's "booboisie" and "Philistines," hating beauty, the sublime, and the rational precisely because, when they are combined, they offer possibilities for new worlds, for thought that could eventually lead to economic and political equality for African Americans.[100] If Schuyler failed himself to see how a group identity, or at least alliances along "racial" lines, could lead to this same end through circuitous and tortured routes, his place as an *agent provocateur* in the midst of his peers at least ensured that the movement toward that space would continue. "The Negro-Art Hokum" purposely brought about Langston Hughes's famous rejoinder, "The Negro Artist and the Racial Mountain,"[101] while Schuyler's columns for the *Messenger* and other publications had a profound, if controversial, effect upon his readers. Schuyler would report decades later that "from what others have told me through the years . . . appearing in [H. L. Mencken's] *The American Mercury* was regarded as something, and if a Negro was good enough to appear in *The American Mercury,* then there must be other Negroes who could write as well or better, and so they did. So many Negroes wrote for *The American Mercury* . . . that can't help but influence the minds of enlightened and liberal people. All this, I think was a contributory factor to the development of the Negro renaissance or writing group."[102] Making such gradual, careful inroads into a larger, national consciousness remained at the heart of Schuyler's philosophy. Proclaiming the superiority of black art and culture could never obtain the same results, as it lacked the simple power of the forceful, if rational, intellect invading the old, and replacing it with the modern new.

3

Wallace Thurman, Richard Bruce Nugent, and the Reification of "Race," Aesthetics, and Sexuality

Their laughter struck me for perhaps the first time. It was not the
joyous laughter which—God knows why—one associates with children. It was mocking and insular, its intent was to denigrate. It was
disenchanted, and in this, also, lay the authority of their curses.

James Baldwin, "Sonny's Blues"

In early 1928, Wallace Thurman sent a letter introducing himself to Jamaican émigré poet Claude McKay, one of the leading lights of the New Negro Renaissance.
After thanking McKay for admiring his contributions to *Fire!!*, the magazine Thurman edited a little more than a year earlier, the young writer surmised that McKay
"must either think me a highly conceited ass or just a plain damn fool" for attempting to challenge the dominant course of African American literature and art.[1]
Although Thurman's modest self-assessment is quite facetious, it also resembles the
view some of his contemporaries held of him. At times, Thurman provided considerable evidence to support such estimations. He indulged liberally in many of the
Harlem Renaissance's sensual, sexual, and artistic excesses even as he publicly decried these same problems in scathing essays and novels, and privately professed his
lack of faith in the idea of the New Negro. Thurman directed no small amount of his
antipathy towards himself, whether through coded terms in his published critiques,
or in haunting unpublished essays that reveal a writer simultaneously desirous of
fame and success, yet utterly convinced that such lofty goals were beyond his powers and native abilities.

Unsurprisingly, Thurman's vehement cries of protest against the excesses of his peers did little, if anything, to help cut him an impressive figure in African American literary history. By all accounts, including those friends who criticized him, few other young New Negroes had as great an influence upon their generation of literary peers as did Thurman, but this has not translated into the general fame that came to Thurman's close friend, Langston Hughes. As Amritjit Singh and Daniel Scott claim, Thurman "developed the critical vocabulary and theoretical frameworks that would make him an indispensable part of the African American critical tradition," but that part has remained largely the understudy waiting in the wings, eclipsed by the enormous reputation of the star players.[2]

Nevertheless Thurman's own reputation has grown in recent years as more of his contemporaries have attested to their complicated friend's importance to the era in which, to reiterate Langston Hughes's oft-quoted assessment, the Negro was in vogue. Hughes himself stressed in *The Big Sea* that Thurman was "a strangely brilliant black boy" who could read eleven lines at a time, criticize anything and everything he read, and display his encyclopedic knowledge of American and continental literature.[3] Hughes goes on to detail Thurman's deep angst over his abilities as a novelist and poet, difficult history as an editor, simultaneous affinity and antipathy for gin, and demise in the charity ward at Bellevue. Hughes's portrait of Thurman has become iconic, often the first cited in retrospectives on the Harlem group of writers.

Compared to the vision of Thurman that their mutual friend Richard Bruce Nugent repeatedly and consistently conjured in interviews, though, Hughes's portrait fades somewhat, resembling more closely a faintly penciled sketch in dire need of color and chiaroscuro. The difference is understandable; as close as Thurman and Hughes were, Nugent and Thurman formed a bond as roommates and mutually admiring intellects who shared passions for art and literature. Equally important, perhaps, was their shared interest in "rough trade," or sexual relations with "straight" men. As Nugent's friend and biographer Thomas Wirth has documented, both men indulged in the fluid sexual atmosphere in Harlem and other sites in New York City, even as they cultivated the circle of artists that Thurman and Zora Neale Hurston later dubbed the "Niggeratti."[4] This is not to suggest that each author's sexuality precipitated his sense of aesthetics; little evidence may be found to support this notion, especially in Thurman's case. Wirth emphasizes as well that Nugent considered his sexuality very much a personal matter, although an intrinsic part of his being.[5]

Thurman and Nugent's immersion in all that the New Negro Renaissance in Harlem had to offer, whether in intellectual, artistic, or sexual terms, illustrates their steadfast belief in democratic expression of their individual selves. Little space stands between Langston Hughes's arguments for free artistic expression for Negro artists in "The Negro Artist and the Racial Mountain" (June 23, 1926) and those that Thurman and Nugent expressed in their own writings. The philosophical connection between these three writers underscores a common thread among satirists of the Harlem Renaissance: total artistic freedom, not a race-based pragmatism, is the ideal. Nowhere is this more evident than in *Infants of the Spring* (1932) and *Gentleman Jigger* (composed 1928–33; published posthumously in 2008), the novels that Thurman and Nugent wrote in tandem about many of the same events. Taken together, Thurman's now-celebrated, if controversial, novel and Nugent's heretofore lost masterpiece offer the most detailed, complex, and luxuriantly colored portraits of an artistic movement in the making. Moreover, the two *romans à clef* arguably retire the most common derisive view of the younger generation of Harlem Renaissance artists (one that Thurman bitterly supported himself), replacing it with a perspective that fully acknowledges the group's flaws but reveals their seriousness in creating a new space for their own aesthetic ambitions, as well those of subsequent generations. As Abby Arthur Johnson and Ronald Maberry Johnson have argued, *Fire!!*, the emblematic magazine that Thurman, Nugent, Hughes, and other young artists envisioned and published, "deserves a place in surveys of American cultural history" as "the first black magazine that was both independent and essentially literary."[6]

Perhaps needless to say, the Johnsons' description befits the authors themselves. The term "Bohemian" invariably finds its way into descriptions of Nugent, as either an adjective or a noun, and with considerable justification. Like Stuartt, the protagonist of *Gentleman Jigger* and an extremely close analog for his creator, Nugent was completely devoted to the arts as a painter, graphic artist, poet, and prose writer, to the point of seldom holding down any sustained form of employment for the entirety of his adult life. Thurman was a bit more pragmatic than his friend, which helps account for the slightly greater renown his career now enjoys, but no less iconoclastic. Both had a deep and lasting influence upon their friends, but until recently only Thurman's significance has been plumbed close to the depths it ought.

Thurman and Nugent's desire for democratic forms of artistic expression found their way into two of the greatest satirical novels of the period—the *Infants of the Spring* and *Gentleman Jigger*—as well as in Thurman's more subtle, earlier novel *The Blacker the Berry* . . . (1928), essays, and criticism. As a result, I hope that Nugent and Thurman will emerge as two sources that all students of the Harlem Renaissance will need to consult to get at the movement's vast riches. Whether considered separately or in tandem, Thurman and Nugent appear to be exemplars of the New Negro movement's modernity equal to their contemporary Jean Toomer. As Karen Jackson Ford argues, Toomer's seminal work, *Cane* (1923), comprises everything that made him the most hauntingly modern writer of the movement; it is an "attempt to summon future possibility as an epilogue to tragedy."[7] Thurman and Nugent evince different degrees of optimism about those future possibilities, but their accord regarding the tragedy inherent in the black artist attempting to capture the beauty and realism of disparate and corporate black experiences cannot be overestimated. Through their major writings, published or unpublished, each influenced his generation.

Quoth Wally Thurman: Harlem Is the Place

Thurman's influence had little to do with his native artistic skills or repertoire of fiction and poetry; few would attest that his artistic talents equaled his significance. Thurman's talents were both social and visionary. He capably forged alliances among disparate authors and writers, knew through experience far more about editing and publishing than virtually all African Americans of his generation, and had the will to assemble projects long after logistical and financial support had evaporated, especially in the case of *Fire!!*. Although less well known than his contemporary and close friend Langston Hughes, and despite his own rejection of the faddishness of interest in the Negro, Thurman's contributions to his peers' artistic efforts enabled these New Negroes to comprise a Harlem Renaissance *movement*, rather than a mere gathering of artists. Until recently, such scholars as David Levering Lewis, Nathan Huggins, and Houston A. Baker Jr. have repeatedly underestimated Thurman, whose career has been relegated to brief assessments or mere footnotes within longer studies of the Harlem Renaissance. Their studies routinely describe Thurman's books in harsh, frequently dismissive terms, as little more than hack writing, while the author is portrayed as little more than a depressed, confused, and somewhat neurotic young man. David Levering Lewis notes, for example, that Thurman's *Infants of the Spring* "was recognized as the mediocre work of a writer who no longer believed in himself as a man, an Afro-American, or an artist" (279).

To be fair, no one can reasonably argue that Thurman was among the most *artistically* advanced or accomplished writers of the Harlem Renaissance, especially when compared to the modernism of Jean Toomer, Nella Larsen and Jessie Redmon Fauset's modern and occasionally understated investigations of gender and class issues, the innovative blues and folk aesthetics of Langston Hughes and Zora Neale Hurston, or Rudolph Fisher's groundbreaking detective fiction. By all accounts, past and present, Thurman was at best an amateur poet, an assessment he eventually came to share. Yet Thurman's oeuvre, while not as spectacular as those of his contemporaries, remained as influential and innovative as the publications he helmed. No *petit magazine* of the period is quite as storied as the ill-fated single issue of *Fire!!*; no novel took on intraracial color prejudice as openly as *The Blacker the Berry . . .* ; no one, with the possible exception of Kansan Langston Hughes, held a perspective as unusual as the Utah émigré, who recognized fully that he was an African American, yet resisted the limits such an identity implied at the time, in both his life and art. Although Nugent's *published* depictions of homosexuality made him the most daring of the group, his sexuality was hardly unique. Thurman had the advantage of being from a state no one associated with a black *presence,* much less black achievement in culture and intellectual life. In Harlem, which Rudolph Fisher dubbed the City of Refuge, Thurman was the ultimate refugee.

As Amritjit Singh and Daniel M. Scott argue, the more disparaging view of Thurman's life and achievements arose from gross reductions of his life and views to those of the protagonists within his novels. If Emma Lou Morgan of *The Blacker the Berry . . .* and Raymond Taylor or Paul Arbian of *Infants of the Spring* seem hopelessly neurotic, cynical, or pathological, it does not follow that their personae are direct analogues of their creator.[8] Thurman's personal beliefs and actions, in fact, frequently clashed with his intellectual positions and artistic creations. He was less concerned with such consistency than with creating and maintaining links to and friendships with the so-called "Niggeratti" for the sake of shoring up their individual talents and aspirations. Along the way, Thurman might fulfill his sincere, unstinting desire to produce and perform as a writer. As Eleonore van Notten argues, Thurman acted as a leader, resource, and frequent if ambivalent ideologue. Through his efforts, "some of the younger black artists and writers began to reject linking the arts to the struggle for racial advancement as championed by W. E. B. Du Bois."[9] What separated Thurman from many of his peers, and therefore marks him as a leader of sorts, is the ambivalence van Notten highlights. Thurman commented often on his polyglot beliefs, the products of many years of reading and the autodidact's common error of imprecision. None of the other members of the "Niggeratti" possessed the degree of naked ambition that Thurman embodied in his intellectual pursuit of a more viable aesthetic for the renaissance. Although he alternately churned out work at a prolific rate and languished in creative despair, Thurman's involvement in and work with several major publications placed him squarely in the movement's center.

Unfortunately, due in part to Thurman's early death at thirty-two and resulting abbreviated output, histories of the Harlem Renaissance have often overlooked this central role. Deeply divided as to the movement's total worth, Thurman nonetheless attempted to provide it with an artistic vision that could allow writing by African American authors to become central parts of the American literary scene while remaining subversive. Thurman's aesthetic consciously steered away from W. E. B. Du Bois's arguments in his controversial address, "Criteria of Negro Art," precisely because of Du Bois's assertion that African American literature is "propaganda, and ever must be, despite the wailing of the purists."[10] Thurman hardly qualified as one of the purists that Du Bois dismisses; in fact, Thurman took great pains to recognize, as Du Bois stresses elsewhere in "Criteria," that the purpose of all art is "the creation of beauty, of the preservation of beauty, of the realization of beauty" using "truth . . . as the highest handmaid of imagination."[11] In many letters, essays, and stories, Thurman casts art within the same general mold. His difference with Du Bois rests, in part, upon a tenuous generation gap that Thurman had little remorse in widening, but it may be read more sensibly as a call to modernism to which Du Bois did not always respond. In his editorial for the first issue of *Harlem: A Forum of Negro Life,* Thurman crafts a dramatic arc of the evolution of Negro writing, in which the older generation that Du Bois represented "was interested only in making white people realize what dastards they were in denying him equal economic opportunities or in lynching him upon the slightest provocation." "This," Thurman continues, "was all right for a certain period," but the activist writers and journalists of the past may still be "blamed for not changing their journalistic methods when time and conditions warranted such a change, and for doing nothing else but preaching and moaning until they completely lost their emotional balance and their sense of true values."[12] African American writers who saw themselves and their "race" primarily as problems could only produce limited art, with the potential for beauty curbed in quest of unalloyed "truth," while those wishing to write in other ways or on other subjects simply had no viable or consistent outlets for their expression. Thurman would have none of this; he intended his efforts—including, of course, *Harlem*—to supplant the "old propagandistic journals" that "had served their day and their generation well," such as the *Crisis* or perhaps Thurman's former employer, the *Messenger.* Thurman's dream was to provide a "forum in which all people's opinions may be presented intelligently and from which the Negro can gain some universal idea of what is going on in the world of thought and art."[13]

Thurman's appeal for an intellectual and artistic democracy reveals the thread that he wove throughout his critical and artistic output. Although Thurman never shied away from political opinion—he was nothing if not an unrepentant Menckenian iconoclast and cynic—he considered anathema the possibility that fellow critics and readers would always consider his work a vehicle for political propaganda dictated by an older generation. That generation remained mired in a rhetoric designed to attest to the humanity of the Negro, but for Thurman the humanity of the Negro was a given. While his folk art was a treasure to be cautiously studied, his culture was also one that should be pushed towards modernity if enough diverse voices had the opportunity to be heard and cultivated. For this position, Thurman's peers revered him, and often cited several key reasons for their admiration and friendship:

~ Thurman was decidedly unwilling to be subject to the literary advice of the older generation, most of whom were still influenced—Thurman might say enthralled—by Victorian ideals.

~ While hardly less impoverished than his fellow "Niggeratti," Thurman was the only member of that fraternity with regular employment and experience in the publishing industry. In fact, at one point he was a pioneer in this regard, when he later found a job at Macaulay's as a reader, which made him "the only Negro . . . to be employed by any of the larger publishing firms."[14]

~ Thurman's connections within and knowledge of the publishing world allowed such journals as *Fire!!* and *Harlem*, both of which showcased some of the "Niggeratti's" edgiest work, to see print, even if both were extremely short-lived publications.

Despite these virtues, Thurman inspired a few tensions among his friends during his life, as well as detractors after his demise. His friends found his aesthetic simultaneously liberating yet uncompromising to the point of brusque dismissal. Given Thurman's notoriously poor skill in poetry, no one missed the irony of an amateur poet criticizing Langston Hughes.

In *Gentleman Jigger*, Thurman's counterpart relishes the idea of creating and publishing art that he and his compeers "might even be censored for, yet so sound it can be defended honestly on artistic grounds."[15] According to Langston Hughes, this agenda alone inspired little conflict within the group; "for artists and writers," Hughes muses, "we got along fine and there were no quarrels" during the creation of *Fire!!*[16] Hughes is unquestionably too generous; in fact, *Infants of the Spring* and *Gentleman Jigger* reveal a number of quarrels among the artists, a few of which grew into major breaks, or in Thurman's case, alienation from his comrades and blunt judgments regarding their contributions to the New Negro movement and to the artistic world as a whole.

Thurman's greatest virtues were also his worst faults; his brazen willingness to try new ventures, combined with deleterious ennui and impatience with the dearth of innovation and free thought among the masses of African Americans, produced prose with an acidic mix of enormous ego and arrogance stemming from deep self-doubt. Like so many of his contemporaries, Thurman came to Harlem with high hopes that the "New Negro" would be able to create art that would establish a new standard, one that would satisfy the African American intellect even as it turned human experience into beautiful and pleasurable reading. When Thurman later determined that pleasure was about the only element existing in excess within the "Niggeratti," his already strong admiration of Mencken got some exercise, as he cynically lamented the improbability of Harlem and African Americans producing art that equaled the "New Negro's" vaunted opinion of himself without sufficient provocation. Musing to friend Hughes, Thurman protested that he did not "enjoy carping and caviling," but needed to "get some things off [his] own chest, and perhaps beget discussion, which will perhaps be of some aid to those of us who wish to make the most of our talents."[17] Branding himself "somewhat of a crusader" cursed with ennui, Thurman argues that, since "there is so little to do in life that is interesting," then "certain Negroes as well as certain whites, have to be pricked to develop," characteristically including himself among those needing a provocateur.[18]

To this extent, Thurman's writings reveal an intellectual alliance with George Schuyler's iconoclasm. Neither author missed many opportunities to blast the pretensions of the New Negro Renaissance's leaders, designating them members of an insufferable bourgeoisie that allowed white faddists, in the benevolent guises of patrons and publishers, to flatter and exploit them. Thurman's August 1927 essay, "Negro Artists and the Negro," offers his most complete and precise incision into the *corpus literati*. "When the Negro art fad first came into being and Negro poets, novelists, musicians and painters became good copy," Thurman begins,

> literate and semi-literate Negro America began to strut and to shout. Negro newspapers reprinted every item published anywhere concerning a Negro whose work had found favor with the critics, editors, or publishers. Negro journals conducted contests to encourage embryonic geniuses. Negro ministers preached sermons, Negro lectures made speeches, and Negro club women read papers—all about the great new Negro art.
>
> Everyone was having a grand time. The millennium was about to dawn. The second emancipation seemed inevitable. Then the excitement began to die down and Negroes as well as whites began to take stock of that in which they had reveled. The whites shrugged their shoulders and began seeking some new fad. Negroes stood by a little subdued, a little surprised, torn between being proud . . . and being angry because a few [artists] had ceased to be . . . "respectable."[19]

Thurman's sardonic, anecdotal review of the very young renaissance's history reveals not only his obvious disdain for the Negro masses' tendency to go for any sign of "emancipation" from the inferior status that marked black life; it also indicates the general populace's skittishness, its nervous tendency to mine any sensation in the 1920s. Out of this mood, Thurman contends, the only material that receives the highest praise is inevitably "considerate of the Aframerican's *amour proper*, soothing to his self-esteem and stimulating to his vanity," and "designed to prove to the American white man that the American Negro [is] not inferior *per se*."[20] Predictably, such works are "honored and blessed by Negroes," regardless of their literary merits, since they serve the propagandistic order of the day.

Thurman's skepticism towards the literary tastes of his intellectual contemporaries leads him to echo George Schuyler's denial of the existence of "racial" literature. In "Nephews of Uncle Remus," his September 1927 article for the *Independent*, Thurman essentially rehashes the sentiments Schuyler expressed in his most famous essay, "The Negro-Art Hokum."[21] After bringing his reader up to date on the controversy between two schools of thought that argue over the question of the existence of a "negro literature," Thurman rests in favor of the "latter school," which "contends that there can be no such thing in America as an individual negro literature; that the Afro-American is different from the white American in only one respect, namely, skin color, and that when he writes he will observe the same stylistic conventions and literary traditions."[22] Both Thurman and Schuyler rejected intellectually the notion of a "racial" literature on the grounds that people of African descent varied widely in their sentiments, origins, histories, and ideologies worldwide. The classification, they feared, served only to reify the racist notion that people of color were inherently different, and therefore inferior, as well as definitions of group identity that did not allow for free, democratic expression. In August 1929, Thurman wrote to Hughes about his own reluctance to use the term "Negro" too broadly in Thurman's unpublished essay collection, *Aunt Hagar's Children,* fearing that the individualism that Thurman cherished for himself and others would be subsumed under his desire to take an objective critical look at the status of African American culture.[23]

In staking out his position on the role of African American literature and art in the struggle for black freedom, Thurman staunchly defended a liberal conception of "black," even as he recognized the alliances fostered among young black artists by their circumstances. His ultimate goal was to get black artists beyond both mimicry of the various literary predecessors under which they operated and the ideological caretakers that were attempting to keep these artists under their wings. Thurman's major flaw was that he did not know what lay beyond these limitations. This flaw might be attributable to a lack of vision or what Thurman called "genius." When he illustrates his own artistic frustrations and anxieties in the following well-quoted passage from *Infants of the Spring,* Thurman could be talking about the Harlem Renaissance itself: "He wanted to do something memorable in literature, something that could stay afloat on the contemporary sea of weighted ballast, something which could transcend and survive the transitional age in which he was living. . . . He did not doubt that he had a modicum of talent, but talent was not a sufficient spring board to guarantee his being catapulted into the literary halls of Valhalla; talent was not a sufficient prerequisite for immortality. He needed genius and there was no assurance that he had it, no assurance that he had done anything more 'than learned his lessons well.'"[24] Thurman filled many of his articles about the renaissance's artists with this type of judgment, one that reflected the sort of modernistic impulse that haunted contemporaries, such as T. S. Eliot, on the other side of the color line.

That Thurman doubted his own genius is not particularly striking; it is a rare artist indeed who does not have moments of doubt in his career, and the "Niggeratti" were rife with artists brimming over with self-doubt, anxious to measure their work against the traditional past. In his celebrated 1926 *Nation* essay, "The Negro

Artist and the Racial Mountain," Langston Hughes decries those black artists who are reluctant to embrace their identity as African Americans, for fear that the label of "Negro artist" will connote both inferiority and topical limits for creative spirits.[25] Although Hughes's essay obliquely countered some of the claims of George S. Schuyler's "The Negro-Art Hokum," published in the preceding issue of the *Nation,* it also aimed a thinly veiled barb at Countee Cullen's reluctance to be known as a "Negro poet," a reflection of Cullen's doubts about the meaning of racial categories. Thurman had his own thoughts about Cullen, both in support of his ambitions and as one of his sharpest critics. In his 1928 essay "Negro Poets and Their Poetry," Thurman praises Cullen as "the symbol" and "the apogee" of "a fast disappearing generation of Negro writers" for his success in translating "into lyric form the highly poetic urge to escape from the blatant realities of life in America" and, contra Hughes, Thurman compliments Cullen for "fleeing from the stigma of being called a *Negro* poet" by "ignoring folk-material and writing of such abstractions as love and death."[26]

Yet Thurman chides Cullen for being "too steeped in tradition, too influenced mentally by certain conventions and taboos," which keep his work from advancing beyond its early promise.[27] Thurman uses this limit to create a segue into his assessment of close friend Hughes, whom he admires for his ability to succeed where Paul Laurence Dunbar, as the nineteenth and early twentieth centuries' preeminent poet of African American folk culture, failed in the Joycean task of "interpret[ing] 'the soul of his race.'"[28] For Thurman, Hughes's success may be found in his avoidance of stock types and emotions in his depictions of common black folk in favor of "dark-skinned symbols of universal characters."[29] Again, the "lampblacked Anglo-Saxon" of Schuyler's "Negro-Art Hokum" reappears, elevated to an ideal form. Even as he shares Cullen's antipathy for adherence to group identity at the expense of the individual, Thurman finds himself attracted to universal, transcendent types in literature, those who cannot be forced into a single identity, even as they rely upon a specific one.

Thurman owes an equal amount in his comparison of these young poets to W. E. B. Du Bois's definition of "double-consciousness" in *The Souls of Black Folk* and to Friedrich Nietzsche, whose writings H. L. Mencken translated and interpreted in 1908. Du Bois's oft-cited description of the Negro limns "a sort of seventh son of a seventh son, born with a veil, and gifted with second-sight in this American world," which yields "a peculiar sensation, this double-consciousness, this sense of always looking at one's self through the eyes of others, of measuring one's soul by the tape of a world that looks on in amused contempt and pity."[30] Du Bois goes on to stress that the goal of the Negro is to "attain self-conscious manhood, to merge his double self into a better and truer self" without losing either of the identities that define him.[31] To do so, the Negro must "husband and use his best powers and his latent genius" to rise above the limits of the American milieu, which "yields him no true self-consciousness."[32] For both Du Bois and Thurman, the Negro cannot afford to wait for America to yield that self-consciousness. In a modern world—in all eras, really—greatness and transcendence would be defined and seized by great men, akin to the "Talented Tenth" that Du Bois championed in his 1903 essay. "The Negro race, like all races," Du Bois writes, "is going to be saved by its exceptional men," the Talented Tenth whose problem is "developing the Best of this race that they may guide the Mass away from the contamination and death of the Worst, in their own and other races."[33]

As Cornel West, Arnold Rampersad, and George Hutchinson have noted, Du Bois's vision of African Americans' collective future relied heavily upon William James's theories of pragmatism espoused while Du Bois studied at Harvard, as well as *fin de siècle* theories of the destinies of great "races" and peoples, the nature of democracy, and art's connection to all of these entities.[34] As a result, Du Bois saw African Americans discovering and implementing what Nietzsche would call "the will to power" through individuals who could transcend the petty, often superstitious and avaricious concerns of the masses for the sake of opening avenues to culture, economic empowerment, full exercise of the franchise, and parity with other "races" via cultural pluralism.[35]

Although occasionally critical of Du Bois's views of African American art, it is difficult to find much difference from Du Bois in Thurman's own theories of African Americans' corporate future. In his own way, each was equally critical of the wasted potential amongst the "Niggeratti." Where Du Bois chided the younger generation for failing to produce an aesthetic and a literature that pragmatically combined beauty and the broader causes of African America, Thurman demanded that black authors play an even greater game by refusing to restrict their art to what was "Negro." To *be* "Negro," for Thurman, was to strive for greatness without boundaries, whether generated by the "race" or the self. To be such an Übermensch meant transcending the corpus of definitions placed upon black thought; to define, simply put, is to limit. Thurman's projection of his own doubts upon his compadres is remarkable because he had no concrete plan to break African American authors out of the trap of "racial" or propagandistic writing save for eschewing all moralizing agendas and pressures. Thurman functioned, not unlike Schuyler, as something of a Menckenite gadfly to the New Negro, even as he ensconced himself fully in the movement.

Of Gadflies and Sweet Berries

Thurman began making his mark upon the renaissance's literary scene shortly after his arrival in the Mecca of the New Negro on September 7, 1925. After publishing a poem, "God's Edicts," and a critical essay, "This American Negro Renaissance" in *Opportunity* magazine in 1926, this particular gadfly found employment at the

Messenger magazine as a contributor and eventually George Schuyler's temporary replacement as managing editor when Schuyler left on assignment for the Pittsburgh *Courier.* Few better substitutes for the magazine's resident satirist may be imagined. Thurman shared with Schuyler not only general disdain for the pretensions of the New Negro movement, poor literature, sloppy thinking, and group ideology, but also a command of language and literature equal or superior to any of his peers. Thurman was an egoist, to put it simply; he states in numerous places in his writings that, for him, "race is nothing. It has its importance perhaps to [his] environment and to [his] physical and psychological structure," but he is "an individual of no race, creed, color or country."[36] Similar to Schuyler or Mencken, Thurman perceived great art to emerge not from any artist's group consciousness or appeals to common ethnic traditions, but instead as an individualistic force of will. He intentionally minimized the environmental—read: group affiliations—and "physical and psychological" aspects of race to clear opportunities to speak his mind. To accede to a particular creed would mean instituting a limit standing in the way of free and truthful expression. In view of Thurman's desultory youth in Utah, group identification and self-imposed limits would perhaps be anathema. As one of a minuscule number of African Americans in a state dominated by the Church of Jesus Christ of Latter-Day Saints—which did not accept African Americans as members until 1978 and decreed them cursed for well over a century—Thurman's eagerness to eschew limits should be self-explanatory. In his 1926 *Messenger* essay, Thurman indicated that Utah, despite its tiny black community and legal opposition to miscegenation, remained virtually free of legal segregation until his adulthood, when he was refused taxi service while visiting his relatives.[37] Thurman had enjoyed early years relatively free of legal segregation and social discrimination that southern African Americans endured as a matter of course.[38] Why would he or any of his fellows wish to have limits on their art or other expression imposed by anyone within or outside African American communities? Such concessions would implicitly grant a stereotypically Victorian idealism and Puritanism upon art, rather than the modern realism that Thurman craved.

Thurman also moved in publishing circles unknown to all but a handful of African Americans at that time. Beyond his early work as an associate editor at an African American newspaper, the *Pacific Defender,* Thurman had read voraciously the black-centered magazines of his day and later worked at such magazines as the *World Tomorrow,* the *Messenger,* and Theophilus Lewis's *The Looking Glass,* where he gained experience assembling a little magazine that would serve him well, *Fire!!.*[39] Later, in 1932, Thurman earned an appointment as editor-in-chief at the Macaulay Company, which published various types of nonfiction and fiction, including Thurman's own *Infants of the Spring.* His extensive experience resulted in that latter position as did a pragmatic attitude towards the publishing world.

Thurman's early work as a journalist freed him from most illusions about the possibilities of a black-owned and -edited magazine featuring the arts, even if the story behind *Fire!!* might seem to belie it. As a little magazine that sought to weave "vivid, hot designs upon an ebon bordered loom" and satisfy "pagan thirst for beauty unadorned,"[40] *Fire!!* succeeded artistically but failed miserably as a financial concern, despite Thurman's efforts to cut costs by reducing the numbers of pages, illustrations, and all color. In October 1926, Thurman wrote Langston Hughes that "we wont be able to use Bruce's drawings. It will add at least $75 to the cost. It will mean 25% added to the press work because the whole magazine will have to be ran [sic] thru the press twice. I just had an idea when I wrote that. Why should we have to run them thru the press twice when we merely want them pasted in. Yes we will be able to do it after all. I must have been dumb when the printer was telling me that. As things are now we have only 32 pages of material. Instead of 48 pages we will have 44. You see I am trying my damdest [sic] to cut the price down."[41] Keeping the price of publishing *Fire!!* within reason had everything to do with the lack of financial support among Thurman's peers, none of whom had employment prospects as steady as their editor, who nearly lost his position at the *World Tomorrow* as the personal and financial strain of *Fire!!* affected his work.[42]

Why did Thurman go to such lengths to see to completion a publication that placed him in debt for years and severely strained his relationships with peers who seldom made good on their financial commitment to an African American literary and artistic magazine? To take Thurman at his word, it could not have been due to race loyalty; he expressed his antipathy towards group identity and politics on numerous occasions. It could not have been because of the promise his fellow editors exhibited as supporters; as Thurman wrote Langston Hughes in the midst of the editorial process, after staying up all night dummying the proofs, "Zora [Neale Hurston] had a date. Jeanette [Randolph] was in South Norwalk. Bunny [Jan Harold Stephansson] could not be found. Neither could [Richard] Bruce [Nugent]. Aaron [Douglas] eluded [Thurman]." His conclusion? "God damn Fire and all the editors."[43] With such supporters, no detractors were necessary, even if the magazine attracted those as well.

Thurman's determination, of course, seems no different from that of any other editor of an independent publication who must deal with conflicting and unreliable personalities. Certainly several other successful black-run and -supported magazines existed and thrived. That it was an African American publication does not make it inherently more significant. Rather, the magazine's editorial goals reveal its historical centrality, regardless of its decidedly abbreviated life. The contributing editors wanted all material to be written by African Americans and for the financial support to come primarily from African Americans, with full editorial control in black hands. When one of the initial contributors, Harvey Carson Crumbine, turned out to be white, his material was removed and the proofs reset.[44] Thurman's motivation resided in his desire to see a magazine devoted strictly to the arts that would make no pretense to social propriety and respectability, much less propagandistic purposes. Thurman's position regarding his own membership in a "race" must be separated from his recognition that no precedent for *Fire!!*—an artistic magazine by and for a younger, modern set of artists—could be found in American literary history. As Thurman told Granville Hicks the following year, "we've done more for the race in five or six years than [the old guard of writers] have accomplished in a generation. We have shown people that the negro can do something instead of telling him that he can."[45] Although Thurman remained skeptical of the New Negro movement he helped to lead, the true spirit of the movement could be found in efforts like *Fire!!* Unlike such spectacular failures as Marcus Garvey's ill-fated Black Star Line, this representation of African American industry allowed no ambitions greater than artistic independence, nor did it impoverish anyone who believed in it —save for Thurman.

Fire!! did affect Thurman's finances and state of mind, of course, adding to his skepticism toward the New Negro movement as a movement. His experiences revealed that few movements survive intact the transition from exuberance to pragmatism. Realizing this problem, Thurman began planning *Fire!!*'s successor soon after its demise. The result, *Harlem,* was less ambitious artistically, but more catholic in format. As he wrote Alain Locke in the fall of 1928, "Harlem is to be a general magazine, containing verse, fiction, essays, articles on current events and debates on racial and non racial issues. We are not confining ourselves to [a]ny group either of age or race. I think that is best. The Crisis and The Messenger [a]re dead. Opportunity is dying. Voila here comes Harlem, independent, fearless and general, trying to appeal to all."[46]

Harlem, like *Fire!!,* lasted for only one issue. If Thurman hoped to generate greater interest than in the explicitly Bohemian *Fire!!,* he hadn't found the formula. He also underestimated the *Crisis* and *Opportunity* as outlets for African Americans' intellectual discourse. As editors, W. E. B. Du Bois and Charles S. Johnson, respectively, were certainly more conservative than Thurman, and certainly held even tighter reins on their publications than their younger would-be competitor. But their magazines held a distinct advantage: links to national organizations working for social justice. *Crisis* or *Opportunity* readers throughout the United States, in the Caribbean, in Africa, or wherever people of African descent gathered could encounter poetry and prose by new or younger artists while remaining abreast of recent developments in African American politics, culture, and civil rights. *Fire!!* and *Harlem* lacked both a distribution system and a central ideological argument that the more established organs posited on a regular basis. Even if the *Messenger* changed its perspective multiple times under its ever-shifting finances and editors, by the late 1920s it had also established firm links to the Brotherhood of Sleeping Car Porters. Thurman, for all of his advanced thinking on African American artistic freedom, never cultivated the firm, consistent base for a black cultural magazine. He spent his career fighting against established categories for black art that few would reconsider.

Little wonder, then, that both of Thurman's satirical novels, *The Blacker the Berry . . .* and *Infants of the Spring,* reflect upon and satirize the predominant assumptions about racial categories held by African Americans and their curious onlookers. Although Harlem's writers and graphic artists were profiled many times by reviewers and critics, none but Thurman created an extended satirical assessment, the medium of the satirical novel or the roman à clef. Rudolph Fisher certainly wrote Langston Hughes into his *The Walls of Jericho* through his character "Langdon, an innocent looking youngster who was at heart a prime rascal and who compensated by writing poetry," but that was the extent of his focus on the *artists* of the Renaissance.[47] Schuyler's *Black No More* barely mentions art at all, although Schuyler repeatedly focuses upon art and literature in his many columns for the *Messenger* and the Pittsburgh *Courier.* Thurman's *The Blacker the Berry . . .* also focuses on the Harlem literati for most of its fourth section ("Rent Party"), upon which *Infants of the Spring* is clearly based, but Thurman does not sustain this focus for the novel's duration.

The Blacker the Berry . . . concerns itself primarily with color caste among African Americans nationwide from Thurman's home state, Utah, to Los Angeles and eventually Harlem. As a typical semi-autobiographical first novel, *The Blacker the Berry . . .* reproduces many incidents Thurman experienced firsthand as a dark-skinned African American man from Salt Lake City's tiny black community. Just as Thurman matriculated at the University of California, Los Angeles, so does Emma Lou Morgan arrive at UCLA's arch-rival, the University of Southern California, to begin her studies, only to discover that the other black students and the city's middle-class black elite repeatedly and systematically exclude those of darker hue. This follows Emma Lou opening the novel musing like a sable, latter-day Tristram Shandy on what her mother had been about in selecting a "black" (that is, dark-skinned) man for her father. "Not that she minded being black," our narrator stresses, "[as] being a Negro necessitated having a colored skin, but she did mind being too black. She couldn't . . . comprehend the cruelty of the natal attenders who had allowed her to be dipped . . . in indigo ink. . . . Why *had* her mother married a black men? Surely there had been some eligible brown-skin man around."[48] Like blacks in Schuyler's dystopian *Black No More* (1931), Emma Lou and her family bemoan and try to dilute her color to prevent the "sorrow and disappointment" that befall darker girls, eternally doomed to be without a reliable mate and shunned socially, unlike their male counterparts.[49]

Infants of the Spring poses numerous seemingly irresolvable questions about the directions African Americans, especially African American intellectuals, should take in view of their political and social ties to other racial and ethnic groups in the United States. Thurman's primary question revolves around the possibility of group and individual identities that will simultaneously avoid being essentialist even as those identities carry the vast majority of African Americans forward. In that sense, it is but an extension of Thurman's deep-seated concerns about the construction of "race" and color-caste distinctions that dominated much of his journalistic work and *The Blacker the Berry* . . . .

In *The Big Sea,* Langston Hughes illustrates how whites frequently responded to Harlem's thriving black cultural institutions and entertainment, where they would go "in droves" to patronize the Cotton Club and other venues. "But," Hughes adds, they were not cordial to Negro patronage, unless you were a "celebrity. . . . So Harlem Negroes did not like the Cotton Club and never appreciated its Jim Crow policy in the very heart of their dark community. Nor did ordinary Negroes like the growing influx of whites toward Harlem after sundown, flooding the little cabarets and bars where formerly only colored people laughed and sang, and where now the strangers were given the best ringside tables to sit and stare at the Negro customers—like amusing animals in a zoo."[50] When whites began to circulate heavily among the Harlem literati—the "Niggeratti"—their hosts and peers received them with a mix of caution and democratic openness, both of which found sufficient justification via earnest patronage and often irritating paternalism. In a few cases—most notably Charlotte Osgood Mason's strict management of Zora Neale Hurston's career—these interactions fulfilled the cynical predictions of *Infants of the Spring*'s protagonist, Raymond Taylor. Eventually, Harlem Renaissance artists had to investigate their own culpability in allowing whites to dominate their circles, to find a framework that would reveal the stratifications along class and color lines separating black people from each other socially, economically, and often physically.

In Alain Locke's literary and critical anthology *The New Negro* (1925), the editor's crucial opening essay, "The New Negro," posits the audaciously powerful argument that a greater consciousness spurred by racial progress is supplanting previous thoughts and images about black people. In the same volume, Charles S. Johnson describes the transformation in black culture as an evolutionary process in which the new form of life is "a city Negro" who is "being evolved out of those strangely divergent elements of the general [that is, rural] background" (285). Harlem's racial admixture simultaneously helped introduce black artists to the marketplace and pushed understanding of inter- and intraracial politics forward. In spite of this progress, though, a barrier still stood between and within the races: a series of basic assumptions about what constituted race and of essentialist racial differences. Both blacks and whites could be and were guilty of perpetuating these reductive assumptions. *Infants of the Spring* reveals a singular frustration with the inability of both the "New Negro" and contemporary whites to recognize the intricate and ultimately delimiting system of racial difference overpowering the United States and, moreover, to perceive and pursue the best means to destroy that system.

The novel's satiric thrust is directed primarily toward those African Americans, and their allies or sycophants, who allow themselves to be deluded by ideals and dreams based upon an unquestioned belief in an all-encompassing collective identity. More specifically, the novel questions whether the artistry emerging from Harlem will have any lasting ideological or epistemological impact upon African Americans. Furthermore, the novel argues that the black artist cannot ever be a "leader of the race" when she or he is consumed by the type of idealistic, Bohemian atmosphere found among the renaissance's writers and artists; s/he must pursue a political life and artistry beyond the Bohemian, one which inspires other black people to completely alter existing sociopolitical structures rather than work from a privileged position within them.

Most of *Infants of the Spring*'s plot transpires within the milieu of "Niggeratti Manor," the name Thurman and Zora Neale Hurston coined and assigned to the townhome at 267 West 136th Street in Harlem where many of the younger New Negroes lived and gathered to socialize in a carnivalesque atmosphere enhanced through seemingly endless gin parties. The manor's inhabitants' decadence and isolation from other people and activities not only locates them in an escapist Bohemia, but also makes the manor a metaphor for Harlem itself. James de Jongh's description of Harlem in the 1920s virtually matches that of Niggeratti Manor; "its creation corresponded, in dramatic ways, to historical alterations in the lives of black and white Americans in the early decades of this century; its mystique was intoxicating; it symbolized the very quality of black life," to the extent that the new concentration of blacks in a cosmopolitan city, in a space removed from yet conversant with other cultures allowed unprecedented production of art and culture.[51] Neither environment succeeded fully in producing cultural riches and changes to the degree its leading lights had hoped. The manor's inhabitants produce more heat than light as they become captivated by their own novelty.

In fact, the novel fully engages its satirical purposes as protagonist Raymond Taylor (virtually analogous to Thurman) parses his alleged "decadence" with his companions Stephen Jorgenson and Samuel Carter, of whom the latter finds Raymond's apartment "'all rather flamboyant and vulgar,'" a sign that African Americans' "taste is naturally crass and vulgar." Raymond "must not go in for loud colors," as it's "'a confession of [his] inferior race heritage.'"[52] Raymond's ironic genuflection before Sam's critique highlights the paternalistic faddishness of liberal white assessments of black culture, frequently without appreciable contact with actual black people. Raymond questions notions of a syncretic, "natural" black culture, widely accepted at the time ("my taste is naturally crass and vulgar"), notions that ignore the continuous construction of cultural differences.

As the novel's resident white liberal, Sam provides a personal history with countless opportunities for some of Thurman's most ferociously barbed satire. A former elite college student, Sam comes to New York City (specifically Greenwich Village) "intent upon becoming a figure in the radical movement" after being "seduced into radicalism by a Jekyll and Hyde professor of economics, who mouthed platitudes in the class room, and preached socialism in private séances to a few [carefully] chosen students. Samuel was one of the professor's mistakes."[53] Unfortunately, "nature had stamped [Sam] an indelible conservative . . . obsessed . . . with the idea of becoming a martyr," sycophant, and hysterical supporter of any and all radical causes.[54] Sam "ultimately allied himself with every existing organization which had the reputation of being red or pink, no matter how disparate their aims and policies. He was thus able to be in sympathy both with anarchists and pacifists, socialists and communists. He went to the aid of any who called, and was unable to understand his universal unpopularity."[55] A classic naïf, Sam eventually realizes "that he was and probably would remain a mere nobody in the radical movement," leading him to Harlem, "an arena in which his mediocrity was overlooked because he had a pale face," where he quickly becomes a "white hope, battling for the cause of the American Negro."[56]

For his efforts, the "American Negro" blindly lavishes acclaim upon this new Great White Hope, inspiring "grateful darkies from coast to coast [to send] him letters of appreciation or appeals for help. The Negro press eulogized him both in the news columns and on their editorial pages. Negro leaders were proud to be associated with him, and to grant him any assistance he might need." Best of all, "what made the rôle eminently satisfying was the vilification and abuse visited upon him by certain cliques of his fellow whites. At last Samuel [became] a martyr."[57] In contrast to Raymond, the one African American who pleases Sam is Niggeratti Manor's Pelham Gaylord, who "was servile, deferential, and quite impressed by Samuel's noisy if ineffectual crusade"; only a stereotypical Uncle Tom should be satisfied with Samuel's activism.[58]

Raymond and flamboyant artist Paul Arbian (that is, Nugent)[59] serve as Sam's irreverent nemeses seeking to debunk blacks' implicit acceptance of their own inferiority in the presence of white patronage, the "Old Negro's" equally stifling paternalism, or their own lack of an intellectual center. If African Americans believed as strongly in ideals of racial and social equality as they profess, they would have no need of the Samuels of the world, in either political or social settings. On the other hand, if Samuel and his ilk took their sociopolitical theories to their logical ends, such actions would manifest themselves fully and positively in all areas of their lives. During an argument over Niggeratti Manor's reliance upon Pelham Gaylord as a de facto servant, Raymond explains to Sam why his "socialistic theories won't work? Treat Pelham as an equal and he would be perfectly miserable. Allow him to do our cooking, washing and ironing and he is happy. He's just a born domestic." Sam argues that the Niggeratti are "subjugating a member of [their] own race" and forgetting that "all humans are equal, prompting Raymond to conclude, "the more you reiterate that, the less I believe you believe it."[60] Samuel's belief in his inherent superiority to evaluate African Americans' problems—in short, his paternalism—makes him more an ally of the contemporary white supremacist, as it reasserts the notion of whites' superior cognitive abilities. Later, Raymond's Danish immigrant friend Stephen criticizes Samuel's hypocrisy from his perspective as a "white" foreigner: "Get this straight, Sam, I'm no hypocrite. I like Ray. I like his friends . . . and none of my likes are based on color. I know nothing about your damn American prejudices, except what I've read in books and been told. A person is a person to me. . . ."[61]

Stephen's argument that the United States' racism is exceptional rather than universal is naive, of course, but it stands as part of the novel's greater metaphor of specific categories and discourse making sense within only one locale, such as Harlem or Niggeratti Manor. We are treated to numerous instances in which the manor's tightly knit Bohemian atmosphere becomes too confining and tense to its inhabitants, especially Raymond, who seeks a solution to his racial conundrums within the manor's creative milieu, ironically finding Stephen, the foreigner and outsider, the only other dweller who fully shares his musings on the compound's absurdities and their similarities to the black community's more pressing issues of poverty, insufficient education, and racism. In what acts as perhaps the novel's most telling trope, Raymond outlines his view of African Americans' intrinsic problems in the United States in answer to Stephen's uncertainty about the two friends' respective futures. Raymond avers that

> I'm going to write, probably a series of books which will cause talk but won't sell, and will be criticized severely, then forgotten. Negroes won't like me because they'll swear I have no race pride, and white people won't like me because I won't recognize their stereotypes. Do you know, Steve, that I'm sick of both whites and blacks? I'm sick of discussing the Negro problem, of having it thrust at me. . . . I'm sick of whites who think I can't talk about anything else, and of Negroes who think I shouldn't talk about anything else. I refuse to wail and lament. My problem is a personal one, although I most certainly do not blind myself to what it means to be a Negro. . . . I have a sense of humor. That's all that saves me from becoming like most of the Negroes I know. Things amuse me. They don't make me bitter.[62]

This conversation occurs after the carnivalesque party at which Raymond rejects Samuel's patronizing view of black culture and Niggeratti Manor's denizens engage in a donnybrook over white women, convincing Raymond that "ninety-nine and ninety-nine hundredths per cent of the Negro race is patiently possessed and motivated by an inferiority complex," the only explanation for Samuel's acceptance and popularity among Harlemites.[63]

Via Raymond, Thurman resists any and all circumscriptions of African Americans' personal, cultural, and intellectual pursuits similar to Schuyler's famous assertion in "The Negro-Art Hokum" that the Negro is "merely a lampblacked Anglo-Saxon." He posits a version of Emersonian individualism as his solution to the problem of black disenfranchisement:

Anything that will make white people and colored people come to the conclusion that after all they are all human, all committed to the serious business of living, and all with the same faults and virtues, the sooner amalgamation can take place and the Negro problem will cease to be a blot on the American civilization. . . . A few years ago it was the thing for all Negroes who could get an education to be professional men, doctors, lawyers dentists, et cetera. Now, they are all trying to be artists. Negroes love to talk, love to tell the stories of their lives. They all feel that they are so different from the rest of humanity, so besieged by problems peculiar only to themselves. And since it is the fashion now to be articulate either in words, music or paint brush, every Negro . . . is tempted to act according to the current fad. . . . [The individualist] is the only type of Negro who will ever escape from the shroud of color . . . who [will] go on about [his] business, and do what [he] can in the best way [he] can, whether it be in business or art. . . . The rest [of the Negroes] must wait until the inevitable day of complete assimilation.[64]

Raymond completes a political program for African Americans that is remarkable for its opposition to the popular progressivism and group-identity politics widely accepted at the time by Harlemites, especially the intellectuals of the renaissance. Raymond also reveals, however, that he'd like to spread dissent among black people with the aid of communistic and leftist rhetoric "'just to see if their resentment is near enough the surface to be inflamed. I'd like to see them retaliate against the whites in their own sphere. For every lynching, I'd like to see Negroes take their toll in whites."[65] When Stephen questions Raymond's conflicting and iconoclastic views, wondering how he "can . . . fight both for the masses and for the individual," Raymond answers, "you have to improve the status of the masses in order to develop your individuals. It is mass movements which bring forth individuals. I don't care about stray darkies getting lynched, but I do care about people who will fight for a principle. And if out of a wholesale allegiance to Communism, the Negro could develop just a half dozen men who were really and truly outstanding, the result would be worth the effort."[66]

Thurman engages in *reductio ad absurdum* in these passages, using Raymond's lack of compassion for "stray darkies getting lynched" to be as shocking as a call for complete assimilation. Raymond embodies the role of the satirical jester, signifying and playing the eternal role of Devil's Advocate to push African Americans away from eternal *talk* about solutions and towards concrete actions. As Raymond wearily tells Stephen, "I suppose I'm bound to thrive on antagonism. . . . I'll probably spend my life doing things just to make people angry. . . . It will be some years before the more forward [blacks] will be accepted as human beings and allowed to associate with giants. The pygmies have taken us over now, and I doubt if any of us has the strength to use them for a step-ladder to a higher plane."[67] African American culture's growth depends precariously on its ability to continually investigate and question itself and recognizing when, precisely, its greatest leaders and ideas are at hand, and devising institutions that support action, rather than abstract culture building.

This view later informs Raymond's reaction to a meeting of Harlem's black writers called by one Dr. A. L. Parkes, Thurman's pseudonym for Alain Locke. This meeting draws together most of the major black voices of the Harlem Renaissance, as well as some of the minor ones, "for the purpose of exchanging ideas and expressing and criticizing individual theories," with the possibility of bringing "into active being a concerted movement which would establish the younger Negro talent once and for all as a vital artistic force."[68] This meeting is based upon salons that various Harlem Renaissance writers had with Locke and upon Thurman's general attitude toward the sort of political mission that Locke, as editor of *The New Negro,* represented. Each of the characters present at Parkes's meeting represents a major artistic or intellectual figure of the Harlem Renaissance hidden beneath a pseudonym that plays on either the initials, rhythm, or other characteristics of the historical figure's name. "Sweetie May Carr," for example, is Zora Neale Hurston; "Doris Westmore" is Dorothy West; "Tony Crews" is Langston Hughes; "Dr. Manfred Trout" is Rudolph Fisher; and so on.

Unfortunately, neither Parkes's verbiage nor his agenda at the actual meeting effectively matches his noble purpose; he "perorate[s]" numerous disapproving allusions to the "decadent strain" running through the artists' work and cajoles them to cultivate "a healthy paganism based on African traditions."[69] Given Parkes's purported openness to the artists' ideas, Raymond and others find Parkes's exhortations patronizing, if they can comprehend them at all. When "DeWitt Clinton" (a pseudonym for Countee Cullen, who attended De Witt Clinton High School)[70] agrees with Parkes, Raymond imagines "that poet's creative hours—eyes on a page of Keats, fingers on a typewriter, mind frantically conjuring African scenes. And there would of course be a Bible nearby."[71] Raymond and Paul then ask Parkes and Clinton, respectively, if "'there really [is] any reason why *all* Negro artists should consciously and deliberately dig into African soil for inspiration and material unless they actually wish to do so,'" and "'how can I go back to African ancestors when their blood is so diluted and their country and times so far away.'"[72] Raymond and Paul thus consider the idea of a syncretic black culture and literature as, at best, a myth. The discussion goes on heatedly until "Sweetie May Carr"/Zora Neale Hurston calls Cedric Williams "a polysyllabic expletive" and the room devolves into a carnivalesque state of "pandemonium," thus erasing the gathering's intellectual discourse, which is never fully regained. The meeting's attendants subsequently disperse, with no consensus attained as to what the responsibilities, goals, and obligations of black artists might be.[73]

Parkes's literary summit thus becomes a metaphor for the state of black art in the renaissance. Raymond reflects soon thereafter that "it was amazing how in such a short time his group of friends had become separate entities, wrenched apart, scattered" by interests in matters both within and outside of Niggeratti Manor. Not unlike the pragmatic endings found in much satire, the latter portion of *Infants* finds the various members pursuing careers that put their talents to more profitable uses than those found within the manor's confines. The manor itself follows this rubric, inasmuch as its landlady, Euphoria Blake, decides to convert it from, in Thurman's euphemisms, "a congenial home for Negro artists to a congenial dormitory for bachelor girls."[74] Soon thereafter, Paul, the novel's quintessential symbol of flamboyant Bohemianism, commits suicide, prompting Raymond to ask if "Paul the debonair, Paul the poseur, Paul the irresponsible romanticist, finally faced reality and saw himself and the world as they actually were? Or was this merely another act, the final stanza in his drama of beautiful gestures," his final means "to make himself stand out from the mob."[75] Raymond's ponderings frame Paul's death as a synecdoche for the disintegration of Niggeratti Manor; in life, he "wooed the unusual, cultivated artificiality, defied all conventions of dress and conduct," and consequently had "nothing left to do except execute self-murder in some bizarre manner," not unlike the Niggeratti's heavy flirtation with the flamboyant and subsequent dissolution in the cascade of economic necessity that overwhelmed any aspirations to a unique society within both Harlem and American culture in general.[76]

Paul leaves behind the manuscript for a novel, but it is accidentally destroyed in the process of his suicide, except for one page that includes a drawing of "a distorted, inky black skyscraper, modeled after Niggeratti Manor, and on which were focused an array of blindingly white beams of light. The foundation of this building was composed of crumbling stone. At first glance it could be ascertained that the skyscraper would soon crumple and fall, leaving the dominating white lights in full possession of the sky."[77]

The Reification of "Race," Aesthetics, and Sexuality

Herein lies a final irony. In lived history, Paul/Nugent's destroyed manuscript was never destroyed, but made untenable by *Infants of the Spring*'s publication. The alleged failure of one of the Harlem Renaissance's greatest artistic minds had more to do with others' ambitions rather than Bohemian ennui. Publication of *Infants of the Spring* precluded *Gentleman Jigger;* Alain Locke's notorious choice to supplant Nugent's art with Aaron Douglas's *The New Negro* compromised both Locke's integrity and Nugent's artistic vision no less than Locke's alteration of the title of Claude McKay's "White House" to "White Houses," thereby undermining both the artist and the fire to be found in black expressions. *Fire!!* emerged to correct this imbalance, but could not compete in the cultural marketplace without the support of the artists, patrons, and other "midwives" of the movement. The high aspirations of the Niggeratti and, by extension, Black Harlem in general, are built upon a foundation of Bohemian, carnal desires and excess that, while amusing in and of themselves, will contribute little or nothing towards solving African American problems without an increasingly exploitative, or at least unreliable system of patronage from different quarters. Under the pressure of white racism and black middle-class aspirations, which respectively seek to destroy African Americans and their culture and fail to patronize it without ideological or other restrictions, black Bohemians will end up consuming themselves, leaving no structure upon which to ensure the future of African America. A possible solution may be a group identity based upon respect for individuality, which offers a way out of an unacceptable dilemma.

Nugent later dismissed Thurman's ending as a half-hearted attempt to draw his novel to a neat conclusion, even as it reflected Thurman's own pessimism regarding the younger New Negro's artistic achievements.[78] If Paul Arbian were Nugent, then his demise is multiply ironic. Nugent, of course, outlived his friend Thurman by more than five decades, and evinced very little of the tragic nihilism that marks Paul's life. The Nugent/Stuartt of *Gentleman Jigger* not only survives, as his real-life counterpart did, but thrives, despite the Bohemianism of both Stuartt and Nugent. The crux for Stuartt/Nugent is the decoupling of his art and life from commercial concerns altogether, as well as from the uplift narrative that the black bourgeoisie represents. Capitalism and uplift both interpolate the black artist in a system in which his individual expression suffers under a quietude that others outside of, but not anterior to, the self mandate for their own benefit. The publisher or the patron of the arts might be able to afford the means to release the artist's creativity, but such control over the means of production requires a diffusion of art.

Does this make Thurman and Nugent vulgar Marxists? In one respect, yes; as Raymond tells Stephen, "if out of a wholesale allegiance to Communism, the Negro could develop just a half dozen men who were really and truly outstanding, the result would be worth the effort."[79] Thurman, however, has no more interest in

Marxism and communism than does George Schuyler. He is a pragmatist who sees the growing influence of the Marxist project as but one means to create the dynamic tension that would allow black creativity to flourish. An essential component of that tension would be satire, as it both demands and creates tension through irony. The laughter it inspires rests upon anger, the same anger that will light the "dynamite" that Raymond/Thurman would like to see in African Americans' artistic and cultural lives. In *Gentleman Jigger*, his own account of this period, friend and compatriot Nugent expressed considerably less anger towards the black literary and artistic scene, and more ironic dismay that so many talented creators granted so many opportunities could produce so little.

Gentleman Jigger Redux, or the Lost History of the "Niggeratti"

Richard Bruce Nugent's *Gentleman Jigger* remains one of the New Negro Renaissance's few significant lost novels despite finally being published in 2008 by Thomas Wirth, Nugent's friend and most thorough amanuensis. Composed coincidentally with Wallace Thurman's *Infants of the Spring*, Nugent never completed a final draft; Wirth notes that he found several partial manuscripts in Nugent's papers and assembled the published text from the latest versions of the novel's various sections and chapters. Despite this status, the novel generally coheres, at least to the extent that its quasi-autobiographical protagonist, Stuartt Brennan, anchors the plot.

As any reader will notice, though, *Gentleman Jigger* comprises two books. The first follows a basic plot nearly identical to *Infants of the Spring*, depicting many of the same events during the most crucial period for the young Harlem Literati circa 1925–27. These include the first encounters among Thurman, Nugent, Langston Hughes, Rudolph Fisher, Eric Walrond, Aaron Douglas, Zora Neale Hurston, Louise Thompson, Helene Johnson, Jessie Redmon Fauset, Nella Larsen, Carl Van Vechten, Alain Locke, and W. E. B. Du Bois as they sought to invent, cement, and define the New Negro Renaissance as a foundation for black artistic expression for the twentieth century.

Detailing Stuartt's evolving queer sexuality and exploits as a lover and companion both to Italian gangsters and an actress/singer, the second half departs from the first plot almost entirely, with the Harlem group virtually absent. If *Gentleman Jigger* had been published in the early 1930s in its current form, this portion would have been an innovation that guaranteed controversy. In nearly every respect an example of erotica—albeit not an explicit one—it extends Nugent's innovations from 1926's story "Smoke, Lilies, and Jade" by analyzing sexuality, race, gender, and ethnicity in overlapping relationships. Nugent's earlier story stands as the first work by an African American to feature an openly bisexual character; *Gentleman Jigger* would have been the first novel to do the same if it had beaten *Infants* into print. It certainly merits analysis under a queer studies or lesbian/gay/bisexual/transgender aegis, to say nothing of Nugent's probably unique analyses of New York's organized-crime underworld.

Unfortunately for our purposes, *Gentleman Jigger's* second half contains very little satire in any appreciable form. Once the novel dispenses with the Harlem literati's artistic successes and failures, it focuses entirely on Stuartt's interest in recreating himself as a sexual being and artist, one that initially had little "homosexual experience," despite boasting of his interest in women and men to the Harlem circle.[80] While I have no desire to minimize the novel's general significance, this shift removes the second half to an entirely different genre and mode. No longer does the novel—and in this case, Nugent as author—seem interested in understanding the New Negro movement's flaws. Having thoroughly made the case that the New Negro fell victim to a lopsided ratio of loquaciousness over action and artistic integrity, Nugent has other topics to unpack.

As does *Infants of the Spring, Gentleman Jigger* Book 1, "Washington to Harlem," details the New Negro movement's inherent flaws, leading to its dissolution as a coherent and consciously purposeful cultural statement. Dwelling on the artists' personalities, Nugent blames their own egotism and apparent dearth of coherent definition among themselves rather than any external influences from powerful patrons or midwives. Unlike *Infants of the Spring's* severe criticism of Raymond Taylor/Wallace Thurman's own failings, *Gentleman Jigger* offers a slightly more generous view of Nugent's close friend and erstwhile roommate, explicitly casting him as the movement's intellectual center. In effect, this counters common narratives that the movement's purported "midwives"—Du Bois, Van Vechten, Locke, Charlotte Osgood Mason, Charles S. Johnson, and Fauset—possessed as much agency in defining that center as scholars have commonly credited. In the novel, Nugent identifies seven young artists as the movement's true nexus, the "Niggeratti," "New Sepia Literati," and the "Negrotesque":

~ Henry Raymond "Rusty" Pelman (Wallace Henry Thurman), the brilliant, dark-skinned writer, intellectual, editor *pro tem* of *The Porter* magazine (aka *The Messenger*), and devotee of H. L. Mencken;

~ Stuartt Brennan (Nugent), the color-conscious, "queer," Bohemian graphic artist, writer, and "vagabond poet" from Washington, D.C.'s elite black bourgeoisie;

~ Anthony "Tony" Brewer (Langston Hughes), celebrated poet and Rusty's close friend;

~ Nona (Zora Neale Hurston), the "student of anthropology" working with Columbia University's Franz Boas and purveyor of "loquacious dialect witticisms" from her native southern background;

~ Howard (Aaron Douglas), an "excellent artist" who draws heavily upon west African figures and Pablo Picasso's African-influenced modernism to become the movement's "'Race Artist'";

~ Paul (John P. Davis), another Menckenite writer and Harvard Law student who writes occasional short stories;

~ Theresa (Gwendolyn Bennett), native Harlemite and short-story author.

Although many other figures from the New Negro movement appear in *Gentleman Jigger*, we can easily argue that Nugent identifies these seven—the number itself signifies an ironically and profanely sacred coterie—as its center not only because they were somewhat sympathetic as creative spirits, but also stood as contributing editors to *Currents,* the novel's analogue for *Fire!!*. Noticeably absent from this group are Rudolph Fisher, whom Thurman and Hughes both revered, and Countee Cullen (immortalized as "Burton Barclay"), though most accounts of the Harlem Renaissance stress that Cullen never identified as one of the "Niggeratti." Eleonore van Notten notes, for example, that Cullen "never felt quite at ease with [the Niggeratti] as a group, socially or artistically," primarily due to the "racial" themes he saw his peers exploring at the expense of being "artists pure and simple."[81] Although *Fire!!* published Cullen's "From the Dark Tower," Thurman considered Cullen's talent wasted and misdirected, a sign that he lacked "originality of theme and treatment, and the contact with life necessary to have had actual, rather than vicarious emotional experiences."[82] In simpler terms, Cullen could not stand the Niggeratti's grotesqueness and vitality. Ironically, despite or due to their association, in *Gentleman Jigger* the young lions' bonds never fully form, nor does the movement ever produce a reason for its existence other than a desire to challenge its elders' ideas about art and exploiting the faddishness of interest in African Americans and their art, an interest that seldom exists outside of New York.

Without question, *Gentleman Jigger* lampoons these artists for the same reasons that preoccupy Thurman in *Infants of the Spring,* but this is to be expected. Thurman and Nugent roomed together for a time and, in Nugent's words, complemented each other artistically. Thurman would help Nugent with his writing, while Nugent would critique and edit his roommate and friend's work. The line dividing Thurman's authorship of *Infants of the Spring* from Nugent's composition of *Gentleman Jigger* remains entirely fluid to this day; as Thomas Wirth notes in his introduction to *Gentleman Jigger,* "Nugent and Thurman were working on their novels at the same time; Thurman finished his first. Its appearance in 1932 effectively blocked whatever prospects for publication *Gentleman Jigger* may have had. . . . The fact that Thurman's novel was published first does not necessarily mean that Nugent imitated Thurman. Indeed . . . Nugent alleged the opposite: that Thurman copied from him" to create a superficially similar roman à clef, but one with a different tenor and emphasis.[83] For his part, Nugent allowed that he bore no ill-will towards Thurman and any unacknowledged use of his work; according to David Levering Lewis's notes from his 1974 interview with Nugent, both "were borrowing from one another and knew it. . . . [Nugent] in fact suggests that [Thurman] appropriated much of his novel—but it was ok."[84] Nugent would have to accept Thurman's borrowing, as he freely took some of Thurman's personal family history—already recounted in more oblique form in *The Blacker the Berry . . .*—to create Salt Lake City native Rusty Pelman's scandalous background, replete with a mother with questionable morals and a grandmother who owned a saloon.[85]

Regardless of Nugent's stance or any plagiarism allegations, the novels' common origin and overlapping plot points corroborate and reify other accounts of the movement's history fictionalized in Rudolph Fisher's *The Walls of Jericho,* Countee Cullen's *One Way to Heaven,* and Thurman's *The Blacker the Berry . . . ,* not to mention Hughes's nonfictional account in *The Big Sea* (1940). Needless to say, the novels put paid to Hughes's assertion in his memoir that *Infants of the Spring* was "the only novel by a Negro about that fantastic period when Harlem was in vogue."[86] Even if Hughes counted only those novels that focused primarily upon the New Negro Renaissance, each mentioned here would easily qualify. We can only conclude that Hughes's memory of events that had recently passed was puzzlingly selective given his friendships with these authors, or he simply never read any novel but Thurman's. Either possibility confirms Thurman's needling of "Tony Crews" (Hughes) in *Infants* as someone with "either . . . no depth whatsoever, or else . . . too deep for plumbing by ordinary mortals."[87] Thurman also considers his friend as lacking, "where his own work is concerned, that discriminating sense of selection which makes the complete artist as critical as he is creative."[88] Although Thurman writes here specifically of Hughes's discrimination and taste in choosing his subjects and editing his own poetry, it is a criticism that Thurman carried over to his personal correspondence, often lambasting Hughes for his inscrutability.

If this issue seems pedantic, let us recall that Nugent and Thurman's frequently charged their fellow "Niggeratti" with failing to care sufficiently about their own art or each other's work to the extent that the former roommates once had. Both Thurman and his avatar Rusty in *Gentleman Jigger* consider themselves intellectual leaders for the younger New Negro set precisely because they think and care deeply about African American literature and literary history far more than for the gin-infused atmosphere that fueled the New Negroes' salons. In one crucial scene from *Jigger,* Rusty expounds on Negro art and his place in the movement: "He was the leader of the Niggeratti, and the Niggeratti led the New Negro. But except for Rusty, they were all rather apathetic leaders. Rusty was the only one of them who had the initiative to push things to the fore—anything, everything—and shade them with black. He was the superb showman—the black Barnum, the opportunist par excellence. He was also vain and had decided that the group was to be recognized as important, and that he was to be recognized as the most important of the group. He was."[89]

Considering how often scholars have cast the movement's midwives as more instrumental than the artists themselves, it might seem odd that Nugent would elevate Rusty/Thurman as the "most important of the group." Even stranger is Stuartt/Nugent as a necessary complement to the brilliant young writer. Thurman's centrality, however, had virtually nothing to do with chronological primacy or whoever made the first mark upon the New Negro Renaissance, much less published the first remarkable poem, story, or novel. Thurman's willingness to define unflinchingly where he and his peers had succeeded and failed *artistically* made him a prime mover, one that Nugent, Hughes, and other authors praised. Unlike Jean Toomer—analogous here to messianic Aeon, the "greatest of living American poets"—Thurman never eschewed his identity *as* a Negro artist, even if he could not accept easy definitions for the term.[90]

To be specific, Rusty/Thurman *can't* eschew his identity; as Sterling—nearly identical to the historical Sterling Brown—tells Rusty, he "can't forget [he's] black" due to his dark skin and marked difference from his fellow Americans, but it "annoys" him that other people "give a damn" due to those differences when he would prefer African Americans to hurry down the path to assimilation. The same holds true for Stuartt.[91] Since neither cannot escape that identity, they "fall back on . . . standards" of literary excellence that appear universal. Through their discussions, the Niggeratti challenge simultaneously "universal" standards and definitions of Negro Art linked to Africa and African aesthetics. At one of the group's gatherings, Stuartt contests whether mere signs—icons—of "African" art make art African, much less African American/Negro. "Well, what do you know about African art?" Stuartt rhetorically asks of his compatriots, answering, "Nothing. Or you wouldn't say so pompously and glibly 'African Art.' One doesn't say 'German art' or 'Italian art' unless it is understood what is meant by such general classification. . . . In most art the feeling that pervades and influences one country is usually felt in other countries. . . . And you don't know a damned thing about African art. Emotionally, psychologically, intellectually, categorically or any goddamned way at all, except in that everlasting dilettante way that's so fashionable these days."[92] To drive home the point, Stuartt argues his friends "couldn't tell a Gabun [*sic*] piece from an Ivory Coast or a Sudan or a Congo or a Benin. In fact, I doubt if you knew there were great enough differentiations in African art to allow for any classification."[93] The fact that Howard/Aaron Douglas draws figures of African Americans "with thick lips and pointed elbows" no more makes his work the "essence of African art . . . converted . . . into modern form" than would *Kente* cloth.[94] Howard/Douglas creates but a pastiche or simulacrum of West African artistic forms, not African art itself.

Aaron Douglas, "Play De Blues," from *Opportunity* magazine, 1926. Art © Heirs of Aaron Douglas, licensed by VAGA, New York, N.Y..

"Negro Art," by extension, can no more exist as anything than a pastiche of different styles. In Stuartt's particular arguments—and here Nugent and Thurman overlap—that art could not stand pat. "The artist," Stuartt contends, "is continually evolving from what he has created in the past. He is a sieve through which all things pass, and only the finest remains to be used and sieved again."[95] From this sieve comes the true artist's modernity; he makes these past influences new. If Aaron Douglas's work fails to obtain this stature, in Stuartt's view, it is due to its superficiality with regard to Sub-Saharan African forms.

Ironically, by this measure we might consider Douglas's art more postmodern than modern primarily because it intentionally creates a pastiche of African art and borrows from multiple sites and influences. And to be fair, Douglas's early work indicates as well a desire to link African Americans as much to the folk culture that emerged in the South as to an African past. Like Zora Neale Hurston, Douglas sought to capture the "*angularity* in everything, sculpture, dancing, abrupt story telling . . . restrained ferocity in everything," and "tense ferocity beneath the casual exterior that stirs the onlooker to hysteria" that both perceived in African American cultural expressions.[96]

Moreover, Douglas's art did indeed evolve over time, taking on additional influences. By the time of 1966's *Song of the Towers* (below), Douglas had expanded his

Spoofing the Modern

repetoire to depict African American culture—specifically jazz—as forged from a barely suggested, perhaps hellish southern, agrarian past, indicated by flames and cotton bolls, and migration to the modern urban towers. He eschews the sort of sharp angles, static figures, and pastiches of African masks and figurines that defined much of his work in the 1920s in favor of softer angles and motion. Whether Douglas ever took Thurman and Nugent's criticism to heart is unclear, but he unquestionably developed his signature mode to fulfill the promise his friends saw. Stuartt rightly criticizes superficial appropriation of African art, whether for the sake of a "Negro" aesthetic or any other reason, but also reveals the general flaw in *Gentleman Jigger* and *Infants of the Spring's* spoof of black modernity.

In "This Negro Literary Renaissance," Thurman argues that the New Negro's rise has resulted in "certain Negroes" becoming "more articulate and more coherent in their cries for social justice, and a few have also begun to appreciate the advantages of racial solidarity and individual achievement," but the movement's results "have been sad rather than satisfactory, in that critical standards have been ignored, and the measure of achievement had been racial rather than literary."[97] Although Thurman obviously restricts these remarks to literature, he extended some aspects

Aaron Douglas, "Song of the Towers," Acrylic on canvas. 1966. Art © Heirs of Aaron Douglas, licensed by VAGA, New York, N.Y..

of his assessment—which resembled Nugent's perspective—to Douglas and other artists. In a 1929 letter to Langston Hughes, Thurman declares that "Aaron [Douglas] needs a change of scenery and a psychic shock," in reference to the younger artists' lack of fresh artistic production.[98] Earlier, however, Thurman had praised his friend's work as "advanced modernism" that featured "raw caricatures of Negro types," thereby indicating a future direction for African American art.[99] Perhaps Thurman and Nugent objected to Douglas's friendship with and informal apprenticeship under Winold Reiss, who "urged Douglas to think of himself as a black artist" and asked him "what kind of picture, what kind of world does a black artist see and transcribe must be responsible for transcribing" over Douglas's preference for landscapes.[100]

If Nugent and Thurman held such reservations, they contradicted public and private compliments toward Douglas's work as well as his obvious inclusion as a contributing editor for and cover artist to *Fire!!*'s sole issue. Since Thurman and the other editors had included Douglas and his work from the project's inception, their regard for his talent is clear. None of Douglas's three pencil-and-ink drawings featured in the magazine's center, moreover, exhibits any obvious African influence, though his incidental illustrations do. Nugent's criticism and Thurman's concern regarding African influences reflect no appreciable sustained evaluation of Douglas; they were among his strongest admirers. Their lampoon is rhetorical, aimed at the same facile Afrocentrism that defined the Garvey movement, which conflated the African continent with a mythical "Africa," one that looked more like an amalgam of Liberia, Sierra Leone, and the Congo than anything real. While Thurman's Raymond Taylor dismisses Garveyism as a "wholesale flight back to Africa" that is as "futile and unintelligent" as Carl Denny's (Douglas's) defense of American blacks' "spontaneous and individual" dancing and singing, Nugent's Rusty and Stuartt defend blacks' "drawing on the culture of Africa—to borrow its forms as we have borrowed our forebears' pigmentation," but only if they truly believe "African art is beautiful" and "consider it art."[101]

The New Negroes' insincerity, rather than a lack of talent, thus emerges as their greatest sin. If Nugent or Thurman disliked African themes and influences in their peers' work, it had little or nothing to do with a revulsion towards Africa itself or as a subject *qua* subject, and everything to do with artistic and intellectual independence that would produce a free, modern sensibility. In "Negro Poets and Their Poetry," Thurman offers Cullen a decidedly backhanded compliment as the "literary apogee" and "symbol of a fast disappearing generation of Negro writers," one "trying to translate into lyric form the highly poetic urge to escape from the blatant realities of life in America into a vivid past" while "fleeing from the stigma of being called a *Negro* poet" by "ignoring folk-material and writing of . . . love and death," thereby making "the banal sound . . . beautiful."[102] Cullen achieves little more than doing what his elders and the poetic tradition expect him to do, dutifully writing about being black in Keatsian lines, rather than upending the tradition or making anything new. His sin? A nearly pure conservatism masking itself with protest lyrics, rather than the radical conservatism found in Claude McKay's "racial" sonnets that simultaneously excoriated racism in a form commonly associated with love, the passage of time, and death rather than defending the barricades.

Yet Thurman feels that McKay's choices restricted him as well, marring his latter poetry with "bombast" in his search for an "emotional depth and spiritual fire" that his peers could not match. The result comprises "mature and moving" verses that indicate McKay really has "something to say," albeit in frames "either stilted, choked, or overzealous." Nevertheless, McKay's triumph is in his unapologetic "revolutionary or protest" work.[103]

Although McKay's "revolutionary" tenor attracted Nugent, Thurman, and other New Negroes, their interest differed from the explicitly radical views that Langston Hughes would express in the 1930s as the Great Depression deepened. For that matter, their appreciation of McKay's "revolutionary" tone had relatively little to do with McKay's own radical political views as he expressed them as an editor and contributor of Max Eastman's the *Liberator* journal in the 1910s and 1920s. Nor did their interest have to do with an abstract or sloppy understanding of revolution as a political act. No, the New Negroes' interest in "revolutionary or protest" material resided squarely in writing as a performative act, language that actually changes the world via the artist's mostly conscious manipulation. It requires understanding the subject empirically. McKay later wrote in his autobiography, *A Long Way From Home*, that the militant sentiment of his most famous poem, "If We Must Die," bore greater relevance to workers' struggles—and therefore was more revolutionary— than Communist critics of the time would allow:

> I did not come to the knowing of Negro workers in an academic way, by talking to black crowds at meetings, nor in a bohemian way, by talking about them at cafés. I knew the unskilled Negro worker of the city by working with him. I lived in the same quarters and we drank and caroused together in bars and at rent parties. So when I came to write about the low-down Negro, I did not have to compose him from an outside view. Nor did I have to write a pseudo-romantic account, as do bourgeois persons who become working-class for awhile and working in shops and factories to get material for writing dull books about workers, whose inner lives are closed to them.[104]

The year 1919's "If We Must Die," moreover, emerged directly from McKay's experiences working as a waiter on railroad dining cars crossing the United States, where "Negro railroad men were nervous" and "stuck together, some . . . armed" to protect each other from the violence against African Americans that exploded in American cities and the South in general that summer.[105] The authenticity of "If We Must Die"—one of many poems McKay produced from this feeling—led to "the Negro people unanimously hail[ing McKay] as a poet" once Eastman, Frank Harris, and other American editors recognized and published his talents. Equally important, McKay's passionate verses collected in *Harlem Shadows* (1922) realized the various aesthetics that black critics would later elucidate in the special issue of *Survey Graphic* that became Alain Locke's anthology, *The New Negro* (1925).[106] Articulating a fighting spirit in which embattled "men" would "face the murderous cowardly pack" of violent mobs, "If We Must Die" obliterated the image of the timid, genteel, long-suffering Negro so familiar to the broader American public. In its place McKay offered personae that would inspire his fellow workers to agitation and tears,[107] and won praise from Thurman, the Niggeratti's most severe critic.

We might attribute some of McKay's favor in Thurman and Nugent's eyes to his somewhat closer ties to the Harlem group compared to other *causes célèbres,* such as Cullen and Jean Toomer. Despite his residence in Greenwich Village's artistic circles, ongoing ties to radicalism, and notoriously difficult personality—Nugent said that McKay "would pick [verbal] fights" frequently, and considered him "an intensely subjective person"—he also thought well of *Fire!!,* which prompted Thurman's February 3, 1928, introductory letter and a brief correspondence.[108] In an October 4, 1928, letter, Thurman solicited McKay's work for the equally short-lived *Harlem* magazine before summarizing his balanced assessment from "Negro Poets and their Poetry."[109] "What I said about you," Thurman writes exasperatedly, "has aroused much antagonism. I contended that you had more . . . depth than any of your contemporaries and that you were the only truly revolutionary poet of the lot . . . . Despite some other things which I have said about you which were not quite so complimentary, I have been accused of being your press agent. Can you beat it? Countee was so upset about the whole matter that he wrote a special paragraph to be included in the *Dark Tower* 'laying me low.'"[110] If Thurman and McKay appear to have formed a mutual admiration society, it's worth recalling that Thurman argued that McKay had, in fact, earned his praise. Like so many other satirists, particularly those in the New Negro period, Thurman, Nugent, Schuyler, and Fisher mourned the dearth of merit among their fellow writers and lampooned their peers' every attempt to embrace the black bourgeoisie's efforts to promote the movement.

Ultimately, Thurman and Nugent's shared efforts in *Infants of the Spring* and *Gentleman Jigger* reveal how much the New Negroes disdained their own press. The lights shining upon the former Niggeratti Manor at the conclusion of *Infants* reveal not only a failed enterprise, but also an edifice constructed with a decidedly contingent aesthetic foundation. When the manor's denizens go their separate ways in *Gentleman Jigger,* their dispersal results directly from the only prodigious issue of

Spoofing the Modern

their associations and salons: talk. "In a moment of clarity," Stuartt muses, Rusty "had summed up the great doings of the Niggeratti, and discovered that they mostly existed in talk. Rusty had written four articles that had been published and paid for. Nona had written any number of short stories, one of which had been published. She then had disappeared—gone South to further her studies in anthropology. Theresa had written one story since the appearance of the *Current,* had been kicked out of her position, and then had married. She was now somewhere in Georgia, either having a child a year or abortions."[111]

Stuartt wishes for Rusty to write the great book he has always aspired, but what finally emerges is the quasi-plagiarized manuscript analogous to *Infants,* "a play that had been produced on Broadway"—analogous to Thurman and William Jourdan Rapp's *Harlem* (no relation to the magazine)—that "was not a particularly good play."[112] Meanwhile, "all of the [other] promising young Negroes wrote. Bad books, but books. Stuartt himself had done one or two illustrations for magazine articles. That was all. Paul had gone back to Harvard, where he studied law." Worst of all, Stuartt's brother Aeon—equivalent to Jean Toomer—dies, leaving the movement without a truly great, modern poet.[113] Toomer had renounced his identity as an African American for the sake of being an American, despite his earlier inclusion in the movement's publications, and soon disappeared, for all intents and purposes, from the literary scene in Harlem and elsewhere.

Of course, the New Negro movement's death has been slightly exaggerated, even if Thurman and Fisher's very real demises robbed it of two immensely intelligent and talented lights. We know that, once freed of her contract with Charlotte Osgood Mason, Hurston (Nona), who began publishing books and worked as a folklorist and anthropologist under Mason and Franz Boas's aegis, went on to become—albeit posthumously—the Niggeratti's most celebrated author after Langston Hughes. Along with so many other black artists, Cullen and McKay's written output declined in the 1930s, but their work remains heavily anthologized and quoted today. In the 1930s in general, black writers produced far more books than had emerged during the 1920s alone, though far too few gained the stature that Richard Wright—Hughes's protégé and nearly the Niggeratti's contemporary—would enjoy by the 1930s' conclusion.

None of this is to argue that Nugent and Thurman's concern regarding their fellows lacks merit, only that both their contemporary and retrospective views on the movement they spurred and developed did not allow for one possibility: that the movement's seemingly excessive "talk" would become the very foundation that Niggeratti Manor seemed to lack. In Langston Hughes's words, the Niggeratti did, in fact, build their "temples for tomorrow, as strong as [they knew] how."[114] *Infants of the Spring* and *Gentleman Jigger* ask us to reconcile an individualistic group consciousness, normally considered an oxymoron in the context of the United States' traditional antipathy towards group cohesion, when it stands in the way of assimilation. In Thurman and Nugent's highly contingent shared sense of modernity, with its deep debt to the pragmatism of William James, this dilemma finds a complex pair of voices struggling with its implications. Through Raymond, Thurman tempts us to dismiss his ideological underpinnings as inherently unrealistic in view of the nationalism that Richard Wright argues is a natural, if problematic, step towards the liberation of African American art and culture. If a nationalist consciousness requires at least a minimal degree of subsumption of the individual will to that of the loosely unified polity, how could the individual and his art *not* be conscripted into the forces of propaganda? As Thurman's complement, Nugent demands that these dueling imperatives remain ever in tension, with one side of the dichotomy ascending as necessary to resolve the question at hand. Both argue that common American principles upheld by masses of African Americans are the crucial links to African Americans' cultural and political progress.

4

Dickties vs. Rats

Class and Regional Differences within the New Negro Movement

In 1920s black Harlem, class differences were impossible to ignore. Walking down a sidewalk meant coming into contact with members of the "Talented Tenth" (as W. E. B. Du Bois identified the black bourgeoisie), "kitchen mechanics" (cooks), maids, Pullman porters, panhandlers, hustlers of various goods (legitimate or contraband), messengers, entertainers, ministers, pimps, prostitutes, teachers, civil rights leaders, political activists, writers, artists, sculptors, poets, policemen (black and white), day laborers, construction workers, doctors, nurses, and representatives from virtually every profession in which African Americans managed to compete. While such an occupational mix was not unusual in itself, least of all in New York City, the *novelty* of black people from so many professions and occupations being able to gather and live together in attractive real estate near the heart of the nation's greatest city—a truly cosmopolitan city—cannot be overstated. Harlem looked like the future of modern black America.

That apparent future remained far from a classless utopia. As the "City of Refuge," as Rudolph Fisher called it, Harlem attracted not only a diverse, eclectic citizenry, but also its class aspirations, affectations, and prejudices, regardless of whether the newly arrived came from Birmingham, Alabama; Waycross, Georgia; Kansas City, Missouri; Los Angeles, California; Eatonville, Florida; Port-au-Prince, Haiti; Chicago, Illinois; Durham, North Carolina; Washington, D.C.; Kingston, Jamaica; San Juan, Puerto Rico; Havana, Cuba; Port-of-Spain, Trinidad and Tobago; or any number of islands, cities, towns, and villages throughout the Americas. Though desires for modernity and economic and cultural freedom brought together people from such disparate backgrounds and careers, the beliefs they held also separated them socially, sometimes as rigidly as the barriers of legal segregation—Jim Crow—that those from the South had left behind as they crossed Mason-Dixon

Line. The community's very geography seemed to reinforce this gap. The masses of black Harlemites lived mostly in the flat grids between the southwestern boundary of 125th Street to the Harlem River in the north-northeast. Between Seventh and Eighth avenues—today's Adam Clayton Powell and Frederick Douglass Boulevards, respectively—could be found Strivers' Row, the elegant array of brownstones on West 138th and 139th streets, where Harlem's wealthy professionals, artists, and aspirants resided. Several blocks' walk due north leads to Sugar Hill, overlooking Harlem and St. Nicholas Park. On Sugar Hill, especially in the apartments at 409 Edgecombe Avenue, could be found the community's wealthiest or most storied elite; "sugar" is slang for money.

Black Harlem's existence and rapid growth during the New Negro movement were, in a sense, direct products of African Americans' desires for class mobility. Although African Americans had lived in Harlem since at least the late nineteenth century, most historians of the period agree that Harlem started its transformation into the Black Mecca in 1904, when African American real estate developers, most notably Phillip A. Payton Jr., began stealthily to buy up buildings on 134th and 135th streets between Lenox and Fifth avenues, then "block-bust" whites out of the neighborhood by renting to blacks.[1] Whites would flee surrounding buildings, and property owners would sell at reduced prices. The vacated properties could then be rented and sold to black applicants at higher prices. Harlem's abundant stock of superior real estate constituted its major draw for newcomers from the South, or even from southern parts of Manhattan. Those African Americans from rural areas accustomed to living near or below the poverty line with access only to inadequate housing viewed Harlem's brownstones with heat and running water as ideal sites in which to realize visions of opportunity and wealth. Even the high rents and slow, inexorable movement towards squalor in many buildings converted to tenements were not enough to dissuade the new migrants and established tenants. Moreover, though Strivers' Row and Sugar Hill were the provinces of the wealthiest, the enterprising working-class Harlemite could achieve them via a combination of heavy work, rent parties, and luck.

Income and distance, of course, were not the only barriers separating the average Harlemite from the ranks of the elite. College or university educations, work in the more lucrative professions of medicine and law, and the traditional businesses and occupations of the African American middle class—insurance, funeral homes, fraternal orders, the ministry—created a cultural gulf that separated the Talented Tenth from the masses. E. Franklin Frazier argues in *The Black Bourgeoisie* that "higher education [for African Americans] has become devoted chiefly to the task of educating the black bourgeoisie," primarily in the fields of business and the professions.[2] Frazier found particularly alarming the black bourgeoisie's dedication to the idea that "money will bring them justice in equality in American life, and they

Spoofing the Modern

propose to get money."[3] The ethos of thrift, industry, and pursuit of business and wealth that Booker T. Washington posited in his long tenure as the leading African American of this time remained vibrant long after his death, extending easily to our present. Though he is better known as Washington's chief ideological rival and as an advocate for civil rights for all African Americans, even W. E. B. Du Bois—the black bourgeoisie's most progressive stalwart—remained as wedded to the material and social trappings of that class as any other. All but the most radical members of the black middle-class dreamed of or remained captivated by residences on Sugar Hill, salons and formal balls, membership in social and philanthropic organizations and networks, and entrée to the best schools and political appointments. To that extent, they differed little from the "Old Negro" invested in premodern Victorian values, save for the promise that modernity held.

Although writing in the late 1950s, Frazier's observations came from both his own researches conducted in the 1940s and 1950s, and his own experiences as a lesser-known, yet significant member of the younger generation of the New Negro movement. Moreover, Frazier's analyses and arguments could be found echoed in a great deal of support in the writings of the time. We have already seen how George S. Schuyler and Wallace Thurman revealed the middle class's unstinting obsession with showing the best of "the race" to the ever-present white world. For both Schuyler and Thurman, such a portrait could never hold, as the troubling diversity of the masses, in all their glory and folly, would inevitably emerge, either by the democratic will of those masses, or through the efforts of the writers and artists, black and white, who would manifest it in their work. The efforts of members of the black bourgeoisie to restrict and control the images of African Americans found in art and literature, therefore, interfered with the democratic impulse that blacks shared with their fellow citizens. What group could be a better source of satire? It collectively desired freedom and democracy for African Americans—in particular, those like itself—yet a substantial number within it feared a democratic vista of free expression.

The New Negro movement's lesser-known satirical authors were equally apt to investigate this disconnect in their works as their more celebrated and cynical peers Schuyler and Thurman. Although both Florida's Zora Neale Hurston and Rhode Island's Dr. Rudolph "Bud" Fisher were members of the black literati, or "Niggeratti," and enjoyed great respect among their peers for their rich wit, storytelling skills, and intelligence, each also stood apart from the rest of the group. Besides her 1891 birth—a decade earlier than most of the literati, and a fact she kept hidden in her autobiography *Dust Tracks on a Road* (1942)—Hurston stood apart as a woman from the deep South, a heritage she wore proudly and assertively as she told endless stories with a witty flair reflecting her background and genius.

As a medical doctor specializing in radiology and roentgenology, Fisher stood apart in occupation alone, as did his residence in suburban Long Island instead of Harlem. Yet his passion for reading and prolifically writing literature, his accomplished musicianship, and incredibly quick wit made Fisher a revered member of the Harlem group. Both Hurston and Fisher wrote and published astounding numbers of short stories during the New Negro movement's height and earned considerable if varying degrees of respect from their peers. Both saw their careers interrupted or cut short in mid-stride: Hurston, due to a crippling and ill-advised patronage contract, condescension, and abiding sexism in the black artistic and intellectual circles; Fisher, by his untimely death in 1934 at the age of thirty-seven.

Though Fisher remains little known outside of a few of his most prominent essays and short stories, even the most casual student of the African American literary tradition now recognizes Hurston as a major author, thanks primarily to author Alice Walker and other scholars who revived interest in Hurston beginning in the 1970s. Yet during the New Negro movement, Hurston never received her due, despite close friendships with the movement's patrons and leading figures. In her fiction and essays, we see glimpses of Hurston's wryly bitter bemusement as a southern black woman with talents barely acknowledged or understood. In few places is this more evident than 1939's retelling of the biblical Mosaic myth and Exodus, *Moses, Man of the Mountain,* in which hapless and obtuse male leaders routinely deny women due credit for their abilities. But Hurston could also write satire equaling anything Schuyler, Thurman, or Nugent created, as in her unpublished mock encomium, "The Emperor Effaces Himself," and the recently discovered "Monkey Junk: A Satire on Modern Divorce," originally published in an obscure newspaper in 1927.[4] The former lampoons Marcus Garvey for his flamboyance, while the latter offers a cynical take on romance, marriage, cuckoldry, and divorce in Harlem. Notably, "Monkey Junk" reveals Hurston's early penchant for parodying biblical narratives, as she does in *Moses, Man of the Mountain* and numerous essays and stories. Hurston places herself squarely within a long African American folk tradition that translates scripture into contemporary terms, but with a significant twist; as "Monkey Junk's" subtitle indicates, Hurston's text is *modern* divorce in the African American community. Both "The Emperor Effaces Himself" and "Monkey Junk" imply a simple truth: it matters little how well black folks assume modernity's trappings and technology; they remain as susceptible to flimflammery and balderdash in the city as in the South.

Though no record exists of Fisher receiving any inspiration or assistance from Hurston for his 1928 novel *The Walls of Jericho,* it relies upon the same motif, riffing off of the biblical account of Joshua at the battle of Jericho, to say nothing of the spiritual "Joshua Fit the Battle of Jericho." A roman à clef similar to Thurman's *The Blacker the Berry . . .* (1929) and *Infants of the Spring* (1932) or Nugent's *Gentleman Jigger* (2008), *The Walls of Jericho* preceded all of these and stands as the first glimpse in fiction of the black literati's divisions by a member of that group. Fisher lampoons the powerful and influential members of the black bourgeoisie, their white patrons, and—briefly—the artists enjoying a moment of glory in the Jazz Age. Although decidedly less biting than Hurston (to say nothing of Thurman or Nugent), Fisher clearly perceived various regional and class prejudices that threatened to drive apart African American community and stop progress towards modernity.

Both authors warn of deleterious snobbery and cynicism across class and regional lines that threaten to calcify and hobble black progress. Only by acknowledging and eliminating these divisions will African American leaders, artists, and working-class folk find a common path to a truly modern, more open future in which African Americans accept regional, class, or gender differences as assets for mutual benefit instead of liabilities holding back the "race." Fisher and Hurston's satirical observations construct Harlem as a site where the modern New Negro constantly struggled to escape a feudal past only to confront his or her own cultural prejudices.

Effacing the Once and Future Empress

Modern literary history is peppered with cases of authors who were grossly underestimated in their time, but later—often posthumously—found a new audience that appreciated their work as literary standards, interests, and tastes broadened. Nearly all of the authors studied here fit that description. Few stories have been so wondrous as that of Zora Neale Hurston, who died almost penniless in Fort Pierce, Florida on January 28, 1960, with her books out of print, nearly forgotten by the coterie of friends with whom she conversed and corresponded over four decades. Until Alice Walker led a successful campaign in the 1970s to bring back into print Hurston's masterwork, *Their Eyes Were Watching God,* the literary world was poised to lose the New Negro Renaissance's most unusual author deep within a pit of obscurity. Unlike such peers as Wallace Thurman and Rudolph Fisher, of course, Hurston lived to an advanced age, and wrote and published excellent work at a respectable, even prolific clip, in some of the better venues for African American authors in the 1920s, 1930s, and 1940s. She did share with her contemporaries, however, criticism that was either dismissive or derogatory, and—in Hurston's case—tainted with sexism. As Alice Walker writes in her preface to Robert S. Hemenway's biography, Hurston was "funny, irreverent (she was the first to call the Harlem Renaissance literati the 'niggerati'), good-looking, and sexy. . . . Her critics disliked even the 'rags' on her head. . . . With her easy laughter and her southern drawl, her belief in doing cullud dancing *authentically,* Zora seemed—among these genteel "New Negroes" of the Harlem Renaissance—*black.*"[5]

Walker's assessment of Hurston's critics understandably focuses upon their disdain for Hurston personally and as a woman, but she gives little attention to the substance of assessments that nearly wrote her out of serious consideration as a novelist, folklorist, and essayist. Perhaps this is an unfortunate consequence of Walker's desire to make Hurston more *authentic* than some of her contemporaries. When Walker wrote her introduction in the late 1970s, that authenticity as a black woman, with both aspects of that identity emphasized equally, was crucial, lest Hurston's iconoclasm and political heterodoxy—she objected to the 1954 *Brown v. Board of Education of Topeka, Kansas* U.S. Supreme Court decision—keep her from regaining a foothold in African American cultural and literary history. This is not to say that contemporary animus towards Hurston was not personal; retrospectives from the late 1930s and early 1940s undeniably attack Hurston as a person. Richard Wright's excoriation of Harlem Renaissance authors as "prim and decorous ambassadors who went a-begging to white America" who "entered the Court of American Public Opinion dressed in the knee-pants of servility, curtsying to show that the Negro was not inferior, that he was human, and that he had a life comparable to that of other people" and who "were received as though they were French poodles who do clever tricks" reads as a thinly veiled attack upon Hurston for enjoying white patronage and supporting the cult of primitivism.[6]

The result for Wright was "humble novels, poems, and plays" that failed to challenge the existing social order.[7] In his equally negative review of *Their Eyes Were Watching God,* Wright charges that Hurston "*voluntarily* continues in her novel the tradition which was *forced* upon the Negro in the theater, that is, the minstrel technique that makes the 'white folks' laugh. Her characters eat and laugh and cry and work and kill," revealing a "sensory sweep" that "carries no theme, no message, no thought." Finally, Wright concludes, Hurston's novel "is not addressed to the Negro, but to a white audience whose chauvinistic tastes she knows how to satisfy."[8] This last comment matches Wallace Thurman's assessment of Hurston as an opportunist who relates folklore to whites for entertainment so she can eat.[9] Similarly, Langston Hughes's portrait of Hurston in *The Big Sea* (1940) praises her for her storytelling abilities and friendship, but also reduces her to being a "perfect 'darkie'" who "was always getting scholarships and things from wealthy white people, some of whom simply paid her just to sit around and represent the Negro race for them, she did it in such a racy fashion."[10]

As John Lowe argues, Hurston's critics, whether her contemporaries or those who later decried her relationships with white patrons and friends, were hypocritical, disingenuous, or sexist in their attention to the sensuality in her work.[11] As we have seen, Hughes also received scholarships, gifts, and other funds from Charlotte Osgood Mason, with whom both Hughes and Hurston arguably played the role of the African American primitive. In slightly different ways, the same was true for Alain Locke, who cultivated a close personal and financial relationship with Mason, yet also minimized Hurston's talents to those of an author of "folklore fiction at its best," and pressed her to write "social document fiction," which would take her afar from her "cradle gift" as a writer, implying that Hurston simply was not trying very hard, and was stuck in a primitivism that failed to move African American fiction forward.[12] Wright, of course, had no relationship to Mason, but benefited directly from another sort of patronage via the publications of the Communist Party USA's front groups.

My purpose here is not to place these authors in a game of one-upmanship in which the artist with the greatest amount of white patronage loses his or her authenticity and right to speak. That would fruitlessly reproduce the same dynamic that drove apart the era's writers. Moreover, the artist completely free from a white gaze or bank account simply did not exist among the New Negroes of the 1920s and 1930s. Rather, I wish simply to demonstrate that these accusations and implications served to turn attention away from careful assessments of Hurston's work and toward the vexed relationship between the African American author and her or his eternally present "white" audience. Such a careful assessment would reveal Hurston's consummate skill not only as a storyteller, but also as a humorist of the first order, one who imbued her short stories, essays, and novels with picaresque heroes, irony, and satire. Her detractors' failure to grasp this view stems from a marked "sexist, anti-Southern bias," one that nearly agrees with primitivists such as Mason in consigning Southern African Americans to the role of backwards primitives who have failed to achieve the beholder's definition of modernity.[13]

Walker's last comment above hints at a significant reason Hurston fell into disfavor. While the New Negro Renaissance represented an opportunity for African American intellectuals and authors to appreciate folk cultures that form what we now recognize as the heart of African American expression, many did not. Of those who did, very few were actually from the South that produced the blues and jazz that Langston Hughes drew upon for his poetry, especially in the earliest days of his career. Lowe argues further that for her harshest critics, Hurston's employment of humor in both her life and her writings was done without the irony and signifying tropes that would have qualified it as the sort of expression that would be deemed acceptable: as satire.[14] That such critics as Wright and Locke failed to detect the extent of Hurston's irony raises a perennially troubling component of the production and reception of satire. To put it bluntly, readers and critics—often male—seldom expect a woman author to produce satire in any sustained, written form. Satire's tendency to employ aggressive forms of irony tends to be gendered male, a skill accorded those expected to go for the jugular, whether writing in a surgically precise rhetorical mode, or in the type of content to be included.

When Hurston began publishing her fiction in New Negro magazines of the mid-1920s, literary examples of satire, irony, and parody by African American women were difficult to find, even if the ironic tropes of black folklife—tropes Hurston mastered—were well known. Criticism across gender lines, of course, has been part of African American literature since Phillis Wheatley's debut, but the type of acerbic wit Hurston possessed found few antecedents in print; primarily such activists as Sojourner Truth and Ida B. Wells-Barnett attacked their opponents with witty approbation. Only Pauline Hopkins's serialized novel *Of One Blood* (1903) appropriated satirical modes of criticizing racism. Hurston thus faced an extraordinarily difficult set of circumstances in garnering respect for her particular brand of wit, much less establishing a reputation as a humorous or satirical writer. A crucial component in this set may be found in this devastating caricature in Wallace Thurman's roman à clef, *Infants of the Spring*: "Sweetie May Carr [Hurston] . . . was a short story writer, more noted for her ribald wit and personal effervescence than for any actual literary work. . . . [She] was a master of southern dialect, and an able raconteur, but she was too indifferent to literary creation to transfer to paper that which she told so well. The intricacies of writing bored her, and her written work was for the most part turgid and unpolished."[15]

Beyond implying that Hurston lacks the competence to write due to a lack of focus, Thurman asserts that she lacks the skill to tackle literature. Ironically, Thurman was one of Hurston's first editors. Even if the sole issue of *Fire!!* (1926) had the appearance of a group effort, Thurman functioned as its primary editor. Hurston's provocative story "Sweat" was among the magazine's features alongside contributions by Hughes, Richard Bruce Nugent, Aaron Douglas, and Thurman himself. Thurman's own literary output in novels, short stories, and poetry was both somewhat limited, and by his own assessment, evidenced lack of polish and skill. Why, then, would he dismiss his peer so cavalierly?

One of their respected fellows, writer and artist Richard Bruce Nugent, made clear that "only two, maybe three, of that Niggerati group felt anything more than this surface business of 'how can I make a splash.'" Those two or three consisted of Thurman, Hughes, and Hurston, and "more than any other people, Zora and Langston were the ones who gave *Fire!!* any of the artistic solidity that it had."[16] For Nugent—the most Bohemian of all the "Niggeratti"—to assert that Hurston and Hughes showed the clearest promise of artistic achievement makes Thurman's dismissiveness somewhat questionable; the fact of her eventual output virtually obviates it.

At the time he wrote *Infants of the Spring*, of course, Thurman had seen little of what we now know of Zora Neale Hurston, the author. Soon after Hurston published under Thurman's editorial eye, she made the acquaintance of Mrs. Mason, who required Hurston to enter into a binding agreement that placed her work under controls that severely damaged and slowed the progress of Hurston's career as a writer and contributor to the spirit of the New Negro Renaissance. Hurston met Mason on September 20, 1927, via Alain Locke, for the sake of securing support for the black folk opera—the ill-fated "Mule Bone"—that Hurston was planning with Langston Hughes.[17] As the bonds between Hurston and Mason developed, the latter became

Spoofing the Modern

"Godmother"—the name she required those under her patronage to call her—and Hurston's patron. Two and a half months later, on December 8, Hurston signed an employment contract with Mason that required Hurston to conduct anthropological research on Mason's behalf.[18] Like Rudolph Fisher's caricature, Agatha Cramp, Mason had long been interested in the lives of "primitive" peoples, but as an elderly, arthritic, hearing-impaired white woman, she possessed neither the physical means nor cultural cachet to investigate the foci of her curiosities firsthand. Due to her own intense interest in collecting folklore, Hurston was a willing agent in the agreement. The contract's perniciousness developed as Hurston's scientific and literary interests coalesced. Mason had total contractual control over any material Hurston collected as her agent. In effect, if Hurston wished to make use of the folklore she discovered, whether in the form of scholarly publications or as part of short stories and novels, she could not legally do so until the contract expired at the end of 1928, or if the contract was extended, as it was through 1929.[19]

In effect, Mason wholly owned the products of Hurston's genius for the remainder of the New Negro's zenith. Hurston's voice was effectively silenced in the crucial years that such peers and occasional collaborators as Thurman and Fisher—neither of whom accepted Mason's largess—and Claude McKay or Hughes—both of whom did—wrote and published some of their best work. That she was silenced by willingly entering into a contract with a powerful *white* patron with condescending views of African Americans and others further compromised her standing in some of their eyes. Thurman's assessment of Hurston, while pointedly cruel, had its basis in the simple fact that Hurston, once the New Negro movement's most inspired and prolific author, published virtually nothing from the moment she signed her contract until its expiration. From late 1924 through October 1927, Hurston published an average of five pieces per year. Other than a rich correspondence with patrons, close friends, and a diverse assortment of acquaintances, only the merest hints of Hurston's genius emerged from the once prolific artist's desk between November 1927 and the release of *Jonah's Gourd Vine* in 1934, and then only surreptitiously, with Mason exercising her control through Alain Locke, also one of her beneficiaries. As Carla Kaplan recounts, when Hurston delayed and abandoned a biography of Cudjo Lewis, the last African survivor of slavery in the United States, in favor of writing and producing her folk play *The Great Day* (1930), Mason and Locke upbraided Hurston by declaring the play's successful debut a "failure," reminding her of her contractual obligations, rewriting her contract, and otherwise attempting to bring her back under Godmother's control.[20] In a grand ironic twist, Hurston saw her creative efforts, particularly *The Great Day* and *Mules and Men*, then in progress, as "a way to get away from 'the oleo-margarine era in Negro writing . . . everything butterfish about it except butter.'"[21] At a point when Hurston's peers wanted black writing to escape faddism, primitivism, and white domination and control, Mason and Locke actively quashed Hurston's efforts to fulfill that promise and to revive a voice her friends had heard clearly but a few years earlier.

These friends could not have let this difference go unnoticed. Thurman's remarks above indicate that one of the most respected "Niggeratti" took Hurston's dearth of new material as proof of her inadequacies and apathy as a writer. Thurman apparently neither knew nor appreciated that his peer was all too conscious of the price she paid. Hurston's frustration with Mason's restrictions is palpable in multiple letters to her peers. In April 1928, Hurston tells Hughes "I could *really* write a Village Anthology now, but I am wary of mentioning it to Godmother for fear she will think I am shirking but *boy* I think [I] could lay 'em something now. I told you I must publish without her consent."[22] On December 5, 1928, Hurston told fellow author Dorothy West, "Wish I could help out on 'Harlem' but it is impossible at present. I'm heartbroken over being bound to silence [by Mason's contract]."[23] Finally, in a mid-1929 letter to Hughes, Hurston writes, "NO, I haven't told [Godmother] that I sent you the material [from Hurston's folklore-collecting activities]. I wanted to get your reaction before sending it to her. I have been full of fear and trembling for what I have done. I feel that I have been honest, but the question [that prompted Hurston to send the material] was, how will it strike others. I started out to manufacture some conclusions and found that I didnt have to. There is too much that is true to say."[24]

Two years later, in 1931, Hurston's inability to publish her material contributed to the conflict over authorship of the play *Mule Bone* that effectively ended her relationship with Hughes. In a letter dated March 8, 1928, Hurston informed Hughes that she had "the street scene still & 2 others [from their collaboration on the folk opera] in my mind—if you want them you can use them for yourself and its O.K. by me. Godmother asked me not to publish and as I am making money I hope you can use them."[25] Although Hurston appears to cede authorship of this material to Hughes, she would later argue that she not only had no intention of surrendering the project to Hughes, but also that her collaborator had abandoned *Mule Bone.* The issue arose when Hughes discovered that the Charles Gilpin Players in Cleveland, Ohio, were staging what Hughes had known as *The Bone of Contention,* the folk opera he and Hurston had labored over in 1928–29. Furious, Hughes confronted Hurston, accusing her of theft. In January 1931, Hurston countered that Hughes had attempted to steal the play from her by dividing authorship with Louise Thompson, whom Hughes had appointed as a typist. "Not that I care what you give of yourself and your things," Hurston writes, "but I do object to having my work hi-jacked. There is no other word for it."[26]

The timing of the conflict could not have been worse. After years of having her creative output strictly controlled (Hurston was still under Mason's contract), her two fellow protégés and friends—Thompson was also in Mason's employ, had once been married to Wallace Thurman former wife, and part of the now-fractured Nig-geratti—disputed Hurston's claim on some of the rich material she had collected. Af-ter attempts at a rapprochement, the various parties remained divided two months later when Hurston wrote Hughes's attorney (and Harlem Renaissance patron), Ar-thur Spingarn, "I think it would be lovely for your client to be a play-wright but I'm afraid that I am too tight to make him one at my expense. You have written plays, why not do him one yourself? Or perhaps a nice box of apples and a well chosen corner. But never no play of mine."[27] Hurston would never work with Hughes as a friend and collaborator again. She would also cut off her links with Alain Locke, who became one of Hurston's strongest critics, while Godmother would end her support in 1933.

Hurston's absence from the active literary scene, as well as her conflicts with Hughes, Thompson, Locke, and others meant that Hurston missed an opportunity to help define African American literature in the 1930s with the ironic sensibility that would have placed the tropes at the heart of African American folklore in the literature's center. This gap appears wider given Hurston's reports of her findings while under Mason's contract. In the same letter to Hughes of April 1928 in which she expresses her desire to write a "Village Anthology," Hurston outlines seven "gen-eral laws" regarding black cultural forms that would eventually be incorporated into her essay "Characteristics of Negro Expression," published in 1934. They include "drama" (that is, "mimicry" of the external world); a tendency to be "lacking in reverence"; "angularity in everything, sculpture, dancing, abrupt story telling"; "re-dundance" and "repetition" of elements in stories and music; "restrained ferocity in everything," a "tense ferocity beneath the casual exterior that stirs the onlooker to hysteria," especially if those onlookers are "nordic"; certain forms of "dialect" with varying rules; the observation that "Negro folk-lore is *still* in the making[;] a new kind is crowding out the old."[28]

Of these laws, Hurston's assertion of the "angularity" of black expression and insistence upon its protean nature are striking, as they refuse to accept a single approach to African American culture. In "Characteristics of Negro Expression," Hurston expands her definition of "angularity" by offering a few examples: "Every posture is another angle. Pleasing, yes. But an effect achieved by the very means which an European strives to avoid. The pictures on the walls are hung at deep an-gles. Furniture is always set at an angle."[29] Angularity as both a literal characteristic and a metaphor reinforces the aesthetic that Hughes outlines in "The Negro Artist and the Racial Mountain," while further widening the space for African American literature and culture to stand apart from and comment upon the culture of Euro-peans or America's white majority. It describes the "swing" and syncopation of jazz, whether in Hurston's time or later eras. More significantly, it undergirds the ironic expression found in literature of the New Negro Renaissance, including Hurston's own satirical works. To be angular is to be iconoclastic in some degree, to avoid the straight shot at a subject, to resist the superficial, straightforward interpretation.

Satire in the Harlem Renaissance reifies Hurston's assertion, which makes her enforced silence on this point more unsettling. The radicalism among black and white Americans that grew with the desperation of the Great Depression also made possible the rise of Richard Wright as a literary force. As Wright's star rose, so did Hurston's, but her chance to establish an intellectual basis for black expression was eclipsed in part by Wright's own interpretation of black folk culture, an explicitly political reading of everyday life in the Jim Crow South, as well as the deeply segregated North. Hurston's more oblique interpretations found in *Mules and Men,* while still powerful and well received, did not possess the blunt force that Hughes had been writing into his own poetry and prose, and that Wright would soon turn into his trademark. Hurston, to be certain, never denied the reality of racism, nor did her characters ignore it. As Hurston's most accomplished collection of African American folklore, *Mules and Men,* framed in the lens of her anthropological training, offers countless examples of tales—many with roots in slavery—that explicitly satirize the precarious position of blacks under the brutalities of slavery and racist oppression. Equally important, these tales enjoin listeners and readers in the way of common sense and communal understandings of morality.

Hurston's attraction to the folk extends beyond the moral cautionary narrative found in so many tales. Before the long silence in her early publishing career, Hurston's short stories and essays revealed a singular wit, an ironist no less skilled than contemporaries Fisher, Schuyler, and Thurman, albeit less prolific than that trio. Only recently, in fact, has the general public had access to the most devastating satirical work in Hurston's written oeuvre, excluding her letters. Hurston's 1925 lampoon of Marcus Garvey and the UNIA, "The Emperor Effaces Himself," remained unpublished for eighty-five years, finally seeing print in Henry Louis Gates and Jennifer Burton's anthology *Call and Response* (2010). Although several Hurston scholars have mentioned the essay briefly, the most extensive analysis to date—about one short paragraph—may be found in Robert Hemenway's *Zora Neale Hurston: A Literary Biography* (1978). Save for the inevitable errors of an early draft, Hurston's essay equals any of George Schuyler's columns excoriating the "Emperor Marcus Garvey."

The essay's pretense is simple, contained within the title itself: Garvey, well known for his bombastic writings and declarations, unprecedented pomp and flamboyance among leaders of the Black Diaspora, and bewildering incompetence in most business matters, is in fact a man of "overwhelming modesty," who on August 1, 1924, could be found "sneaking down [Lenox] Avenue [in Harlem] in terrible dread lest he attract attention to himself," succeeding "nobly, for scarcely fifty thousand persons saw his parade file past trying to hide itself behind numerous banners of red, green, and black."[30] The event Hurston describes is the UNIA's 1924 convention, the organization's last great hurrah before Garvey, the organization's president, supreme potentate, and provisional emperor of Africa—all self-bestowed titles—began serving his prison sentence at the federal penitentiary in Atlanta for his 1923 conviction for mail fraud. Garvey's prison term was followed by the Jamaica native's deportation and consequent disappearance from the forefront of African American politics.

Hurston's lampoon focuses upon Garvey's propensity to assume titles and comparisons to great figures in world history. "On the walls of his living room in 129th Street," Hurston writes, "there hung a large picture of Napoleon. On the opposite wall hung one, still larger, of himself. It is evident he wished no comparisons drawn. If he had, he would have caused them to be hung side by side."[31] As Colin Grant notes, Garvey's tendency to admire such legendary leaders and strongmen as Napoleon, Otto von Bismarck, Toussaint L'Ouverture, and Benito Mussolini was more than the embarrassing pretense that his critics leapt upon; it signaled his canniness in marketing his organization for public consumption by blacks with high expectations after centuries of oppression and uneven leadership.[32] Garvey's genius was in adopting the structures of past and present institutions that had successfully provided organized bases for African American social and cultural life in the brutal face of Jim Crow and in the absence of any real civic equality. Hence the UNIA's titles, such as "high chancellor," "chaplain general," "potentate," "or supreme commissioner," as well as more exotic appellations such as "Duke of the Nile," "Duke of Uganda," and "Baron of the Zambezi" emulating those found within such black fraternal organizations as the Prince Hall Masons.[33]

The paramilitary organization of the UNIA's African Legion, with their crisp uniforms, perfectly drilled cadence, and internal security function made the association appear fully equipped to recolonize the African continent, if only the masses had the will. Moreover, Garvey could later claim with some accuracy—and without any appreciable irony—that "We were the first Fascists. . . . When we had 100,000 disciplined men, and were training children, Mussolini was still an unknown, [and] Mussolini copied our Fascism. But the Negroes sabotaged it."[34] Garvey's oratorical skills, eye for promotion, and frequent self-aggrandizement made for extremely good copy in black and white newspapers alike, ensuring the UNIA's exponential growth in the early 1920s and the establishment of a strong personality cult around its leader. Although the spectacular failure of the Black Star Line and Garvey's attempts at rapprochement with the Ku Klux Klan facilitated the provisional president's fall, he never ceased to present the image of an eloquent, charismatic, and visionary leader. Photographer James Van Der Zee's images of Garveyites and their leader at the UNIA's conventions in 1920 and 1924 in particular have immortalized him as an exemplar of race pride, one who helped inspire such later, equally controversial groups as the Nation of Islam. After a long period of obscurity[35] Garvey was eventually enshrined as one of the national heroes of Jamaica.

Hurston, like W. E. B. Du Bois, A. Philip Randolph, Chandler Owen, Robert Bagnall, Schuyler, Thurman, and countless other critics, would have none of this. Garvey's garish displays and startling comparisons—easy fodder for satire in their own right—weren't as damnable as Garvey's hoarding of titles, power, and a seemingly endless stream of money from his followers. Garvey's expansive ambition, backed by nothing but the words of his editorials in *Negro World* and the purchase of membership dues and publicity, allowed him to claim in 1920 that "ninety days from now we will have a Black House side by side with the White House in Washington," a claim that Hurston quotes in "Emperor," followed by a gentle remonstrance to the reader that Garvey "might have demanded the entire site on which the White House stands, but . . . he will permit even the conquered whites to have an executive mansion side by side with his."[36]

Hurston goes on to recount in detail select passages from the transcript of Garvey's federal trial, wherein he "invariably . . . knew more about legal processes" than his lawyers, an all too accurate reference to Garvey's decision to fire his attorneys and mount his own defense. Hurston's coup de grace may be found in her final indictment, coinciding with the account of her subject's conviction. Garvey was innocent of fraud, Hurston declares, because, although he "sold a few trifling thousand dollars [sic] worth of Black Star Line stock before he had a ship" and "had sold a few passages to Africa on a ship that did not exist," "what's a few little ships among emperors!" The accusation of fraud is false; Garvey

> had taken the people's money and he was keeping it. That was how he had become the greatest man of his race. Booker T. Washington had achieved some local notice for collecting monies and spending it on a Negro school. It had never occurred to him to keep it. Marcus Garvey was much in advance of the old school of thinkers. Hence he stood in places never dreamed of by Booker T. Washington. There have been some whisperings concerning W. E. B. DuBois on account of his efforts to lower the violent mortality rate among his people, and advance their interests generally, but he never learned how to keep the people's money, and so missed true greatness.[37]

Hurston had no discernible affection for Du Bois, Garvey's best-known nemesis; as she told Annie Nathan Meyer, Du Bois "is a propagadist [sic] with all the distorted mind of his kind. He is doing a great service perhaps for his race, but he must use propaganda methods and those methods never follow actual conditions very accurately."[38] Moreover, Hurston was appalled when an article in the May 1929 issue of *Literary Digest* magazine on the travels of the Harlem literati misquoted Hurston as

Spoofing the Modern

saying that Du Bois "was the greatest, for I do not think so."[39] In fact, Hurston found Du Bois nearly as pretentious as Garvey; later in life she described him as a "goateed, egotistic, wishy-washy" leader who "can endure no one being prominent but himself. He is the same man that spent nearly a generation trying to destroy Booker T. Washington."[40]

Hurston's disgust toward Garvey and Du Bois alike appears rooted in each leader's unwillingness to share power, especially with the bright younger intellects that surrounded them. This antipathy arises repeatedly in Hurston's work; in her most renowned novel, 1937's *Their Eyes Were Watching God*, protagonist Janie condemns her second husband, Joe "Jody" Starks, the self-appointed mayor of Eatonville, Florida (heavily drawn from the historical Joe Clarke, who played a similar role in the town), for silencing her voice through most of their eighteen-year marriage. Similarly, 1926's "Sweat" depicts one Delia Jones sadistically tormented by her husband, Sykes, until she arranges his demise by the same snake she fears.[41] Hurston's well-documented conflict with Alain Locke and the young Richard Wright through their reviews of *Their Eyes* reveals the prevailing condescension with which her contemporaries treated her work. That all of these clashes are between men in powerful positions and a woman who wishes only to speak and be free is no coincidence. While Hurston's personality is not written into all of the women in her fiction, each reveals a singular opposition to men who occupy positions of power above the merits of their talent, but well within reach of their overweening ambition. The path to power was littered with the careers and intellectual efforts of women like Hurston, effectively muted when her voluminous output should have placed her among the most celebrated writers of her generation. Even if she claimed in "How It Feels to Be Colored Me" that she was not of "the sobbing school of Negrohood" that claims victim status,[42] Hurston's letters offer a testament of her frustration with these men belittling their intellectual and artistic equals, if not superiors.

That particular sort of gendered arrogance anchors Hurston's lost parody, "Monkey Junk: A Satire on Modern Divorce." Originally published in 1927, "Monkey Junk" combines the archaic English of the King James Bible, including the verse form, with contemporary Harlem slang to tell the story of a young man that "dwelt in the land of the Harlemites" and "thought that he knew all the law and the prophets," prompting his declaration: "'I know all that there is about the females. Verily, I shall not let myself be married,'" despite his certainty that "merry maidens were like unto death for love of him."[43] Naturally, "none desired him," but soon a "maiden gazeth upon his checkbook and . . . coveted it," charming the unnamed Harlemite into spending vast sums upon her, and tying the knot.[44] The narrative plays out comically, with the brash protagonist at first celebrating his newlywed status to the community, at least until he begins to tire of bestowing his fortune upon his wife. She promptly cuckolds him—frequently—leading to divorce proceedings. Despite his wife's infidelities and her incompetent young attorney, she gets the best of her husband by adorning herself in finery and flirting openly with the divorce court's judge and jury. The result? A large alimony payment from our Harlemite, as his ex-wife was "some kind of brown" (read: a comely woman).[45] Nonplussed and angry at his misfortune, the protagonist confronts and physically threatens his ex-wife, but she remonstrates that he will go to prison if he carries out his threats. He then returns to his native Alabama to pick cotton after his erstwhile spouse sends a letter telling him to "'Go to the monkeys, thou hunk of mud, and learn things and be wise.'"[46]

Although superficially a straightforward morality tale, "Monkey Junk" highlights Hurston's perennial desire to appropriate and update biblical narratives and language for a more modern African American audience. As the story's subtitle indicates, though, Hurston had no interest in celebrating uncritically the New Negro's entrée into the modern, especially if it breeds the arrogance and hubris the protagonist exemplifies. His wife demonstrates quite clearly that he knows virtually nothing about any of the subjects he claims, whether women, the law, or "prophets"; she is the latter, and with a trickster's repertoire—playing upon men's vanity, lust, arrogance, and venality—triumphs. If this moral tale seems somewhat amoral—neither the Harlemite nor his bride exudes any discernible virtue—we should recognize that tricksters seldom exemplify upstanding behavior; they deal in confidence, not ethics, and ultimately reveal how susceptible their victims are because they refuse to admit their own vulnerability. Modern arrogance breeds modern twits lured into altogether modern marriage and divorce, with contemporary laws rewarding the person best able to control the narrative, not the one necessarily at fault. The Harlemite fails because he has knowledge, not wisdom, and presumption rather than experience. His former bride manipulates the law in her favor, using her equally inexperienced attorney as a mere proxy for her machinations. Men in power, it seems, have very little.

"Monkey Junk" reveals Hurston's skepticism toward and angular approach to the idea of modern progress. Gender differences, exploited properly, may trump the rule of law, thereby sending the newly urbane Harlemite packing back to the same rural South that spawned Hurston. Instead of celebrating the modern, sexually liberated woman, Hurston casts human vanity as its own worst enemy. Harlem has no magical properties, other than to turn new migrants from the South into dupes and cuckolds, not aspiring Horatio Algers. The story constructs a seamless pastiche of contemporary slang with simulacra of biblical language and situations to underscore how men attempt to arrogate to themselves all authority to control their narratives, but find themselves ever vulnerable to irony, to the trickster, to angularity.

In *Moses, Man of the Mountain* (1939), Hurston offers her lengthiest critique of the status of African American male leadership, told through a complex allegory that relies upon one of the most enduring mythological tropes in African American cultural history: the story of Moses and the Hebrews' exodus from Egypt. Hurston draws upon the Mosaic legend "not so much to debunk a Judeo-Christian prophet as to remove him from scripture in order to relocate him in Afro-American tradition."[47] The novel revises Hurston's September 1934 short story, "The Fire and the Cloud," which posited Moses as "half man, half god," a figure standing halfway between the divine and the earthly.[48] This role is identical to Moses's place in the Vodun (Voodoo) practices that Hurston had studied in *Tell My Horse*, her 1938 anthropological study of Haitian and Jamaican syncretic religious practices. *Moses, Man of the Mountain* remains among Hurston's least-studied works, perhaps as a result of its unusual position straddling satire, folklore, romance, and the picaresque; it is therefore difficult to classify. Moreover, its ambition to update the Mosaic myth and the Exodus from Egypt to extend its resonance within African American cultural traditions present Hurston with a challenge at which she does not always succeed. The story of enslavement and the Exodus has held a permanent berth within African American music and folklore as a thinly veiled analogue to American chattel slavery; besides the many slave narrators and black leaders who drew explicit comparisons between themselves and Moses, such spirituals as "Go Down, Moses," "Didn't Old Pharaoh Get Lost," "Ride on Moses," and "Turn Back Pharaoh's Army" explicitly refer to the Hebrews' triumph over slavery and oppression. Hurston's attempt to rewrite this tradition consciously as an allegory for African Americans' status in the 1930s often reduces some of the Exodus's legendary images and moments—Moses's confrontation of Pharaoh, the parting of the Red Sea, and the bestowment of God's commandments—to background material, with the voice and petty politics of the Hebrews in the foreground.

The novel's Hebrews—anachronistically called Israelites—speak in black English and contemporary slang, are kept in slavery, must withstand various forms of overt racist oppression, and are more deeply tied culturally to the land of their oppression than they would like to admit. Invariably, racism is portrayed as utterly irrational, yet possessing absolute hegemony over the Israelite body. "The Hebrew womb," for example, "had fallen under the heel of Pharaoh. A ruler great in his newness and new in his greatness had arisen in Egypt and he had said, 'This is law. Hebrew boys shall not be born. All offenders against this law shall suffer death by drowning.'" Hebrew women consequently begin shuddering with "terror at the indifference of their wombs to the Egyptian law."[49] Hurston's spoofing of the contingent nature of chattel slavery—whether of the Egyptian or American kind—sets a tone of absurdity for the novel that recurs intermittently, often understated. Pharaoh and his Egyptian slaveholders are repeatedly lampooned as imperious, arrogant buffoons building "more government projects . . . than you can shake a stick at" for the sake of a "brand-new Egypt" with slave labor.[50] As a result, Hurston implicitly compares the Egyptians to Roosevelt's New Deal, particularly the Works Progress

Administration that helped put millions of Americans—black and white alike—to work. Egypt resembles a kingdom less than a stifling bureaucracy that rewards technocrats and complacency. When Moses flees Egypt—in the Bible, to escape punishment for killing a slave driver—he is "subject to no law except the laws of tooth and talon. He had crossed over" to become a man freed of wealth, power, and influence, but also the laws of the State.[51] Once out of Egypt, he learns two new laws of Nature that govern his behavior through the rest of the narrative: "It seems like the first law of Nature is that everybody likes to receive things, but nobody likes to feel grateful. And the very next law is that people talk about tenderness and mercy, but they love force. If you feed a thousand people you are a nice man with suspicious motives. If you kill a thousand you are a hero. Continue to get them killed by the thousands and you are a great conqueror. . . . Oppress them and you are a great ruler. Rob them by law and they are proud and happy if you let them glimpse you occasionally surrounded by the riches that you have trampled out of their hides."[52]

Moses learns during his time in the wilderness how to become the HooDoo Man that Hurston favored as a folk hero, but his observations about leadership reveal as well a strain in Hurston's thought that surfaced in "The Emperor Effaces Himself" and much of her correspondence. It is a profoundly skeptical, if not cynical view of the perils of government. To be a hero is to kill; to be a beneficent leader is to risk being an outcast, *homo sacer*. Even as a leader within his future father-in-law Jethro's tribe, the Midianites, he notices that "people treated him like he was some great lord. They were too deferential and impressed," failing to see Moses as a flawed, normal human who enjoys the same pleasures as those surrounding him.[53] Although Moses eventually takes up Jehovah's charge to tell Pharaoh to free the Hebrews, his legendary reluctance owes as much to his stammer as his distance from the people, whose language and thoughts he doesn't speak or know.[54]

Hurston's text inserts both dramatic tension and greater irony into the legend by noticeably minimizing the role of God and raising Moses from his role as a mere spokesperson for God to a true leader, one fraught with realistic problems with his own ego and self-importance. Moses's *humanity* as a leader is Hurston's focus; his adopted siblings, Aaron and Miriam, frequently chide him for his arrogance, which they believe to be a product of his mysterious heritage, which could be either Hebrew or Egyptian. As Hemenway recounts, "In 1937, two years before *Moses* appeared, Freud had published two controversial essays . . . which drew from sketchy historical evidence to assert not only that Moses was Egyptian, but also that the monotheistic religion he brought to the Hebrews originated with a heretical ruler of Egyptian antiquity."[55] Hurston uses this evidence as another basis to argue that Moses must be considered as both a great prophet, hero, and anti-hero inasmuch as he is a decidedly flawed leader of even more flawed people who both admire and revile him at turns. He is "a two-headed man"—a nod to Moses's status as a HooDoo trickster—and an outcast.

Moses's greatest struggle in the novel, in fact, is not to conquer Pharaoh; it is to find a way to lead the Hebrews, who are as obsessed with skin color as their African American analogues were, as seen in the conflict between the Talented Tenth and Garvey. They resent having a leader whose wife, Zipporah, is dark-skinned, and constantly attempt to wrest power from Moses out of their doubts regarding his leadership abilities and whether he was ever called to lead them in the first place.[56] In casting the Hebrews, especially Aaron and Miriam, as overly ambitious, Hurston suggests a crisis in black leadership that Schuyler also recognized. That is to say, the Hebrews, like African Americans, have been beset with leaders who "are much too sensitive to the wishes of the people but [that are] too unconscious of their needs" and have "a big idea of [their] own importance."[57] This portrait of Aaron is not unlike Hurston's own opinions of leaders ranging from Marcus Garvey to Du Bois and Locke,[58] all of whom struck her as arrogant and self-important. While Moses retains this same flaw, though, Hurston does not necessarily posit him as the object of satire. Rather, she satirizes the unrealistic expectations the Hebrews and, by extension, African Americans, have of their leaders. Just as Du Bois and Garvey struck Hurston as "propagandists," other African Americans evinced a tendency to rely upon a single voice rather than a panoply or chorus. That single voice was almost invariably male, a putative "great man" whose flaws were self-evident: a dearth of common sense, intellectual independence, financial security, and occasionally self-preservation. The masses exist in a symbiotic relationship with these leaders, in which the mere display of eloquence supplants their ability to demand agency and democracy, if we understand the latter to mean that sovereignty lies in the people. To yield that agency to any other sovereign is to guarantee an unbroken cycle of feckless leaders and demagogues, none able to bring about true progress.

In Walked "Bud": Rudolph Fisher vs. Strivers' Row

Of all the Harlem literati, only Dr. Rudolph "Bud" Fisher came close to earning unequivocal praise from both peers and reviewers during his lifetime. His fifteen published short stories and two novels, *The Walls of Jericho* (1928) and *The Conjure-Man Dies* (1932), along with such essays as "The Caucasian Storms Harlem" (1927)[59] won extensive acclaim, and remain among the most anthologized works from the movement. On first glance, Fischer seems the New Negro writer least apt to pursue a literary career. Born in Washington, D.C., in 1897, Fisher was a Baptist minister's son who spent his formative years in Rhode Island. After being one of the first African Americans to earn BA and MA degrees at Brown University in Providence, Fisher returned to his native Washington, D.C., to attend famed Howard

University's medical school, where he taught embryology while earning his MD in 1924. After a brief internship at Howard, Fisher relocated with his new wife, Jane, to New York City for a two-year fellowship at the National Research Council at Columbia University's College of Physicians and Surgeons prior to setting up his practice as a radiologist and roentgenologist in Harlem, where he had an X-ray clinic and later served as superintendent of Harlem's International Hospital.

Throughout this period, Fisher cultivated his writing and occasionally socialized with his peers in the New Negro movement. Fisher's passion, it seems, was his literary career, despite his pioneering effort as a practicing, published physician and scientist. He availed himself most often of the subjects that formed the locus of intellectual discourse, but seldom found a balanced yet sympathetic voice in black literature: the working-class African American. To be certain, working-class and poor black folks had remained within America's consciousness since Reconstruction. Their place had remained one proscribed by fear, stereotype, and superficial observations, marked by apparently ineluctable differences that made them nearly inassimilable, at best, and crude savages at worst. In the 1920s and 1930s, these assessments were not merely the province of grotesque racists and public demagogues; they found sympathetic and prominent intellectual voices in Madison Grant's *The Passing of the Great Race, or, the Racial Basis of European History* (1916) and via the work of Lothrop Stoddard. In *The Rising Tide of Color Against White World Supremacy* (1921) and *Re-forging America: The Story of Our Nationhood* (1927), political scientist and historian Stoddard presents pseudo-scientific arguments that the white "race" was in danger of losing its dominance and purity against the multiplying hordes of non-white peoples, who are culturally and genetically inferior. It is Stoddard's text that Tom Buchanan in F. Scott Fitzgerald's *The Great Gatsby* praises (as "*The Rise of the Colored Empires* by this man Goddard") for its "scientific stuff" offering a desperately needed warning for whites. Grant and Stoddard's works were extremely popular, finding advocates in the U.S. Senate,[60] and in the academic world, where it became a crucial text in the libraries of eugenicists and social scientists sharing Stoddard's views, including Margaret Sanger, with whom he co-founded the American Birth Control League. Such African American intellectuals as W. E. B. Du Bois vociferously responded to the arguments and poor science that Grant and Stoddard employed; Du Bois publicly debated Stoddard in Chicago in 1929, a highly charged event that drew thousands in person and many others over a broadcast. By many accounts, Du Bois resoundingly pummeled his opponent with both logic and impassioned rhetoric, but that hardly ended the ongoing pursuit of scientific bases for racist policies and practices.[61]

Fisher found himself in an intellectual environment that saw little value for African Americans in general, but even less for those representing a "rising tide" of genetically inferior stock. His writings were not, in the main, devoted to disproving explicitly the fallacious claims of racial science, but instead to examining the structures of class and "race" that divided African American communities and threatened to undermine their efficacy as they sought places in all levels of American society. One of Fisher's desired projects, as Margaret Perry emphasizes, was "to become known as Harlem's interpreter," an amanuensis to black Harlemites confronted with a different "rising tide of color" or, to be more precise, colorism and classism, which threatened to reify the arguments of white supremacists and the Talented Tenth elite. Fisher's primary vehicle was the short story, of which he wrote and published dozens, but his two novels, *The Walls of Jericho* (1928) and *The Conjure Man Dies* (1932), reveal a gift for the sustained narrative. In the former novel in particular, Fisher concentrates most of the premises that resounded throughout his fiction: the absurdity of colorism; the vexed relationship between the Talented Tenth and their wealthy Caucasian counterparts; the extensive facades of culture, class, and region found throughout African American communities; and the elusiveness of a core African American identity. For Fisher, that elusiveness arose from interwoven suppressions and repressions of unpleasant controversies among African Americans, forming truths hidden in plain sight. As Michel Foucault writes about sexuality in the Victorian Age, intra-group classism and colorism, often concomitant with regional prejudices, were the "illegitimate" issues that had to "take their infernal mischief elsewhere: to a place where they could be reintegrated, if not in the circuits of production, at least in those of profit."[62] In one way or another, illicit or forbidden sexual transgressions frequently form the subtexts of the repressed issues. Is not colorism a product of the sexual liaisons, whether forced or willing, across the color lines, as well as a synecdoche of the greater problem of white supremacy? Do not class prejudices among African Americans reference the same fear of dissolution of the "better" stock of black folks? Like Foucault's last point, did manufacturers of skin lighteners and hair-straightening products in Fisher's era (and ours) not profit at least in part due to apprehensions regarding the degree of African heritage apparent in the individual's phenotype? Is not one of the greatest fears of the racist and his or her victims alike the invasion or discovery of unwanted, "other" progeny?

In his stories, essays, and novels, Fisher confronts these issues most often by employing a common satirical technique, one that recurs throughout African American literature: reversal. This is not simply a case of the bottom rail, as the folktale goes, always rising to the top; instead, Fisher inverts the conventional situations and sources of tension found in American and African American culture surrounding "racial" distinctions. In Fisher's corpus, the Caucasian storms Harlem; the lower-class "rats" get the better of the middle- to upper-class "dickties"; the "yellow" African American suffers the worst forms of prejudice, not his tragically dark-skinned brethren. Through these reversals Fisher troubles both cultural and literary conventions in subtle ways seldom seen among his peers. While interest in the satirical efforts of Thurman and Schuyler has grown in recent years, to date Fisher's short stories have received far more interest and attention, whether through reprints or as the subjects of scholarly studies. This pattern continues a reputation he earned in the New Negro movement as one of its premiere authors of short fiction. Wallace Thurman gently lampooned Fisher in his novel *Infants of the Spring* as Dr. Manfield Trout, "who practiced medicine and also wrote exceptionally good short stories," and alternately praised and admonished him in his critical reviews "not because he has not been good, but because he has not been good enough."[63] Eight months before Fisher's death, Zora Neale Hurston wrote Dorothy West to express her desire to "be in the [same issue of *Challenge* magazine] with R. Fisher. He is greater than the Negroes rate him generally. That is because he is too honest to pander to our inferiority complex and write 'race' propaganda."[64] To be certain, Fisher fully deserved these notices; his short stories imagine in exquisitely witty terms the situation of Harlem's newer habitués, especially those from the South. Similar to his friend Langston Hughes, Fisher concerned himself primarily with black folklife and the individuals who create and inhabit it. As a consequence, Fisher pushed the "educated and aspiring classes,"[65] with whom he had more common experiences, to the margins of his works, transforming them into caricatures and ciphers, infected with chilling ambition and grossly bereft of any sense of in-group camaraderie that did not veer into condescension.

Both *The Conjure-Man Dies* and *The Walls of Jericho* remain landmark works in African American literary history. Just as Schuyler's *Black No More* is the first novel of speculative fiction in the corpus, *The Conjure-Man Dies* stands as the first detective novel ever published in book form by an African American. *The Walls of Jericho* might also make a legitimate claim to be the first entirely satirical novel by an African American, although it is equally noteworthy for its explicit attempt to examine specifically Harlem's class consciousness. Preceding novels of the movement foreground the exploits of one particular class, whether high or low, in African American culture in general, while others might spend considerable energies and plot space in Harlem alone. Until *The Walls of Jericho,* Harlem's unusual class strata never made up the novel's whole, much less via an explicitly satirical or comic mode.

Immediately dividing Harlem in the opening pages into a community of "dickties,"[66] represented by the very fair-skinned African American lawyer Fred Merrit, and "shines" or "rats,"[67] personified in the comic pair of piano movers, Jinx Jenkins and Bubber Brown, Fisher maps out a city within a city that is in the process of converting into the Black Mecca of legend. When Merrit purchases a house on Court Street in an upscale, predominantly white section of Harlem, the African American community begins to split over whether Merrit's civil rights should be protected, allowing him to move into his dream home, or if it is more important not to raise racial tensions by acquiescing to the established definitions between the races. Using their own form of "signifying," Jinx and Bubber debate among themselves whether it is worth the time and effort of any "rat" to defend the aspirations of "dickties," who "prefer to ignore [their] existence."[68] If such "dickties" as Merrit want to "[bust] into a fay [white] neighborhood," Jinx argues, then it is out of a desire, common among dickties, "to be fay," then "come cryin' . . . fo' help" to the "rats" when whites retaliate. Bubber counters that "fays don' see no difference 'tween dickty shines and any other kind o' shines. One jig in danger is ev'y jig in danger. They'd lick *them* and come on down on *us*. Then we'd have to fight anyhow. What's use o' waitin'?"[69] Explicit here is the rift between the "Talented Tenth" that W. E. B. Du Bois had defined and the other nine-tenths of the black populace. Even if Merrit's intent in the novel is to storm Harlem's many blocks and neighborhoods that remained deeply segregated, this is as invisible to Jinx and Bubber as Merrit's African features are later to white dowager Agatha Cramp.

As Harlem underwent the slow transformation from being a largely white suburb of New York City to a predominantly black city within a city, and as African Americans themselves became more prosperous, this division with roots in slavery began to widen, exacerbated by common notions among blacks of the superiority of light skin. Phenotypical and ancestral proximity to whites equals a desire for social proximity "classing off": rejecting any unnecessary affiliations with the lower classes that might threaten the privileges that came with lighter skin. Bubber and Jinx quite simply care less about any way that Merrit's actions might produce greater equality than they do about the inequality that adds another form of humiliation to everyday black life. To these compatriots, Merrit is like Hurston's Moses, also *homo sacer*, or sacred man, the individual who, because he has transgressed the law, lives outside it and may be killed by anyone. Like *homo sacer*, Merrit—his name a pun on the notion of being a "credit to one's race," and therefore to his society— appears to have violated one of the most sacred taboos within African American society: desiring to *be* white, rather than live and struggle in the world blacks occupy. *Homo sacer* "may be killed and yet not sacrificed."[70] In other terms, he may not be part of the sacred rituals in society, in the eyes of the sovereign ruler and of the law. Jinx and Bubber, of course, are hardly the sovereigns that, according to Agamben, must cast out the individual who is to become *homo sacer*. Nevertheless, they consider him *persona not grata* because of his skin, his apparent motives, and—quite simply— the fact that he is able to hire Joshua Jones's piano-moving company. He possesses access to privileges that should transcend skin color, but seldom do in that era. He has a foot in the white world, so anyone in that world can kill him, but Jinx and Bubbler could not do the same, at least not in any ritualized or socially acceptable form.

Fisher's sympathies for Jinx and Bubber's position remain ironic, though; their antipathy toward Merrit is based upon appearance, not fact, just as the two compadres' ceaseless bickering covers their own homosocial bonds. "The habitual dissension between these two," we learn, "was the symptom of a deep affection which neither . . . would have admitted. Neither Jinx and Bubber nor any of their associates had ever heard of Damon and Pythias, and frank regard between two men would have been considered questionable to say the least. . . . Accordingly their own expression of this affection had to take an ironic turn. They themselves must deride it first, must hide their mutual inclination in a garment of constant ridicule and contention, the irritation of which rose into their consciousness as hostility."[71]

In short, Jinx and Bubber's personal bond of true friendship resembles that between the ancient Greek mythological figures, whose story connotes a homosocial if not homosexual bond. As Stephen P. Knadler indicates, the works of Fisher, Wallace Thurman, and several other New Negro authors contain male characters—Knadler focuses upon the "sweetback" who straddles a line of sexual ambivalence between macho and effeminate.[72] Jinx and Bubber share a common, normally unspoken bond, but cannot allow that bond to evolve into a more deeply emotional exchange. When the pair drink a pint of whiskey in lieu of fighting later in the novel,[73] it is the only incident in which their emotional bond becomes more apparent, even if the comedic moment never implies a sexual component. Nevertheless, this moment of confrontation, mediated and ameliorated by alcohol, allows solidarity while simultaneously foreshadowing the fall of another intraracial wall at the novel's denouement.

The subtle dilemma contained within Jinx and Bubber's relationship finds other analogues, particularly in the cowardice and hypocrisy of the "dickties" themselves when the "Litter Rats Club," a group of dickties with members resembling the "Niggeratti" and their mentors, meets to discuss Merrit's case. Members include "Tod Bruce," whose personality resembles that of Richard Bruce Nugent and Wallace Thurman, and the Langston Hughes–esque "Langdon, an innocent looking youngster who was at heart a prime rascal and who compensated by writing poetry";[74] club president J. Pennington Potter is arguably an amalgamation of renaissance midwives James Weldon Johnson, W. E. B. DuBois, Jessie Redmon Fauset, and Alain Locke. The club's concern, as Potter proclaims, is to make certain that "'this colony . . . should extend itself naturally and gradually—not by violence and bloodshed.'"[75] Merrit, arguably the text's representation of Fisher's voice, responds militantly, arguing that "'the extension of territory by violence and bloodshed strikes me as natural enough. . . . I haven't much of a memory, but I seem to recall one or two instances,'" instances from American history in which the nation expanded its boundaries through murder and deception. Potter's fear is a direct reflection of the more conservative element among the black bourgeoisie, reminiscent of Booker T. Washington, that believes in slow, natural progression of the race, rather than militant protest. As Tod Bruce observes, "Nowadays . . . we grow by—well—a sort of passive conquest. The fays move out, and the jigs are so close no more fays will move in. So the landlord has to rent to jigs and the colony keeps extending. But if Fred wants to return to the older method, I don't think it will do any great harm to the rest of us. He's taking all the risk. And even though he claims a racial interest, he has admitted that the chief motive is personal after all. It's his business."[76]

By attempting to integrate white Harlem, then, Merrit is reaching beyond the boundaries set for African Americans via the example of Booker T. Washington, boundaries still held sacred by the genteel bourgeoisie. He is no less an outlaw to this constituency than to the other "rats" of the working class. Merrit is, as Bruce notes, on a "war," a "conquest of territory" in which the land to be gained is both physical and social.[77] In either dimension of this land, Merrit is *homo sacer,* a status likely to bring the normal doom of the outlaw: "[The white residents of Harlem will] resist. They'll warn you with threatening notes. They'll try to buy you out. If these don't work, they will probably dynamite you."[78] In short, Merrit may be sacrificed at any time, only to be mourned later by the same bourgeoisie apt to benefit from his disappearance or destruction.

We may argue, on the one hand, that Fisher's novel exhibits the influence of H. L. Mencken, whose railings against the "booboisie," the genteel, Victorian influence in American middle- to upper-class circles, were well-loved by many among the Niggeratti, including Fisher. In particular, Mencken's skepticism towards patronizing whites resonates within Fisher's text; Mencken would surely have approved of Fisher's lampooning one figure in particular as a metonym for debilitating and controlling white patronage. The dowdy, stuffy Miss Agatha Cramp—a rich, white philanthropist and patron of the arts—is inarguably meant to represent Charlotte Osgood Mason, the real patron responsible for financing the early careers of Langston Hughes, Zora Neale Hurston, Alain Locke, and other major figures of the Harlem Renaissance. Boasting of Cramp's "sufficiently large store of wealth and . . . sufficiently small store of imagination," Fisher creates a portrait of a hypocritically racist woman who has "been devoting her life to the service of mankind. Not until now had the startling possibility occurred to her that Negroes might be mankind, too."[79] Again, as David Levering Lewis has emphasized, Mason, known affectionately as "Godmother" by her beneficiaries, was a dowager obsessed with "primitives," whether they were of Negroid or Native American stock.[80] She continually sought out the elements in African American culture that seemed to be "pure"; that is to say, she sought the last traces of unadulterated Africanisms in black culture, usually at the expense of noticing the rich amalgam in front of her eyes.

To Agatha Cramp, "Negroes . . . had been rather ugly but serviceable fixtures, devices that happened to be alive, dull instruments of drudgery" until a conversation with her maid, Linda, reveals that some "primitives" might actually be worthy of social work and improvement.[81] Fisher quickly compares Cramp to other whites who come to Harlem and head its civil rights and improvement associations (embodied in the "General Improvement Association," a composite of the NAACP with shades of Marcus Garvey's UNIA) out of paternalistic rather than altruistic impulses, and those who come to gawk shamelessly at Negro life with "gasps, grunts, and ill-concealed squirms, or sighs and astonished smiles.[82] Cramp eventually meets Merrit and, mistaking him for a white man, is delighted to hear that the apartment he has purchased is next to hers. Much of the plot's remainder revolves around Merrit's sardonic attempts to expose Cramp for the fool she is by concealing his heritage, thereby drawing out the witless dowager's prejudices.

The novel interpolates the metaphor of the biblical Joshua and the battle of Jericho through both Merrit and the protagonist, Joshua "Shine" Jones, each of whom struggles with different "walls" within the eponymous city. Merrit gamely assaults the likes of Agatha Cramp by tearing down the walls of prejudice—whether based on race or class—and segregation, while Shine's struggle is to mitigate his own hostility. His victory in this regard is later trounced, however, when, ironically, the black pool-hall owner Henry Patmore burns down Merrit's residence and attempts to rape Linda, with whom Merrit had been involved, as vengeance for a past offense. Given that Merrit was expecting whites to commit such an atrocity, the novel's complex racial politics receives a new twist, one that went behind the sort of stereotypical chauvinism of which African Americans were frequently accused. Intraracial tensions and problems are not merely contentions to be relegated to the margins of African American politics; they are inarguably at the center, and potentially more dangerous than interracial tensions, especially in the purportedly freer North.

Merrit and Shine attempt to resolve these tensions through a business transaction that stands as one solution to the gulf between the classes. Merrit proposes that Shine take over the piano-moving company he works for after Merrit purchases it; "what we Negroes need," Merrit argues, is "a business class, an economic backbone. What kind of social structure can anybody have with nothing but the extremes—bootblacks on one end and doctors on the other. Nothing in between. No substance. Everybody wants to quit waiting table and start writing prescriptions right away. Well, here's a chance for you and a good investment for me. Race proposition, too. How 'bout it?"[83] In this proposed transaction may appear the comity found all too seldom in the rest of the black world. Merrit proposes, quite simply, that he and Shine work together to build an economically viable, pragmatic working class, one that could tear down the walls of racism not by starting enterprising businesses or donating to philanthropic organizations. Rather, investing the black working class with venture capital and business sensibilities would bring a more sober tenor to the quest for progress, one resulting in an independent—and therefore powerful—economic foundation, one that would obviate class divisions through partnerships.

The first components of black life to be sacrificed in this agreement would be naïveté and inexperience. Merrit asks only that Shine invest his "experience" in the

Spoofing the Modern

business. This does not result in instant gratification; when Shine drives out to Merrit's country house in the ultimate chapter to retrieve a recovered Linda, he cynically notes that he doesn't expect a "dickty" to get out of bed early in the morning.[84] Merrit, however, *is* awake, and watches the pair depart, wanting to join them, realizing that his failure had been to recognize the extent of the intraracial tensions that led to his Harlem residence's destruction. As he watches Shine and Linda drive off into the horizon, he recognizes that they are driving into "another land," one in which his past assumptions about his status will have little purchase.[85]

Fisher's *The Walls of Jericho* thus maintains the cultural introspection found throughout the novels of the Harlem Renaissance, additionally imbuing that introspection with the ironic critique found within Schuyler and Thurman's columns and novels. As the New Negro Renaissance fell from the giddy heights of the latter half of the 1920s, authors such as Fisher and his peer Zora Neale Hurston had less value as faddish commodities; in Fisher's case in particular, very little of his work is read or studied outside of academic circles. Their uncompromising desire to focus on the tensions within African American communities, especially from the perspective of the folk, yielded all too little appreciation.

For Hurston and Fisher alike, the tensions between the classes in African America of the 1920s and 1930s could not be resolved with any particular agenda that external forces designed and controlled. Paternalism, whether emerging from liberal whites or middle-class blacks, only served to reify existing models that posited African Americans as a "problem" that needed to be corrected and cared for, without voice or consciousness. A committee of Hebrews notes resentfully that Moses is "going to come along to tell us how to talk," even though the people have known how to "talk"—to express themselves forcefully and effectively—far longer than the ineloquent Moses has. Hurston's Joshua notes, not unlike Fisher's, that the people need to "come on up front and talk [their] big talk to [Moses] instead of to me and the rest of the people. . . . Don't let me hear nothing you don't want him to know."[86] Indeed, moving the talk from the public circle to action remains the great challenge in the long struggle between the "dickties" and the "rats," one that haunted African American literature long after the New Negro Renaissance.

5

Punchlines

For a cultural movement ensconced with conspicuous glamour, the Harlem or New Negro Renaissance didn't inspire too many fond remembrances from its participants. Looking at the literary scene, in fact, it seemed to inspire more bile than *bonhomie* among satirist and sage alike. Forty years after *Black No More*'s publication, George Schuyler recalled that he wrote "The Negro Art Hokum" primarily because "this idea of a special and separate Negro art and literature was very current in those days, and a lot of people were profiting from it. In other words, they were making it a sort of a racket, and [he] felt that this was unscientific and unsound," and in need of an opposing voice.[1] Langston Hughes famously closed his first memoir, *The Big Sea,* with a perfunctory take on the movement's demise: "[The spring of 1930] for me (and, I guess, all of us) was the end of the Harlem Renaissance. We were no longer in vogue, anyway, we Negroes. Sophisticated New Yorkers turned to Noel Coward. Colored actors began to go hungry, publishers politely rejected new manuscripts, and patrons found other uses for their money."[2] The second half of Nugent's *Gentleman Jigger* follows Stuartt after the Niggeratti have dispersed for want of a common purpose, with his former compatriots disappearing almost entirely from the plot. In Thurman's unpublished review of his own *Infants of the Spring,* he castigates himself for assigning his characters—based, of course, on real acquaintances—"an importance which blinded him to their true value," leading to a "bad novel" that did the inexcusable; it dealt with a subject other than the "better class of Negroes," who've never had a novel that "truthfully depict[s]" the "semi-literate bourgeoisie" that dictated the renaissance's tastes.[3] To corrupt King Pyrrhus, one more glamorous literary movement like that, and surely black culture would be undone.

Needless to say, African American art, literature, and culture did not die with the New Negro Renaissance's decline in the 1930s. Its legacies appear in contemporary African American literature, from conflicts over the literature's purposes to black literature's access to publishing. Among African American satirists in particular, the same questions regarding art, commerce, and ideology find fertile ground.

Even if Langston Hughes had been correct to state that something called the *Harlem* Renaissance ended in spring 1930—an assertion we now can now safely dismiss—it is simply and demonstrably untrue that the movement's demise heralded anything more distressing than its creators' eclipsed fortunes. As Cary Wintz puts it, "For the individual writer the end of the Renaissance was a personal event occurring when he or she consciously disassociated from the movement," while some scholars argue that the movement never truly ended, instead continuing in different form into the 1960s.[4] Wintz argues instead that the movement indeed declined and ended, but primarily because it received no *new* ideas or artists. The movement's leading artists tried to publish more substantial works in the 1930s, often successfully. Hughes was quite correct to say that those artists lacked the fanfare that attended a new poetry collection, novel, or anthology just a few years earlier. From 1930 to 1935, at least fifteen major works by artists associated with the New Negro movement appeared; from 1922 to 1930, publishers released about thirty-four equally notable and occasionally less mature books.[5] If that constitutes a decline, most authors would welcome such a dearth of opportunity. While works published during the Great Depression did not sell terribly well, neither did their Roaring Twenties predecessors; once we exclude career journalists like Schuyler, Langston Hughes remains the only New Negro who realized a living wage from his writing.

Scholars who argued that the movement continued until the 1960s in different form are not without merit, especially once we consider the influence the New Negroes held over their descendants. Hughes became one of the most popular poets in African America, if not American history, with a handful of landmark works—"The Negro Speaks of Rivers," "The Weary Blues," "Mother to Son," "Red Silk Stockings," "I, Too," "America," "Let America Be America Again," "The Negro Mother," "Christ in Alabama," "Goodbye Christ," "A Dream Deferred," among others—frequently anthologized, taught, and recited in countless churches, public spaces, and classrooms. Zora Neale Hurston did not begin to exert a measurable or obvious influence until the early 1980s, twenty years after her death in 1960, but like her contemporary and former friend, subsequent movements in African American literature now trace their lineage to her. Countee Cullen and Claude McKay, for that matter, have also received varying degrees of acclaim since the 1930s, even if only for the ambivalence and fire each expressed regarding American blacks' lives. Readers, scholars, and teachers have embraced each of these authors as major voices in African American literature. In short, history has been most kind.

Nevertheless, no one would contend that Schuyler, Thurman, Fisher, and Nugent have achieved similar acclaim or are likely to become as familiar anytime soon. Of these, only Schuyler's legacy has enjoyed a significant boost as *Black No More* has found its way back into print and into college classrooms as the American Right slowly rediscovers an African American who might have been comfortable claiming today's Tea Party as *simpatico*. Unless someone turns the novel into a film, though, Schuyler is apt to remain no more or less notorious than his fellow satirists.

Each author's *influence* on subsequent generations has a different story, one more sanguine, albeit circuitous. As we have seen, New Negro satirists cast skeptical, if not cynical, eyes toward the very movement that defined them precisely because, as a category, "race" alone seemed insufficient to encompass the democratic impulses each possessed or to describe their intellectual scope, much less to define an entire movement. Satire allowed each to lampoon African Americans' apparent tendency to embrace totalizing ideologies, however temporarily, and the general public's long-standing desire to oversimplify, co-opt, or entirely ignore African American culture in every medium available. During the New Negro's ascent and after his demise, satire allowed New Negroes, particularly the Niggeratti, to attack the vacuity they perceived in the heart of American institutions.

As the Great Depression worsened in the first half of the 1930s, though, satire receded as a popular expressive mode for black iconoclasm. With no more novelty to keep the New Negro *new*, an exhausted movement, and economic desperation, satire fell out of vogue, to be supplanted by the socialist or urban realism that Richard Wright, Chester Himes, and William Attaway embodied. In the United States, leftist radicalism gained greater popularity as a possible solution to the dispossessed poor's dire straits; in African American intellectual circles, the Communist Party USA made some of its more significant inroads, attracting black writers in part via opportunities to see their work in print in difficult times, regardless of whether the artists were true fellow travelers. Among white-owned periodicals, only the newer leftist magazines, such as *Partisan Review, New Masses, Midland Left, Anvil,* and *Left Front* made conscious efforts to seek out and publish new black writers. The same African American-owned magazines that had incorporated short stories and poetry by black authors, such as the *Crisis* and *Opportunity,* still sought their material, but with less enthusiasm toward encouraging groundbreaking work.[6] African American literature in general remained vital, if not as flamboyant; as Blanche Ferguson notes, the "opening that had been wedged during the Renaissance period was widening to admit greater numbers of courageous voices." As of the mid-1930s, many "Renaissance figures were still writing, among them Langston Hughes, Zora Neale Hurston, Arna Bontemps, Wallace Thurman, and Sterling Brown . . . [with] new names . . . appearing in the fields of both prose and poetry."[7] Black literary publications became commonplace, rather than "Negro firsts" remarkable simply due to their primacy.

The former New Negroes did not take satire's decline lightly or without resistance. Sterling Brown's 1930 essay "Our Literary Audience," published in *Opportunity,* castigates black readers who perceive black books as "sociological documents," who are "afraid of truth telling, of satire" and too "bourgeois," or who "insist that

Negro books must be idealistic, optimistic tracts for race advertisement."[8] Several of the New Negroes' most accomplished satirical works, of course, appeared or were composed well after Brown's essay: *Black No More* (1931), *Infants of the Spring* (1932), *One Way to Heaven* (1932), *Gentleman Jigger* (ca. 1927–32; published 2010), Hughes's *The Ways of White Folks* (1934), *Moses, Man of the Mountain* (1939), and Dorothy West's *The Living is Easy* (1948). Schuyler continued to publish his "News and Reviews" column in the Pittsburgh *Courier* for many years; it often relied heavily upon satire and irony. Satire lived; it just didn't thrive financially or in publishers' esteem.

We might be tempted to place a modicum of credit—or blame—for this state of affairs at Richard Wright's feet. His influential 1937 essay "Blueprint for Negro Writing" argues for a more radical nationalism among African American authors, one that would produce realistic depictions of the black masses' social and economic situations, rather than the "curtsying" that Wright cast as "the voice of the educated Negro pleading with white America for justice" before and during the New Negro Renaissance.[9] Wright's low opinion of the New Negro movement's accomplishments, at least as he characterizes it here, obviously dismisses the black bourgeoisie's concern with appearing respectable before a totalizing white gaze; moreover, his remark about "Negro geniuses" "curtsying" before white patrons not only disparagingly feminizes the New Negro's efforts, but may also be a vicious swipe at Zora Neale Hurston in particular, given the latter's relationship with Charlotte Osgood Mason. Combined with his novel *Native Son*'s publication in 1940, Wright's call in "Blueprint" for a nationalist, radical literature built upon the richness of black folklore inarguably altered the face of African American literature for the remainder of the twentieth century, if not until the present.

But to force Wright to play the role of villain in this narrative is to fall into a facile melodramatic trap. Wright held many influences in common with his New Negro predecessors and peers; in his memoir, *Black Boy* (1945), Wright famously cites H. L. Mencken's scathing attacks upon southern culture in such essays as the "Sahara of the Bozart" as major catalysts in his desire to write. Wright considered words as weapons at least as much as Schuyler and Theophilus Lewis did. Even if Wright's radicalism stands in contradistinction to Schuyler's growing conservatism—which wouldn't take full flower until the 1940s—we should note that "Blueprint of Negro Writing" dismisses the New Negro movement's literary arm for reasons that hardly differ from Thurman or Nugent's disappointment that their artistic experiments and publishing efforts never yielded the sort of carefully outlined aesthetic that he proposes, one that would have answered fully the challenges Du Bois posited in "Criteria of Negro Art." Wright had more in common with Wallace Thurman than he did with Karl Marx, and never wielded the power that any major publisher held as a matter of course.

Despite rejecting his literary fathers and mothers in quasi-Oedipal fashion, Wright carried forward some of their spirit even as he laid the ground for the realistic fiction that would soon dominate black literature. In so doing, he also made it possible for the African American satirists who arose between 1970 and 1980 to have an awfully fecund source of mirth. During the New Negro movement, the tensions between artists writing social-document fiction and poetry—what Du Bois would call propaganda—and those attempting to further the art for its own sake set the Niggeratti against Du Bois and Charles S. Johnson at times. In contemporary African American fiction circles, this concern remains, underscored by shifts in black politics and economics since the 1960s' civil rights movement that altered *how* black authors wrote about African American literature culture, but not entirely *what* made the literary scene alternately distressing and hilarious.

The stage of the civil rights movement that began after World War II brought African Americans' issues to the national consciousness as never before. Upon a foundation comprising decades of NAACP activism, black struggles for equality in World War II, and Cold War politics, this turbulent period offered countless opportunities to redefine African Americans in the popular imagination. Satire did not figure prominently in the postwar literary scene. Absent were the calls for the sort of iconoclasm that George Schuyler made a matter of course, even if satire itself was far from death. Taking tensions within black communities, racism, and civil rights as their métier, Dorothy West's *The Living is Easy*, Ralph Ellison's *Invisible Man* (1952), and Langston Hughes's "Here to Yonder" newspaper columns featuring Jesse B. Semple (1943–65) offered salient contributions to African American humor in the 1940s and 1950s.

The 1960s and 1970s offered even fewer opportunities for African American literary satirists, despite satire and dark, ironic humor flourishing in postmodern literature in general. As in the 1920s, the modern civil rights movement in those decades would seem satire's ideal location. Movement leaders argued vociferously, as did Martin Luther King Jr. in 1963's famous "Letter from Birmingham Jail," that the arguments against civil rights activism had no ethical or moral bases, depending entirely upon political expediency—if not virulent racism—for their rationales. King confesses that he has

almost reached the regrettable conclusion that the Negro's great stumbling block in his stride toward freedom is not the White Citizen's Counciler or the Ku Klux Klanner, but the white moderate, who is more devoted to "order" than to justice; who prefers a negative peace which is the absence of tension to a positive peace which is the presence of justice; who constantly says: "I agree with you in the goal you seek, but I cannot agree with your methods of direct action"; who paternalistically believes he can set the timetable for another man's freedom; who lives by a mythical concept of time and who constantly advises the Negro to wait for a "more convenient season." Shallow understanding from people of good will is more frustrating than absolute misunderstanding from people of ill will. Lukewarm acceptance is much more bewildering than outright rejection.[10]

King's rhetorical confession hardly constitutes satire. It lacks vitriol, invective, and an openly mocking mode. The letter's overall purpose, in fact, is to cajole the Christian and Jewish ministers whose letter prompted his response.[11]

Yet like his contemporary and distant adversary, Nation of Islam minister Malcolm X, King possessed and displayed a fine sense of irony that recognized a simple fact: the greatest impediments to black progress were not the vile and often buffoonish (albeit still dangerous) open racists, but the moderates and the liberals whose support could evaporate at a moment's notice. Malcolm X's "Message to the Grass Roots," delivered November 10, 1963, mocks the very notion that the civil rights movement constitutes a "revolution," since it espouses nonviolence as its core philosophy. In particular, though, Malcolm X's lampoon of the March on Washington, which went from a grassroots movement to one that cooperated with the Kennedy administration, represents some of his most spectacular satire:

It's just like when you've got some coffee that's too black, which means it's too strong. What you do? You integrate it with cream; you make it weak. If you pour too much cream in, you won't even know you ever had coffee. It used to be hot, it becomes cool. It used to be strong, it becomes weak. It used to wake you up, now it'll put you to sleep. This is what they did with the march on Washington. They joined it. They didn't integrate it; they infiltrated it. They joined it, became a part of it, took it over. And as they took it over, it lost its militancy. They ceased to be angry. They ceased to be hot. They ceased to be uncompromising. Why, it even ceased to be a march. It became a picnic, a circus. Nothing but a circus, with clowns and all. You had one right here in Detroit—I saw it on television—with clowns leading it, white clowns and black clowns. I know you don't like what I'm saying, but I'm going to tell you anyway. 'Cause I can prove what I'm saying. If you think I'm telling you wrong, you bring me Martin Luther King and A. Philip Randolph and James Farmer and those other three, and see if they'll deny it over a microphone. . . . They controlled it so tight—they told those Negroes what time to hit town, how to come, where to stop, what signs to carry, what song to sing, what speech they could make, and what speech they couldn't make; and then told them to get out town by sundown. And everyone of those Toms was out of town by sundown.[12]

The message in Malcolm's diatribe is clear: Black progress is threatened most often by its own champions, including the same Dr. King who authored the devastating "Letter from Birmingham Jail." However unintentional, the threat stems from leaders fearing their own followers' potential, especially when those followers might upset an apple cart built over weeks, months, or years of careful strategizing. In their distinctive ways, both King and Malcolm X saw their adversaries' caution as political expediency, designed to retard or halt the progress they sought. Like the Harlem literati a generation earlier, they recognized that the greatest impediment to progress often remained within the movement, where the tantalizing *idea* of forward movement was more palatable than a fully committed and executed plan.

Even if they occasionally mocked their opponents, neither King nor Malcolm X, of course, attempted *literary* satire in their most prominent speeches and writings. With very few exceptions, satire found a cold reception in an era in which a breathtaking freedom movement, urban violence, and the Vietnam War's deadly toll dominated the popular imagination. Such authors as Ishmael Reed, William Melvin Kelley, Hal Bennett, and Charles Wright were the exceptions that proved the rule; during the Black Arts movement and under the Black Aesthetic that such critics as Addison Gayle, Amiri Baraka, and Larry Neal developed, "revolutionary" writing that would inspire the masses to throw off their psychological and economic shackles trumped writing that might take a different tack, perhaps even questioning the revolution itself. Reed in particular noted in such novels as *Mumbo Jumbo* (1972) and *The Last Days of Louisiana Red* (1974) the similarities between the New Negro Renaissance and the Black Arts movement. Both movements saw black literary and cultural production explode (identified in *Mumbo Jumbo* as the pandemic "Jes Grew"); both saw impressive and promising new talents enter the literary scene; both comprised numerous debates over the aesthetic and cultural directions black art should take.

The Black Arts movement never enjoyed the satirical spirit that the Harlem literati husbanded. If the latter group saw itself bringing black culture into modernity and redefining American identity, the Black Arts movement focused more on rejecting, if not overthrowing, the America that continued to define "American" as white, Anglo-Saxon, Protestant, and often racist and imperialist. It had no place for someone like Schuyler, now a staunchly archconservative, anticommunist writer who defended and spoke for the ultra-right John Birch Society and mocked Martin Luther King Jr. as a "sable Typhoid Mary" spreading discontent and violence as a Red dupe. The feeling, naturally, was mutual; if Schuyler held no brief for the mainstream civil rights movement for inciting "disturbers of the peace," the black power movement and its black arts cultural arm were beneath contempt.[13]

It would take the evolution of the Black Arts movement and the Black Aesthetic into the "New Black Aesthetic" of the 1980s and 1990s for satire to regain its stature in African American literature. First coined by author Trey Ellis in his eponymous 1989 essay, the "New Black Aesthetic" attempts to define the state of African American literature, culture, and art as it stood between the nationalism of the Black Arts movement of the late 1960s and 1970s and an unprecedented future. Ellis pointedly and explicitly allies his generation with that of the "New Negro" or Harlem Renaissance, arguing that a younger generation of artists "misunderstood by both the black worlds and the white" and "[a]lienated (junior) intellectuals" came of age after the civil rights and black power movement of the 1960s. This generation has reached a certain maturity as "cultural mulattoes" who combine "zeal, *Glasnost* ['Openness'], and talent" "across both race and class lines."[14]

If Locke's New Negro arose from several causes, including the national post–World War I zeitgeist that returning black war veterans spurred, along with a new respect for the riches and indelibly *American* quality of African American history and folk culture, then Ellis's "cultural mulatto" has benefited directly from past social-justice movements—including the New Negro Renaissance and the Black Arts movement—but may not feel completely obliged to embody their often conflicting ideals and principles, especially when such efforts circumscribe the concept of blackness. In Ellis's terms, cultural mulattoes "just have to *be* natural" but "don't necessarily have to *wear* one," the latter term indicating the "natural" or "Afro" hairstyle.[15] This generation's ambivalence regarding the black power era's ideals allows it simultaneously to respect its predecessors and lampoon them for their oversights. It also makes it possible for African American artists to work on projects that transcend instrumentalism. That is to say, like certain New Negro or Harlem Renaissance artists before them, New Black Aestheticians create for their own purposes, rather than solely for a white intelligentsia or a particular brand of black nationalism. Ellis ultimately concludes that cultural mulattoes "no longer need to deny or suppress any part of our complicated and sometimes contradictory cultural baggage to please either white people or black."[16] It is Ellis's most overt homage to Langston Hughes's 1926 essay "The Negro Artist and the Racial Mountain," where Hughes declares, "If white people are pleased, we are glad. If they are not, it doesn't matter. We know we are beautiful. And ugly too. The tom-tom cries and the tom-tom laughs. If colored people are pleased we are glad. If they are not, their displeasure doesn't matter either. We build our temples for tomorrow, strong as we know how, and we stand on top of the mountain, free within ourselves."[17] Hughes and Ellis alike envision a future for black art without strict ideological boundaries, agendas, or sociological projects controlling the artist's impulses. Both writers broadly define the black artist to be inclusive and democratic, rather than ideologically hidebound and recherché.

The New Black Aesthetic as Ellis understands it quickly came under scrutiny. In the same issue of *Callaloo,* Eric Lott and Tera Hunter offered pointed responses, with Lott dismissing "commodifiable slogans like 'New Black Aesthetic'" and "false totalizing of a generation of intellectuals" while praising Ellis for smartly identifying within that generation "one of the only postmodernisms with a conscience" and the institutions that support it.[18] Lott goes on to argue that Ellis ignores how black intellectuals from both the previous and current generation have actively engaged in creating African American literary and cultural traditions that simply did not exist until the 1970s and 1980s. Without these intellectuals' rather painstaking work to recover lost texts by black women, gays, and lesbians, and to trouble popular conceptions of gender, no New Black Aesthetic could exist. Moreover, Lott continues, Ellis glibly collapses class divisions among the "buppies, b-boys, and bohemians" he celebrates, as if their generational link trumps all.[19]

Tera Hunter confronts even more pointedly the flaws in Ellis's celebration along gender and class lines. Many of the contemporary rap groups Ellis praises for their authenticity and innovations, such as Public Enemy, "bring with them leftover aspects of cultural-nationalism qua 1960's sexism with a vengeance. Their heroes are Martin Luther King, John Coltrane, Marcus Garvey, Elijah Muhammad, and Louis Farrakhan. Their enemy is not only white, but she is also black and female."[20] Hunter goes on to illustrate how Spike Lee's first commercially released films repeatedly and systematically reduce women to oversexed, frequently objectified ciphers lacking agency (Nola Darling in She's Gotta Have It, 1986) or alternately "shallow" or "dull[,] politically correct . . . appendages to the men of their respective social groups" (School Daze, 1988).[21] Ellis's essay does celebrate women authors and artists as well, including Toni Morrison, Terry McMillan, Lisa and Kellie Jones, the black women's performance art group Rodeo Caldonia, and Joan Armatrading.[22] Of these, though, only the Jones sisters merit more than a mention. Ellis's subsequent reply to his critics offers little more than a token defense of his biases. His response to Hunter's critique simply ignores her careful citation of Public Enemy and Lee's gender problems; instead, he tepidly claims that the former simply had one misogynistic, anti-Semitic minor member (Professor Griff) that embarrassed the rest of the group, and that many of their heroes and associates are women.[23] As defenses go, this does Ellis few favors.

Even if Ellis may not have offered an unassailable definition of the New Black Aesthetic—if such a thing were possible—he succeeded in sketching a rough outline, at least, of a notable shift in African American cultural sensibilities in the post–civil rights era and bringing it to critical attention. Such critics as Bertram Ashe,[24] and Mark Anthony Neal,[25] and Crystal Anderson,[26] among many others, have essayed to give Ellis's ideas greater depth and heft. Ashe in particular offers a richer context for Ellis's exuberant, if flawed, essay by pointing out how such critics and writers as Greg Tate, Nelson George, Terry McMillan, Paul Beatty, Danzy Senna, Touré, Darius James, Emily Raboteau, and Lisa Jones developed in their essays, stories, and novels a critical and cultural vocabulary for what we may now safely call the "Post-Soul" aesthetic.

In satirical terms, the "Post-Soul" generation's concerns may best be summed up by the blogger "Morpheus Reloaded" in his blog, "Pro-Black Thugs, Pimpin' Revolutionaries & Alien Conspiracies: Navigating the Underbelly of the 'Conscious' Community," which satirizes the various political factions within the African American community. Although the entire blog is brilliant, one excerpt deserves special notice for our purposes. The author lampoons "The 1960ers," individuals that either participated in or admire that decade's political movements without sufficient critical distance. They have the benefit of good intentions and "are genuinely concerned with the plight of black people" and "good at organizing protests" and "informing the younger generation [of] the monumental importance of history from half a century ago." But the 1960s were "near [half] a century ago," and "many of the staunch 1960'ers seem unable to deal with the realities of the 21st century; too few understand that different times require different tactics." As a result, they are "generally antiquated . . . and unable to reach the masses" and need to "[a]dapt and change or perish. As the urban philosopher of Shaolin would say, these analog cats need to get digital."[27]

Morpheus Reloaded's perspective on the 1960s generation reflects a sense among the post–civil rights generation that black politics, while ostensibly progressive, has become reactionary with regard to its tactics. No occasion is too small for a protest march; nothing occurs in African American communities today that cannot be explained by something that occurred in the 1950s in the 1960s; the youth of today are woefully misguided. Although no generation can honestly be reduced to a few stereotypes—Morpheus Reloaded's essay freely admits to being satire, after all—members of the post-soul generation may see its elders in the same light that the New Negroes viewed the Old Negro: a generation accustomed to seeing African Americans as a "problem" to be "solved" via the same means that had not brought about full equality. The more things change, the more they stay the same. Or, as Ashe reminds us, Ellis and other post-soul writers and critics would rather have an "anti-aesthetic" than a restrictive, ideologically hidebound norm with little room for irony.[28]

Surveying satire by African Americans from the 1980s until the present also seems to indicate that some aspects of the post-soul aesthetic's moment—"the most exciting period [Ellis] has ever known"—ring true. At the very least, African American fiction writers have embraced the post-soul movement's call for an openness of subject matter, especially when the goal is redefining "race" and African American culture in the wake of 1960s and 1970s black nationalism, along with evolving conceptions of gender and sexuality within African American communities. Taking apparently unintentional yet uncannily similar cues from the typical contents within George Schuyler and Theophilus Lewis's "Shafts and Darts" column to more contemporary authors, we find a number of remarkable parallels.

Percival Everett's breakout novel, *Erasure* (2001), features at several points novelist Juanita Mae Jenkins, author of *We's Lives in da Ghetto,* who learned how to write of black life when she "went to visit some relatives in Harlem for a couple of days" when she was twelve, an oblique swipe at author Sapphire (Ramona Lofton), who taught at the City College of New York (located in Harlem) before writing her novel *Push* (1996), which garnered a $500,000 advance contract. The novel's protagonist, Thelonious "Monk" Ellison, a writer of experimental fiction whose novels sell abysmally, save for the one conventional novel in his *oeuvre* that explicitly focuses upon race.[29] At the novel's opening, Ellison finds that his latest novel cannot find a home; as with his earlier fiction, editors and reviewers allow that it is "finely crafted" but cannot see what it "has to do with the African American experience," which would preclude its shelving in the "African American interest" sections in bookstores. Monk Ellison allows that others have considered him "not *black* enough," despite the fact that he is "living a *black* life, far blacker than [they] could ever know," but he refuses to accept their construction of his subjectivity. Monk's "blackness" has its foundation in his desire to embrace all his complexities, regardless of whether they are "raced" categories. Yet in doing so, his identity constantly risks erasure, precisely because he cannot decide where it does—or should—belong.

Contemporary African American satirists enjoy along with other black authors the benefits of a period in which Toni Morrison, Alice Walker, Gayl Jones, John Edgar Wideman, Edward P. Jones, Terry McMillan, and Colson Whitehead have gained critical and sometimes great commercial success since the mid-1980s. Yet that success has been achieved through a devil's bargain that continues to dog African American literature in general. While publishers opened up more markets for black writing in the wake of Terry McMillan's wildly popular *Waiting to Exhale* (1992), that opening reflected publishers' more benign yet precarious understanding of black writers and readers alike. Mat Johnson's *Hunting in Harlem* (2003) features Bobby Finley, author of *The Great Work,* a novel whose entire plot takes place in a closet in Alaska, who must compete against Bo Shareef, best-selling author of *Datz What I'm Talkin' Bout!,* which shamelessly exploits black readers' apparently unslaked desire for narratives about romantic and sexual relationships. The opening pages of Everett's *Erasure,* Paul Beatty's *White Boy Shuffle* (1996), and Trey Ellis's *Platitudes* (1988) eschew the blues narrative that has become popular in contemporary African American fiction. Fran Ross's *Oreo* (1975) represents a defiant counternarrative to the argument of some proponents of the Black Aesthetic, inasmuch as its eponymous hero, Christine Schwartz, ironically bridges two cultures—black Christianity and Judaism—through her very existence.

Since the late 1960s, novelist and critic Ishmael Reed has explicitly maintained the same defiant stance that Ross presents in her sole published novel. From *The Free-Lance Pallbearers* (1967) until his most recent novel, *Juice!* (2011), about the O. J. Simpson trial and its aftermath, Reed's fiction questions the aesthetics and cultural politics within African American communities, with certain feminists, black nationalists, and tastemakers receiving his most frequent and acerbic critiques. *Mumbo Jumbo* (1972) in particular recognizes what Trey Ellis perceived: the New Negro Renaissance and Black Arts/Black Aesthetic movements bore more similarities than differences, chief among them black and white intellectuals attempting to restrict African Americans' cultural expressions to the most acceptable and least troubling forms. Set during the New Negro Renaissance, *Mumbo Jumbo* revolves around the pandemic Jes Grew, Reed's metaphor for unfettered, ancient, creativity of African origins, manifested as the New Negro *zeitgeist* and surrounding hysteria. Attempting to suppress and cure the pandemic, representatives of the Wallflower Order (read: Ivy League), an affiliate of the Knights Templar, hire a naïve young artist, Nathan Brown, to be the "Talking Android" who will help the order co-opt the New Negro's work. Hired by Wallflower Order head Hinckle Von Vampton (read: Carl Van Vechten and/or George Plimpton) to write for the *Benign Monster* (read: Plimpton's *Paris Review*), Brown is tasked with writing reviews that will suppress any work that threatens the master narrative of white supremacy, and help flush out and squelch Jes Grew. In one crucial passage, we discover that murdered black nationalist Abdul Sufi Hamid's attempt to publish via the *Benign Monster* the ancient Book of Thoth—the text that revived, or conjured the Jes Grew pandemic—failed due to the waning of the "'Negro Awakening' fad." Moreover, the editors inform him that the work is "not 'Nation' enough": lacking in sufficient radical chic.[30] Like Everett's "Monk" Ellison and the historical artists and writers of the New Negro movement, Hamid confronts the reality that black and white arbiters of taste also arrogate to themselves black authenticity not for the sake of advancing creative arts, but controlling them.

Mumbo Jumbo's rather complex plot offers the stakes that Reed and other, more contemporary authors face: African American authors seldom, if ever, enjoy complete autonomy so long as they heed calls for authenticity of any sort. To accommodate a black aesthetic may mean squelching dissent in favor of conformity, but pursuing other agendas may sacrifice truth and accuracy. In Reed's most controversial novel, *Reckless Eyeballing* (1985), protagonist Tremonisha Smarts (a womanist author all too similar to Alice Walker) writes novels that depict African American men unflatteringly as they attack racism. Other authors—several of whom seem to mouth Reed's opinions on contemporary feminists—argue that Smarts unwittingly allies herself with white feminists possessing racist views. Smarts eventually admits that her blues-based narratives reflect the same hazard that Thurman observed among his fellow Niggeratti: "All of us who grew up in the middle class want to romanticize people who are worse off than we are." The time has come for "teen-age mothers" "to begin writing about places like [Brooklyn, New York's] Bed[ford]-Stuy[vesant neighborhood] themselves, and then all of us debutantes will have to write about ourselves, will have to write about our backgrounds instead of playing tour guides to the exotics."[31]

Reed's novel ultimately demands that artists with privileged, middle-class back-grounds clear the space required for others to write their own experiences, inde-pendent of class constructions that ultimately benefit all but the least privileged. Inevitably, this presents a dilemma that confronts contemporary writers and their literary forebears alike: creating that space leads inevitably to critical judgment of the products that fill it. Such judgments rely upon the standards developed by middle-class critics, who may have access to more privilege than their subjects. Sat-ire allows for enough self-consciousness to highlight this difference, but it remains a product of critical and intellectual distance itself. It must remain just aloof enough to criticize while immersed in its subject. Few authors can walk this line skillfully.

Schuyler's condemnation of the purveyors of "hokum," the inauthentic, those intellectual and artistic figures who need an Other to create their own identities, continues to resonate in more contemporary satirical fiction, foregrounding once again the problem of commercial exploitation that confronts the art. If we consider these works as a loosely defined aggregate, products of the post-soul aesthetic simul-taneously based upon yet questioning the black aesthetics that arose in the 1960s and 1970s, then they stand together against a tendency in black cultural movements to worship icons and ideologies for the sake of progress. Instead, these authors, like Schuyler before them, keep the discourse open, saying the impolitic and iconoclastic at will.

These authors form a loose coalition with at least one binding argument: an overdetermined idea of "race" itself confuses and blocks progress toward the Ameri-can ideal of democracy, whether in life or art. Arguments about racial issues were, of course, central to the Harlem Renaissance, but in these authors' works we find some of the more direct representations of the arguments surrounding "race" of the era. Schuyler's purpose was to demonstrate the meaninglessness of "race" itself; Thurman, Nugent, and Hughes reserved the bulk of their disdain for the intellectual decadence, self-hatred, and self-defeating arguments among black creative artists; Hurston distrusted most discussions of "race" as African American leaders advanced them; Fisher was wary of integration and gentrification during the renaissance. All saw the issue as one that also warped the content, appearance, and direction of art by people of African descent.

Contemporary satirists, in turn, have found themselves part of a movement that easily surpasses the New Negro Renaissance in commercial success and cultural im-pact; Terry McMillan, Toni Morrison, Alice Walker, and Sapphire's novels have been adapted into films whose box office receipts and awards have frequently dwarfed their source material. Through much of the 1980s, 1990s, and 2000s, new authors who placed their novels, nonfiction books, and poetry with major publishers enjoyed notices and profiles within such scholarly and popular black-oriented venues as *African American Review, Callaloo, Ebony,* and *Essence,* along with *American Literature, Publisher's Weekly,* and *Poets & Writers.* Their work has been anthologized many times over, assigned in university courses in most cases, and celebrated at academic conferences. But to the contemporary satirist, neither awards nor box office success is expected to last, and publishers' interest in African American literature is equally uncertain. Whereas the publishers of the New Negro Renaissance took risks with African American authors writing both traditional literature and more popular forms, contemporary satirists insist that the contemporary mainstream publishing industry no longer takes any risks, inasmuch as it is dominated by but a few conglomerates. Eight of the most popular African American–oriented imprints, for example, are under the aegis of only five major conglomerates: Amistad (HarperCollins), One World (Ballantine/Random House), Harper Trophy (HarperCollins), Jump at the Sun (Hyperion/Disney), Dafina (Kensington), Walk Worthy (Warner), Strivers Row (Villard/Random House), and Harlem Moon (Broadway/Random House).[32] Very few African American editors work at these publishers, who may very well decide to eschew experimentation in favor of social-document fiction and urban sensationalism. Mat Johnson, Percival Everett, Ishmael Reed, the late Fran Ross, and Trey Ellis, among many others, have had trouble keeping their earlier works in print despite numerous prizes and accolades.

This cautionary narrative might not always sound the most dreary depths, of course. Publishing goes in cycles dictated by more than either unconscious racism, neglect, or ledger sheets. Black authors continued to enjoy access to publishing well after the New Negro's heyday as the nation's continued fascination with African American culture evolved during the Great Depression, World War II, and beyond. The African American satirist also continues to share George Schuyler's memorable remarks upon his era: "I am reading a story about American Negroes. The white author has attempted to catch dialect and convey psychology. He has sketched a racial memory background: Jungles, leopards, crocodiles, tom-toms, and all the rest of which American Negroes know nothing. There is much about primal Instincts and the veneer of civilization. The author's ignorance and the editor's gullibility are equally refreshing. I laugh as you would laugh at the imaginings of a very small child. I laugh too at the thousands who will devour this trash."[33]

Schuyler goes on to note the absolute wonder that his fellow citizens display when they discover that Negroes do, in fact, write novels and poetry and work in occupations other than the manual arts. Like Monk Ellison observing the barbarian hordes of exploitative black fiction writers battering down the literary gates almost seventy-five years later, the younger Schuyler suggests—tongue poking a painful hole through a well-worn cheek—that life as an "Aframerican" affords countless opportunities for amusement: "Negroes, of course, are too thin-skinned to delight in many of the situations in which they find themselves. That requires a developed sense of humor. But nearly all of them get the thrills. It is their social heritage. So they love America and are loyal citizens, ever ready to shed their blood to maintain its independence and the liberties vouchsafed every citizen by the Constitution. For my part, I would never be able to stand all this noise and smoke and stone and steel and machinery, if my blackness did not bring diversion and relief. Thrice blessed are we sons of Ham."[34] Blessed indeed.

Notes

Chapter 1 ~ Toward a Revision of the Harlem Renaissance

1. Martin Japtok, "Pauline Hopkins' *Of One Blood,* Africa, and the 'Darwinist Trap,'" *African American Review* 36.3 (Fall 2002): 404.

2. Ibid., 405.

3. Hazel V. Carby, introduction, *The Magazine Novels of Pauline Hopkins* (New York: Oxford, 1988), xxxi.

4. W. E. Burghardt Du Bois, *Darkwater: Voices from Within the Veil* (New York: Harcourt, Brace and Howe, 1920), 49–50.

5. W. E. B. Du Bois, "Close Ranks," *Crisis* 16 (July 1918): 111. Mark Ellis discovered that Du Bois's critics were justified in accusing him of writing the uncharacteristically accommodationist piece to ensure acceptance of his application to the Military Intelligence Branch. Ellis did not, however, offer a full summary of his stance on the war, as Du Bois saw the conflict as one emerging from colonialism and imperialism from the start. See Mark Ellis, "'Closing Ranks' and 'Seeking Honors': W. E. B. Du Bois in World War I," *Journal of American History* 79.1 (June 1992): 96, 100, 124.

6. George S. Schuyler, *Black No More: Being an Account of the Strange and Wonderful Workings of Science in the Land of the Free,* A.D. *1933–1940* (1931; rpt. Boston: Northeastern University Press, 1989), 90.

7. Ibid., 90.

8. David Levering Lewis, *W. E. B. Du Bois: The Fight for Equality and the American Century, 1919–1963* (New York: Holt, 2000), 258.

9. James Weldon Johnson, "About Poetry and Poetry Makers," *New York Age,* December 16, 1915.

10. James Weldon Johnson, "When Is a Race Great?" *New York Age,* March 11, 1918.

11. James Weldon Johnson, "Views and Reviews," *New York Age,* February 21, 1920, quoted in Charles Scruggs, *The Sage in Harlem: H. L. Mencken and the Black Writers of the 1920s* (Baltimore: Johns Hopkins University Press, 1984), 57–58.

12. Langston Hughes, "The Negro Artist and the Racial Mountain," *Nation* 122.3181 (June 23, 1926): 694.

13. James Weldon Johnson, *Along This Way* (1933), in *Writings.* ed. William L. Andrews (New York: Library of America, 2004), 187.

14. Ibid.

15. Colson Whitehead, *The Colossus of New York: A City in Thirteen Parts* (New York: Doubleday, 2003), 3.

16. Wallace Thurman, "Quoth Brigham Young: This Is the Place," *Messenger* (August 1925): 235.

17. George S. Schuyler, *Black and Conservative* (New Rochelle: Arlington House, 1966), 95; Kathryn Talalay, *Composition in Black and White: The Life of Philippa Schuyler* (New York: Oxford University Press, 1997), 68.

18. Zora Neale Hurston, *Dust Tracks on a Road* (Philadelphia: J. B. Lippincott, 1942): 138, qtd. in Valerie Boyd, *Wrapped in Rainbows: The Life of Zora Neale Hurston* (New York: Scribner, 2003), 93.

19. Wallace Thurman, "This Negro Literary Renaissance," in *Collected Writings of Wallace Thurman*, ed. Amritjit Singh and Daniel M. Scott III (New Brunswick, N.J.: Rutgers University Press, 2003), 241.

20. Hurston was born in 1889, although for many years she claimed she was born a decade later. Thurman was born in 1902, as was Hughes, while Rudolph Fisher was born in 1897. Schuyler, who didn't consider himself part of the Harlem literati, was born in 1895.

21. Lewis, *W .E. B. Du Bois*, 164–65.

22. Richard Wright, "Blueprint for Negro Writing," *New Challenge: A Literary Quarterly* 2.2 (1937): 53. Wright's essay does not confine itself to circumstances unique to the Harlem Renaissance. In fact, most black writers of poetry and fiction were often forced to adopt more conciliatory and less inflammatory politics in their works in order to gain access to the limited publishing venues available to them prior to and after the Harlem Renaissance. I would argue, however, that given the recent memory of the Harlem Renaissance and its writers' actions during the period, Wright's remarks are directed almost entirely to the cadre of authors who were his immediate predecessors.

23. George Hutchinson, *The Harlem Renaissance in Black and White* (Cambridge, Mass.: Harvard University Press, 1995), 276–77.

24. Houston A. Baker Jr., *Modernism and the Harlem Renaissance* (Chicago: University of Chicago Press, 1987), 13–14.

25. Ishmael Reed and Steve Cannon, "George S. Schuyler, Writer," in *Shrovetide in Old New Orleans*, ed. Ishmael Reed (New York: Doubleday, 1978), 203. In this interview with Schuyler, Reed also criticizes Huggins's assessment of the Renaissance, noting "I never heard of anybody describing a movement of white writers as having failed when there could be individual successes in art . . ." (203).

26. Baker, *Modernism*, xv–xvi.

27. Hutchinson, *Harlem Renaissance*, 3.

28. The "Black Press" is a euphemism for the loose network of little magazines, vanity press books, newspapers, pamphlets, and church publications through which African Americans continuously published their work in the decades before the Harlem Renaissance. See Roland E. Wolseley, *The Black Press, U.S.A.* (Ames: Iowa State University Press, 1971); Martin E. Dann, ed., *The Black Press, 1827–1890: The Quest for National Identity* (New York: G. P. Putnam's Sons, 1971).

29. Baker, *Modernism*, xvii.

30. James Smethurst, *The African American Roots of Modernism: From Reconstruction to the Harlem Renaissance* (Chapel Hill: University of North Carolina Press, 2011), 3.

31. Ibid., 7.

32. Scruggs, *The Sage in Harlem*, 181.

33. Sonnet Retman, *Real Folks: Race and Genre in the Great Depression* (Durham, N.C.: Duke University Press, 2011), 5.

34. Ibid., 5.

35. Rudolph Fisher, "The Caucasian Storms Harlem," *American Mercury* 11 (1927): 396–97.

36. Wallace Thurman, *Infants of the Spring* (1932; rpt. Boston: Northeastern University Press, 1992): 240.

37. Ibid., 187.

Chapter 2 ~ The Importance of Being Iconoclastic

1. Alain Locke, letter to Jean Toomer, July 1, 1923, MSS 1, box 5, folder 1, James Weldon Johnson Collection, Yale Collection of American Literature, Beinecke Rare Book and Manuscript Library.

2. Scruggs, *Sage in Harlem*, 8–9.

3. Jeffrey A. Tucker, "'Can Science Succeed Where the Civil War Failed?': George S. Schuyler and Race," *Race Consciousness: African American Studies for the New Century*, ed. Judith Jackson Fossett and Jeffrey A. Tucker (New York: New York University Press, 1997), 137.

4. Scruggs, *Sage in Harlem*, 3.

5. Incidentally, Gates himself is named after Mencken. As chair of the W. E. B. Du Bois Institute at Harvard University, Gates also heads an organization named after one of Schuyler's favorite satirical targets. Both Du Bois and Gates have also become fairly recent foci of Ishmael Reed's withering critical perspective. See Reed's introduction to the 2000 Signet edition of Booker T. Washington's classic *Up from Slavery* (1897).

6. Ishmael Reed, "George S. Schuyler," introduction to George S. Schuyler, *Black No More: Being an Account of the Strange and Wonderful Workings of Science in the Land of the Free, A.D. 1933–1940* (New York: Modern Library, 1999), vii.

7. Schuyler, *Black and Conservative*, 350.

8. Ibid., 195–96.

9. Jeffrey Ferguson, *The Sage of Sugar Hill: George S. Schuyler and the Harlem Renaissance* (New Haven, Conn.: Yale University Press, 2005), 174.

10. Schuyler, *Black and Conservative*, 341.

11. Ibid., 344–45.

12. As an autobiography, *Black and Conservative* provides a strange yet fascinating take on Schuyler's adventures. As Michael Peplow notes in his own biography of Schuyler, *Black and Conservative* combines within its covers two markedly different narrative approaches that cross generic boundaries. The first half of the book contains a supremely rich history of black cultural life in the first half of the twentieth century as seen through the experiences of the younger, more radical Schuyler, as filtered through his older, more mature persona. It succeeds equally as autobiography, travelogue, and history, no less than such predecessors in the African American literary tradition as Booker T. Washington's *Up from Slavery* (1901), Du Bois's *The Souls of Black Folk* (1903), James Weldon Johnson's *Along this Way* (1933), or Hurston's *Dust Tracks on a Road* (1942). The second half consists primarily of Schuyler's inarguably strident and unrepentant Red-baiting, polemics on the hazards of collectivism, and catalogues

of communist dupes exposed for all the world to see. As Michael W. Peplow notes, the tone of the second half occasionally bleeds into the first, and threatens to rob the entire narrative of its power. "Was his first intention to write a highly readable autobiography," Peplow asks, "or a conservative manifesto? We do not find the answer in *Black and Conservative*" (*George S. Schuyler* [Boston: Twayne, 1980], 100–101).

13. Boyd, *Wrapped in Rainbows,* 354.

14. See especially Talalay, *Composition in Black and White;* Oscar R. Williams, *George S. Schuyler: Portrait of a Black Conservative* (Knoxville: University of Tennessee Press, 2007); and Carla Kaplan's *Miss Anne in Harlem: The White Women of the Black Renaissance* (New York: Harper, 2013). Talalay's biography naturally spends considerably more space discussing Philippa Duke Schuyler, but investigates Schuyler's early life as well as his and Josephine Cogdell Schuyler's complex and difficult marriage. Williams analyzes Schuyler's earliest years to an unprecedented extent, while Kaplan offers the closest approximation to a full biography of Cogdell Schuyler to date.

15. David Horowitz, *Radical Son: A Generational Odyssey* (New York: Free Press, 1997).

16. Qtd. in Peplow, *George S. Schuyler,* 30.

17. George S. Schuyler, "The Reminiscences of George S. Schuyler" (New York: Oral History Collection of Columbia University, 1960), 123.

18. Ibid., 116.

19. Ibid., 117.

20. Lewis published a short-lived magazine, *The Looking Glass,* which included some of the earliest work by Wallace Thurman (Elonore van Notten, *Wallace Thurman's Harlem Renaissance* [Amsterdam: Editions Rodopi, 1994], 102–3).

21. Schuyler, "The First *Real* Witch Hunt," undated manuscript, Box 8, folder 10, George S. Schuyler Selections, Manuscripts, Archives, and Rare Books Division, Schomburg Center for Research in Black Culture, New York Public Library.

22. Jervis Anderson, *A. Philip Randolph: A Biographical Portrait* (Berkeley: University of California Press, 1972), 74–75.

23. Ibid., 77.

24. Ibid.

25. Ibid.

26. Ibid., 79, 81.

27. Qtd. in Anderson, *A. Philip Randolph,* 98; editorial, *Messenger* 2.1 (January 1918): 20.

28. Theodore Kornweibel, *No Crystal Stair: Black Life and the* Messenger, *1917–1928* (Westport, Conn.: Greenwood Press, 1975), 4.

29. Anderson, *A. Philip Randolph,* 107.

30. Kornweibel, *No Crystal Stair,* 4.

31. Anderson, *A. Philip Randolph,* 115.

32. Kornweibel, *No Crystal Stair,* 3; Anderson, *A. Philip Randolph,* 108.

33. Anderson, *A. Philip Randolph,* 111–12.

34. The *Messenger* ran ads in support of Socialist Hillquit's New York mayoral campaign throughout its sporadic 1918 run.

35. Anderson, *A. Philip Randolph,* 116.

36. Kornweibel, *No Crystal Stair,* 165–66. Garvey appealed to colorism with regard to the editors in part due to their rather harsh impugning of his color, national origins, and other

aspects of his identity. These very personal denunciations were not justifiable, of course, but neither party was purely the victim in this instance.

37. Craig Gable, ed., *Ebony Rising: Short Fiction of the Greater Harlem Renaissance* (Bloomington: Indiana University Press, 2004), 2, 61, 71.

38. Schuyler, *Black and Conservative*, 52–53.

39. Ibid., 68.

40. Scruggs, *Sage in Harlem*, 54–55.

41. H. L. Mencken, *The Diary of H. L. Mencken*, ed. Charles A. Fecher (New York: Vintage 1991), 382. Mencken wrote elsewhere, "There are few white columnists in fact, who can match [Schuyler] for information, intelligence, independence and courage" (*Diary*, 382 n. 1).

42. Ibid.

43. George S. Schuyler, "Black Supremacy in Love," typescript, Box 8, folder 10, Schuyler Family Papers, Manuscripts, Archives, and Rare Books Division, Schomburg Center for Research in Black Culture, New York Public Library, 1–3.

44. Linda O. McMurry, *To Keep the Waters Troubled: The Life of Ida B. Wells-Barnett* (Oxford, U.K.: Oxford University Press, 1998), 157–58. Per McMurry, the quotation from Wells-Barnett was originally published in a pamphlet entitled *Southern Horrors, Lynch Law in All Its Phases*, collected in *Selected Writings of Ida B. Wells-Barnett*, ed. Trudier Harris (New York: Oxford University Press, 1991), 19.

45. Wells-Barnett, *Southern Horrors*, 159–60.

46. For a richly detailed account of Josephine Cogdell's life and relationship with George Schuyler, see Kaplan, *Miss Anne*, 83ff.

47. This has much to do with Chandler Owen's brother having died in March 1923 after struggling to find employment in New York City in the face of rampant racism by supposedly equanimous labor unions. This tragedy caused Owen to be distracted from his duties as *Messenger* coeditor a few months later to renounce the Socialist Party and radicalism in general before leaving to greener pastures in Chicago, although he remained titular coeditor for the rest of the magazine's life (Anderson, *A. Philip Randolph*, 142–43).

48. Anderson, *A. Philip Randolph*, 139–40; Schuyler, *Black and Conservative*, 138–39.

49. Schuyler, *Black and Conservative*, 136.

50. Ibid., 137.

51. Schuyler and Lewis, "Shafts and Darts," *Messenger*, April 1924, 108.

52. Scruggs, *Sage in Harlem*, 180–81.

53. Langston Hughes, *The Big Sea* (1940; rpt. New York, Thunder's Mouth, 1986), 374.

54. Schuyler, *Black and Conservative*, 141.

55. Robert W. Bagnall, "The Madness of Marcus Garvey," *Messenger*, March 1923, 638.

56. Marcus Garvey, "Prejudice," in *Philosophy and Opinions of Marcus Garvey*, ed. Amy Jacques Garvey (1925; rpt. New York: Atheneum, 1992), 18.

57. Kornweibel, *No Crystal Stair*, 139.

58. Ibid., 140; Anderson, *A. Philip Randolph*, 131–32.

59. Kornweibel, *No Crystal Stair*, 140.

60. Anderson, *A. Philip Randolph*, 132; Randolph, *Messenger*, October 1922, 499–500.

61. Kornweibel, *No Crystal Stair*, 145.

62. Schuyler, "Shafts and Darts," *Messenger*, October 1923, 841.

63. Leon Guilhamet, *Satire and the Transformation of Genre* (Philadelphia: University of Pennsylvania Press, 1987.

64. Schuyler, "A Tribute to Caesar," *Messenger* 6.7 (July 1924): 225.

65. Ibid.

66. Schuyler, "A Tribute to Caesar," 226.

67. Schuyler and Lewis, "Shafts and Darts," *Messenger* 6.8 (August 1924): 238.

68. W. E. B. Du Bois, "A Lunatic or a Traitor," *Crisis* 28 (May 1924): 9.

69. Du Bois, "Marcus Garvey," *Crisis* 21.2 (December 1920–January 1921): 58.

70. Du Bois, "The Black Star Line," *Crisis* 24.5 (September 1922): 214.

71. Du Bois, "Marcus Garvey," 58.

72. Anderson, *A. Phillip Randoph*, 137.

73. Kornweibel, *No Crystal Stair,* 166.

74. Ibid.

75. Ferguson, *Sage of Sugar Hill,* 15.

76. A. Philip Randolph, "Reply to Marcus Garvey," *Messenger* 4.8 (August 1922): 469.

77. Schuyler, "A Tribute to Caesar," 226.

78. Alain Locke, "The New Negro," *The New Negro,* ed. Locke (1925; rpt. New York: Atheneum, 1992), 9, 11.

79. Schuyler, "Shafts and Darts," *Messenger* 9.1 (January 1927): 18.

80. Ibid.

81. Ibid.

82. W. Lawrence Hogue, *The African American Male, Writing, and Difference: A Polycentric Approach to African American Literature, Criticism, and History* (Albany: State University of New York Press, 2003), 8. Hogue argues that, with a "nonfoundational and relativist approach to valuing cultural objects or literary texts, [he] can impute cultural capital to texts from all the various traditions in African American literature. Taking a polycentric approach to the literature, [he] can speak of different African American texts as having contingent value, without getting into the issue of hierarchy, superiority, and inferiority." As a result, measuring the value of African American texts and institutions need not rest upon a single set of criteria, especially those supported by the middle class. A more complete approach requires many different class and ideological perspectives.

83. W. E. B. Du Bois, "The Negro and Radical Thought," *Crisis* 22.3 (July 1921): 103. See also Cornel West, *The American Evasion of Philosophy* (Madison: University of Wisconsin Press, 1989), 138–50, for a detailed analysis of Du Bois's background in pragmatism.

84. George S. Schuyler, "How to Be Happy, though Colored," typescript, Schuyler Family Papers, 1–2.

85. Ibid., 3.

86. Scruggs, *Sage in Harlem,* 53.

87. George S. Schuyler, *Black No More,* 71.

88. H. L. Mencken, "The Sahara of the Bozart," rpt. in *A Mencken Chrestomathy,* ed. H. L. Mencken (1949; rpt. New York: Vintage, 1982), 185–86.

89. Mencken, "Sahara," 184.

90. Schuyler, "Reminiscences," 117–18.

91. Mencken, "Sahara," 185.

92. Schuyler, "Reminiscences," 117.

93. Ibid.

94. George S. Schuyler, "The Negro-Art Hokum," *Nation* 122 (1926): 662–63.

95. Ibid., 662.

96. Schuyler, "Shafts and Darts," *Messenger* 8.9 (September 1926): 271.

97. Ibid., 8.5 (May 1926): 143.

98. Ibid., 8.9 (September 1926): 271.

99. Ibid., 8.3 (March 1926): 72.

100. Ferguson, *Sage of Sugar Hill*, 194.

101. Ibid., 183–84. Editor Freda Kirchwey of *The Nation* commissioned Schuyler's piece to provide a more skeptical look at the New Negro movement, then solicited Langston Hughes's response, which, per Kirchwey's wishes, did not truly refute Schuyler, but instead allowed Hughes to declare African American artists' independence on their own terms.

102. Schuyler, "Reminiscences," 123.

Chapter 3 ~ Wallace Thurman, Richard Bruce Nugent, and the Reification of "Race," Aesthetics, and Sexuality

1. Wallace Thurman, letter to Claude McKay, February 3, 1928, Claude McKay Collection, James Weldon Johnson Papers, Beinecke Library, Yale University, Box 5, folder 14.

2. Singh and Scott, eds., Collected Writings of Wallace Thurman, 177.

3. Hughes, *The Big Sea*, 234.

4. Thomas Wirth, "Introduction" to Richard Bruce Nugent, *Gentleman Jigger* (Philadelphia: Da Capo, 2008), xiv.

5. Ibid., xvii.

6. Abby Arthur Johnson and Ronald Maberry Johnson, *Propaganda and Aesthetics: The Literary Politics of African-American Magazines in the Twentieth Century* (Amherst: University of Massachusetts Press, 1979), 77.

7. Karen Jackson Ford, *Split-Gut Song: Jean Toomer and the Poetics of Modernity* (Tuscaloosa: University of Alabama Press, 2005), 3.

8. Singh and Scott, eds., *Collected Writings of Wallace Thurman*, 14–15. While Singh and Scott allow that Thurman divided aspects of his personality and experiences among these protagonists, they caution against seeking anything more than partial correspondence. This caution particularly holds for Raymond Taylor of *Infants of the Spring*, who holds many of Thurman's views of literature. Thurman distributed other behaviors and quirks among principal characters within the novel.

9. Van Notten, *Wallace Thurman's Harlem Renaissance*, 14.

10. W. E. B. Du Bois, "Criteria of Negro Art," *Crisis* 32 (October 1926): 296.

11. Ibid.

12. Wallace Thurman, "Editorial Essay," *Harlem: A Forum of Negro Life* (November 1928): 1.

13. Ibid., 2

14. Hughes, *The Big Sea*, 375.

15. Nugent, *Gentleman Jigger*, 34.

16. Hughes, *The Big Sea*, 236.

17. Thurman, letter to Langston Hughes, ca. July 1929, in *Collected Writings*, 127.

18. Ibid.

19. Thurman, "Negro Artists and the Negro," *The New Republic*, August 31, 1927, 37, rpt. in *Collected Writings,* 197.

20. Ibid, 39.

21. Schuyler, "The Negro-Art Hokum," 662–63.

22. Wallace Thurman, "Nephews of Uncle Remus," *Independent* 119.4034 (September 24, 1927): 296–98, rpt. in *Collected Writings,* 200–205.

23. Wallace Thurman, letter to Langston Hughes, ca. August 1929, in *Collected Writings,* 124.

24. Thurman, *Infants of the Spring,* 144–45.

25. Hughes, "Negro Artist," 692–94.

26. Wallace Thurman, "Negro Poets and Their Poetry," *Bookman,* July 1928, rpt. in *Collected Writings,* 213.

27. Ibid.

28. Ibid.

29. Ibid.

30. W. E. B. Du Bois, *The Souls of Black Folk* (1903; rpt. New York: Knopf, 1993), 8–9.

31. Ibid., 9.

32. Ibid.

33. W. E. B. Du Bois, "The Talented Tenth," *The Negro Problem: A Series of Articles by Representative American Negroes of To-day* (1903; rpt. New York: Arno, 1969), 33.

34. Hutchinson, *Harlem Renaissance,* 36–37.

35. Du Bois, *The Souls of Black Folk,* 67–68; Hutchinson, *Harlem Renaissance,* 37.

36. Wallace Thurman, letter to Fay M. Jackson, May 5, 1928, Fay M. Jackson Memorial Collection, qtd. in Van Notten, *Wallace Thurman's Harlem Renaissance,* 117.

37. Thurman, "Quoth Brigham Young"; letter to William Jourdan Rapp, n.d., ca. April 1929, qtd. in Van Notten, *Wallace Thurman's Harlem Renaissance,* 80.

38. As but one example, Thurman matriculated at the University of Utah in 1920 as a pre-med student with goals of becoming a medical doctor until he quickly lost interest in favor of journalism, writing, and the arts. He recorded no instances of overt racism during his studies until he enrolled at the University of Southern California in 1922, an event he depicted in the opening chapters of *The Blacker the Berry* . . . . In other words, Thurman had to leave Utah for California to experience overt racism from whites and blacks alike. See Van Notten, *Wallace Thurman's Harlem Renaissance,* 79.

39. Van Notten, *Wallace Thurman's Harlem Renaissance,* 86, 102.

40. Wallace Thurman, foreword, *Fire!!* 1 (November 1926): 1.

41. Wallace Thurman, letter to Langston Hughes, October 30, 1926, MSS 26, Box 155, Folder 2877, James Weldon Johnson Collection.

42. Thurman, letter to Langston Hughes, n.d., ca. October 1926: "Just one more complication and I will be ready to blow up. Have had two bad checks which I had to make good to The World Tomorrow. Fire is certainly burning me" (MSS 26, Box 155, Folder 2877, James Weldon Johnson Collection).

43. Ibid.

44. Van Notten, *Wallace Thurman's Harlem Renaissance,* 152–53.

45. Granville Hicks, "The New Negro: An Interview with Wallace Thurman," *Churchman* 30 (April 1927): 10.

46. Wallace Thurman, letter to Alain Locke, 3 October 1928, Moorland-Spingarn Collection, Howard University.

47. This does not mean, however, that Fisher did not satirize certain figures within the renaissance who were indirectly involved in the movement's literary campaigns. *The Walls of Jericho's* "Agatha Cramp" is almost certainly Fisher's scarcely hidden caricature of Charlotte Osgood Mason.

48. Wallace Thurman, *The Blacker the Berry* . . . (1929; rpt. New York: Scribner, 1996), 21.

49. Ibid., 22.

50. Hughes, *The Big Sea,* 368–69.

51. James de Jongh, *Vicious Modernism: Black Harlem and the Literary Imagination* (Cambridge, U.K.: Cambridge University Press, 1990), 12.

52. Thurman, *Infants of the Spring,* 11–12.

53. Ibid., 27.

54. Ibid., 28.

55. Ibid.

56. Ibid., 30.

57. Ibid., 30–31.

58. Ibid., 31.

59. "Arbian" is a homonym for RBN, or Richard Bruce Nugent.

60. Thurman, *Infants of the Spring,* 49.

61. Ibid., 52.

62. Ibid., 214–15.

63. Ibid., 140.

64. Ibid., 216–17.

65. Ibid., 218.

66. Ibid., 218–19.

67. Ibid., 221.

68. Ibid., 228.

69. Ibid., 233–35.

70. Amritjit Singh, foreword, Thurman, *Infants of the Spring,* xv; Bernard W. Bell, *The Afro-American Novel and Its Tradition* (Amherst: University of Massachusetts Press, 1987), 133.

71. Thurman, *Infants of the Spring,* 236. A reference to Cullen's "ambivalence that vacillates between African ancestralism and Western classicism" in addition to Cullen's skeptical view of religion and superstition in his only novel, *One Way to Heaven;* Bell, *Afro-American Novel,* 134.

72. Thurman, *Infants of the Spring,* 237.

73. Ibid., 242–45.

74. Ibid., 277.

75. Ibid., 280.

76. Ibid., 280–81.

77. Ibid., 284.

78. Nugent explained to Thomas Wirth that Paul Arbian's death was "the only way Wallie could think of to end the book" (Wirth, introduction, *Gay Rebel of the Harlem Renaissance: Selections from the Work of Richard Bruce Nugent* [Durham, N.C.: Duke University Press, 2002], 15).

79. Thurman, *Infants of the Spring*, 218–19.

80. Nugent, *Gentleman Jigger*, 172, 112–13.

81. Van Notten, *Wallace Thurman's Harlem Renaissance*, 145.

82. Thurman, "Nephews of Uncle Remus," 204.

83. Wirth, introduction, Nugent, *Gentleman Jigger*, xiii.

84. David Levering Lewis, Interview with Bruce Nugent, September 11, 1974, "Voices from the Renaissance," David Levering Lewis Collection, Schomburg Center for Research in Black Culture, New York Public Library.

85. Nugent, *Gentleman Jigger*, 13–18.

86. Hughes, *The Big Sea*, 227.

87. Thurman, *Infants of the Spring*, 232.

88. Thurman, "Nephews of Uncle Remus," 203.

89. Nugent, *Gentleman Jigger*, 108.

90. Ibid., 62–63.

91. Ibid., 126–27.

92. Ibid., 110.

93. Ibid.

94. Nugent, *Gentleman Jigger*, 109.

95. Ibid., 112.

96. Zora Neale Hurston, letter to Langston Hughes, April 12, 1928, rpt. in *Zora Neale Hurston: A Life in Letters*, ed. Carla Kaplan (New York: Doubleday, 2001), 115–16.

97. Thurman, "This Negro Literary Renaissance," 246.

98. Wallace Thurman, letter to Langston Hughes, ca. May–June 1929, rpt. in *Collected Writings*, 119.

99. Thurman, "Negro Artists and the Negro," 197.

100. Hutchinson, *Harlem Renaissance*, 398.

101. Thurman, *Infants of the Spring*, 240–41; Nugent, *Gentleman Jigger*, 108.

102. Thurman, "Negro Poets and Their Poetry," 212.

103. Ibid, 211.

104. Claude McKay, *A Long Way from Home* (1937; rpt. New York: Harcourt, Brace, Jovanovich, 1970), 228.

105. Ibid., 31.

106. Ibid.

107. Ibid., 31–32.

108. Lewis, Interview with Nugent.

109. Thurman, letter to Claude McKay, October 4, 1928, rpt. in *Collected Writings*, 165.

110. Ibid.

111. Nugent, *Gentleman Jigger*, 160.

112. Ibid., 160, 162–63.

113. Ibid., 160–61.

114. Hughes, "Negro Artist," 694.

Chapter 4 ~ Dickties vs. Rats

1. De Jongh, *Vicious Modernism*, 5–6.

2. E. Franklin Frazier, *Black Bourgeoisie* (1957; rpt. New York: Free Press, 1990), 84.

3. Ibid., 85.

4. Glenda R. Carpio and Werner Sollors, "The Newly Complicated Zora Neale Hurston," *Chronicle of Higher Education* 57.18 (January 2, 2011): B8.

5. Alice Walker, "Foreword: Zora Neale Hurston—A Cautionary Tale and a Partisan View," in Robert S. Hemenway, *Zora Neale Hurston: A Literary Biography* (Urbana-Champaign: University of Illinois Press, 1977), xiv–xv.

6. Wright, "Blueprint," 53.

7. Ibid.

8. Richard Wright, "Between Laughter and Tears," *New Masses,* October 5, 1937. Emphases Wright's.

9. Thurman, *Infants of the Spring,* 229–30.

10. Hughes, *The Big Sea,* 239.

11. John Lowe, "Hurston, Humor, and the Harlem Renaissance," *Harlem Renaissance Reexamined: A Revised and Expanded Edition,* ed. Victor A. Kramer and Robert A. Russ (Troy, New York: Whitston, 1997), 309.

12. Alain Locke, "Jingo, Counter-Jingo and Us," *Opportunity* 16.1 (January 1938): 10.

13. Lowe, "Hurston, Humor, and the Harlem Renaissance," 309.

14. Ibid., 310.

15. Thurman, *Infants of the Spring,* 229.

16. Richard Bruce Nugent, interview with Robert E. Hemenway, May 1971, Robert E. Hemenway files, qtd. in Boyd, *Wrapped in Rainbows,* 136.

17. Boyd, *Wrapped in Rainbows,* 156–57.

18. Ibid, 158–59.

19. Ibid, 159–60; Hemenway, *Zora Neale Hurston,* 109–10.

20. Kaplan, *Miss Anne,* 244–47.

21. Ibid., 242.

22. Zora Neale Hurston, letter to Langston Hughes, April 12, 1928, rpt. in *Zora Neale Hurston,* ed. Kaplan, 115.

23. Zora Neale Hurston, letter to Dorothy West, December 5, 1928, rpt. in *Zora Neale Hurston,* ed. Kaplan, 134. *Harlem: A Forum of Negro Life* (1928) was the second major effort on the part of the younger New Negroes to produce a magazine representing the group's efforts. Like *Fire!!,* it was edited by Wallace Thurman and was short-lived, with only one issue seeing print; as was not the case with *Fire!!, Harlem's* contributors extended beyond the core group of younger authors (aka the "Niggeratti"), with George S. Schuyler, Alain Locke, and Alice Dunbar-Nelson contributing essays.

24. Zora Neale Hurston, letter to Langston Hughes, ca. spring/summer 1929, rpt. in *Zora Neale Hurston,* ed. Kaplan, 143. Grammatical errors are in the original. Some of the material that Hurston writes of here became part of the manuscript for *Negro Folk-Tales from the Gulf States,* which in turn became *Mules and Men* (1935) much later (Kaplan, ed., *Zora Neale Hurston: A Life in Letters,* 52). In any case, Hurston was forbidden from showing her material to anyone, including Hughes, who was also a beneficiary of Mason's patronage at the time.

25. Zora Neale Hurston, letter to Langston Hughes, March 8, 1928, rpt. in *Zora Neale Hurston,* ed. Kaplan, 114.

26. Zora Neale Hurston, letter to Langston Hughes, January 18, 1931, rpt. in *Zora Neale Hurston,* ed. Kaplan, 202.

27. Zora Neale Hurston, letter to Arthur Spingarn, March 25, 1931, rpt. in *Zora Neale Hurston,* ed. Kaplan, 215.

28. Zora Neale Hurston, letter to Langston Hughes, April 12, 1928, rpt. in *Zora Neale Hurston,* ed. Kaplan, 115–16.

29. Zora Neale Hurston, "Characteristics of Negro Expression," 1934, rpt. in *Sweat,* ed. Cheryl Wall (New Brunswick: Rutgers University Press, 1997), 59.

30. Zora Neale Hurston, "The Emperor Effaces Himself," n.d., Zora Neale Hurston Collection, James Weldon Johnson, Box 1, folder 15, rpt. in Henry Louis Gates Jr. and Jennifer Burton, *Call and Response: Key Debates in African American Studies* (New York: W.W. Norton, 2010), 267–68. Although the essay is undated in Hurston's papers, the topic, Hurston's correspondence, and the dearth of writings after 1927 make a 1925 composition date most plausible.

31. Hurston, "Emperor Effaces Himself," 268.

32. Colin Grant, *Negro with a Hat: The Rise and Fall of Marcus Garvey* (New York: Oxford University Press, 2008), 265–66.

33. Grant, *Negro with a Hat,* 119, 266.

34. Joel A. Rogers, *Additional Facts on Marcus Garvey,* Negroes of New York Writers' Program, 1939; rpt. in Grant, *Negro with a Hat,* 439–40. Garvey, to be fair, also condemned Mussolini's invasion of Ethiopia, declaring him a "tyrant" and a "bully" (Rogers, *Additional Facts,* 439–40).

35. Grant, *Negro with a Hat,* 453–54.

36. Hurston, "Emperor Effaces Himself," 269.

37. Ibid., 270.

38. Zora Neale Hurston, letter to Annie Nathan Meyer, October 27, 1927, rpt. in *Zora Neale Hurston,* ed. Kaplan, 108.

39. Zora Neale Hurston, letter to Langston Hughes, May 31, 1929, rpt. in *Zora Neale Hurston,* ed. Kaplan, 144–45.

40. Zora Neale Hurston, letter to Maxeda Von Hesse, April 7, 1951, rpt. in *Zora Neale Hurston,* ed. Kaplan, 652.

41. Zora Neale Hurston, "Sweat," *Fire!!* (November 1926): 45.

42. Zora Neale Hurston, "How It Feels to Be Colored Me," *World Tomorrow* 11 (May 1928): 215.

43. Zora Neale Hurston, "Monkey Junk: A Satire on Modern Divorce," *Chronicle of Higher Education* 57.18 (January 2, 2011): B8.

44. Ibid., B8.

45. Ibid., B9.

46. Ibid., B10.

47. Hemenway, *Zora Neale Hurston,* 258.

48. Ibid., 256.

49. Zora Neale Hurston, *Moses, Man of the Mountain* (1940; rpt. New York: Vintage, 1991), 1.

50. Ibid., 121.

51. Ibid., 78.

52. Ibid., 79–80.

53. Ibid., 99.

54. Ibid., 129–30.

55. Hemenway, *Zora Neale Hurston*, 257.

56. Hurston, *Moses*, 242–44.

57. Ibid., 245.

58. Hemenway, *Zora Neale Hurston*, 37–38.

59. Fisher, "The Caucasian Storms Harlem," 393–98.

60. On April 9, 1924, Senator Ellison DuRant "Cotton Ed" Smith of South Carolina implored his fellow senators to read *The Passing of the Great Race,* as he expressed his gratitude that "we have in America perhaps the largest percentage of any country in the world of the pure, unadulterated Anglo-Saxon stock; certainly the greatest of any nation in the Nordic breed" (qtd. in André Hoyrd, "Of Racialists and Aristocrats: George S. Schuyler's *Black No More* and Nordicism," in *African American Humor, Irony, and Satire: Ishmael Reed, Satirically Speaking,* ed. Dana A. Williams [Newcastle, U.K.: Cambridge Scholars, 2007], 26).

61. Lewis, *W. E. B. Du Bois,* 235–37.

62. Michel Foucault, *The History of Sexuality, Volume I: An Introduction* (1978; rpt. New York: Vintage, 1990), 4.

63. Thurman, *Infants of the Spring,* 233. Thurman, "High, Low, Past, and Present: Review of *The Walls of Jericho, Quicksand,* and *Adventures of an African Slaver,*" *Harlem: A Forum of Negro Life* (November 1928), in *Collected Writings,* 218–21.

64. Zora Neale Hurston, letter to Dorothy West, March 24, 1934, rpt. in *Zora Neale Hurston,* ed. Kaplan, 297.

65. W. E. B. Du Bois and Alain Locke, "The Younger Literary Movement," *Crisis* (February 1924), 162.

66. The light-skinned, bourgeois black professional class.

67. Working-class African Americans.

68. Rudolph Fisher, *The Walls of Jericho* (1928; rpt. Ann Arbor: University of Michigan Press, 1994), 3.

69. Ibid., 7–8.

70. Giorgio Agamben, *Homo Sacer: Sovereign Power and Bare Life,* trans. Daniel Heller-Roazen (Palo Alto, Calif.: Stanford University Press, 1998), 8.

71. Fisher, *Walls of Jericho,* 10–11.

72. Stephen P. Knadler, "Sweetback Style: Wallace Thurman and a Queer Harlem Renaissance," *Modern Fiction Studies* 48.4 (Winter 2002): 905–6.

73. Fisher, *Walls of Jericho,* 203–14.

74. Ibid., 36.

75. Ibid.

76. Ibid., 43.

77. Ibid., 41.

78. Ibid., 42.

79. Ibid., 58, 61.

80. David Levering Lewis, *When Harlem Was in Vogue* (New York and Oxford: Oxford University Press, 1979, 151–2.

81. Fisher, *Walls of Jericho,* 61–69.

82. Ibid., 73.

83. Ibid., 282–83.

84. Ibid., 290.

85. Ibid., 292–93.

86. Hurston, *Moses*, 203.

Chapter 5 ~ Punchlines

1. Schuyler, "Reminiscences," 77.

2. Hughes, *The Big Sea*, 334. A few pages earlier, Hughes notes that he broke off his relationship with his own unnamed patron, Charlotte Osgood Mason, hence his final poke.

3. Wallace Thurman, "Review of *Infants of the Spring*," unpublished manuscript, in *Collected Writings*, 226.

4. Cary Wintz, *Black Culture and the Harlem Renaissance* (Houston: Rice University Press, 1988), 217.

5. Ibid., 164–65. Wintz omits Schuyler's *Black No More* from his catalog of New Negro works.

6. Johnson and Johnson, *Propaganda and Aesthetics*, 98.

7. Blanche Ferguson, *Countee Cullen and the Negro Renaissance* (New York: Dodd, Mead, and Co., 1966).

8. Quoted in Ferguson, *Countee Cullen and the Negro Renaissance*, 98–99. Slightly altered portions of this paragraph appeared in my essay "African American Literature and the Great Depression," in *The Cambridge History of African American Literature* (Cambridge, U.K.: Cambridge University Press, 2011), 290.

9. Wright, "Blueprint," 53.

10. Martin Luther King Jr., *Why We Can't Wait* (New York: New American Library, 1964), 72–73.

11. "A Call for Unity," American Friends Service Committee, April 12, 1963.

12. Malcolm X, "Message to the Grass Roots," *Malcolm X Speaks*, ed. George Breitman (New York: Grove Weidenfeld, 1965), 16–17.

13. Williams, *George S. Schuyler*, 146–47.

14. Locke, foreword, *The New Negro*, ix; Trey Ellis, "The New Black Aesthetic," *Callaloo* 38 (Winter 1989): 234. *Glasnost* is the policy that former president and general secretary of the Communist Party of the Soviet Union Mikhail S. Gorbachev initiated in 1989 to allow greater transparency in government.

15. Ellis, "New Black Aesthetic," 236.

16. Ibid., 235.

17. Hughes, "Negro Artist," 694.

18. Eric Lott, "Response to Trey Ellis's 'New Black Aesthetic,'" *Callaloo* 38 (Winter 1989): 244–45.

19. Ibid., 245–46.

20. Tera Hunter, "'It's a Man's, Man's, Man's World': Specters of the Old Re-newed in Afro-American Culture and Criticism," *Callaloo* 38 (Winter 1989): 248.

21. Ibid., 248–49.

22. Ibid., 236–43.

23. Trey Ellis, "Response to New Black Aesthetic Critics," *Callaloo* 38 (Winter 1989): 250–51.

24. Bertram Ashe, "Theorizing the Post-Soul Aesthetic: An Introduction," *African American Review* 41.4 (Winter 2007): 609–23. Ashe's introduction opens a special issue of *African American Review* that he edited on the Post-Soul aesthetic. For all practical purposes, the Post-Soul and New Black Aesthetics are synonymous.

25. Mark Anthony Neal, *Soul Babies: Black Popular Culture and the Post-Soul Aesthetic* (New York: Routledge, 2002).

26. Crystal S. Anderson, "The Afro-Asiatic Floating World: Post-Soul Implications of the Art of Iona Rozeal Brown," *African American Review* 41.4 (Winter 2007): 655–65.

27. Morpheus Reloaded, "Pro-Black Thugs, Pimpin' Revolutionaries & Alien Conspiracies: Navigating the Underbelly of the 'Conscious' Community," www.playahata.com/pages/morpheus/blackconscious.htm (accessed February 27, 2013). Other factions lampooned include "The Doom Projectors," "Supa Dupa Afrikans," "The Lumpen-Proletariat Reform Movement," and "We Hate Whitey Federation." The "urban philosopher of Shaolin" alludes to the hip-hop group Wu Tang Clan, which cites kung fu films from the 1970s as its most prominent influence.

28. Ashe, "Theorizing the Post-Soul Aesthetic," 612.

29. "Second Failure: My 'realistic' novel. It was received nicely and sold rather well. It's about a young black man who can't understand why his white-looking mother is ostracized by the black community. . . . I hated writing the novel. I hated reading the novel. I hated thinking about the novel" (Percival Everett, *Erasure* [New York: Hyperion, 2001], 61).

30. Ishmael Reed, *Mumbo Jumbo* (1972; rpt., New York: Atheneum, 1988), 98.

31. Ishmael Reed, *Reckless Eyeballing* (New York: Atheneum, 1986), 131.

32. Paul D. Colford, "Publishers Find It Pays to Do Write Thing," *New York Daily News*, December 11, 2000, 34.

33. George S. Schuyler, "Blessed Are the Sons of Ham," *Nation* 124:3220 (March 23, 1927): 314.

34. Ibid., 315.

Bibliography

Agamben, Giorgio. *Homo Sacer: Sovereign Power and Bare Life.* Trans. Daniel Heller-Roazen. Palo Alto, Calif.: Stanford University Press, 1998.

Anderson, Crystal S. "The Afro-Asiatic Floating World: Post-Soul Implications of the Art of Iona Rozeal Brown." *African American Review* 41.4 (Winter 2007): 655–65.

Anderson, Jervis. *A. Philip Randolph: A Biographical Portrait.* Berkeley: University of California Press, 1972.

Ashe, Bertram. "Theorizing the Post-Soul Aesthetic: An Introduction." *African American Review* 41.4 (Winter 2007): 609–23.

Bagnall, Robert W. "The Madness of Marcus Garvey." *Messenger,* March 1923, 638.

Baker, Houston A., Jr. *Modernism and the Harlem Renaissance.* Chicago: University of Chicago Press, 1987.

Bell, Bernard W., *The Afro-American Novel and Its Tradition.* Amherst: University of Massachusetts Press, 1987.

Boyd, Valerie. *Wrapped in Rainbows: The Life of Zora Neale Hurston.* New York: Scribner, 2003.

"A Call for Unity." American Friends Service Committee, April 12, 1963.

Carby, Hazel V. Introduction. *The Magazine Novels of Pauline Hopkins.* New York: Oxford University Press, 1988. xxix–l.

Carpio, Glenda R., and Werner Sollors. "The Newly Complicated Zora Neale Hurston." *The Chronicle of Higher Education* 57.18 (January 2, 2011): B6-B8.

Colford, Paul D. "Publishers Find It Pays to Do Write Thing." *New York Daily News,* December 11, 2000, 34.

Dann, Martin E., ed. *The Black Press, 1827–1890: The Quest for National Identity.* New York: G. P. Putnam's Sons, 1971.

de Jongh, James. *Vicious Modernism: Black Harlem and the Literary Imagination.* Cambridge, U.K.: Cambridge University Press, 1990.

Du Bois, W. E. Burghardt. "The Black Star Line." *Crisis* 24 (September 1922): 210–14.

———. "Close Ranks." *Crisis* 16 (July 1918): 111.

———. "Criteria of Negro Art." *Crisis* 32 (October 1926): 290–97.

———. *Darkwater: Voices from Within the Veil.* New York: Harcourt, Brace and Howe, 1920.

———. "A Lunatic or a Traitor." *Crisis* 28 (May 1924): 8–9.

———. Marcus Garvey." *Crisis* 21.2 (December 1920–January 1921): 58–60.

———. "The Negro and Radical Thought." *Crisis* 22.3 (July 1921): 103.

———. *The Souls of Black Folk.* 1903. Rpt. New York: Knopf, 1993.

————. "The Talented Tenth." *The Negro Problem: A Series of Articles by Representative American Negroes of To-day.* 1903. Rpt. New York: Arno, 1969, 29–75.

————, and Alain Locke. "The Younger Literary Movement." *Crisis* (February 1924): 161–62.

Ellis, Mark. "'Closing Ranks' and 'Seeking Honors': W. E. B. Du Bois in World War I." *Journal of American History* 79.1 (June 1992): 96, 100, 124.

Ellis, Trey. "The New Black Aesthetic." *Callaloo* 38 (Winter 1989): 233–43.

————. "Response to New Black Aesthetic Critics." *Callaloo* 38 (Winter 1989): 250–51.

Everett, Percival. *Erasure.* New York: Hyperion, 2001.

Ferguson, Blanche. *Countee Cullen and the Negro Renaissance.* New York: Dodd, Mead, and Co., 1966.

Ferguson, Jeffrey. *The Sage of Sugar Hill: George S. Schuyler and the Harlem Renaissance.* New Haven, Conn.: Yale University Press, 2005.

Fisher, Rudolph. "The Caucasian Storms Harlem." *American Mercury* 11 (1927): 393–98.

————. *The Walls of Jericho.* 1928. Rpt. Ann Arbor: University of Michigan Press, 1994.

Ford, Karen Jackson. *Split-Gut Song: Jean Toomer and the Poetics of Modernity.* Tuscaloosa: University of Alabama Press, 2005.

Foucault, Michel. *The History of Sexuality, Volume I: An Introduction.* 1978. Rpt. New York: Vintage, 1990.

Frazier, E. Franklin. *Black Bourgeoisie.* 1957. Rpt. New York: Free Press, 1990.

Gable, Craig, ed. *Ebony Rising: Short Fiction of the Greater Harlem Renaissance.* Bloomington: Indiana University Press, 2004.

Garvey, Marcus. "Prejudice." In *Philosophy and Opinions of Marcus Garvey,* ed. Amy Jacques Garvey. 1925. Rpt. New York: Atheneum, 1992, 18.

Grant, Colin. *Negro with a Hat: The Rise and Fall of Marcus Garvey.* New York: Oxford University Press, 2008.

Guilhamet, Leon. *Satire and the Transformation of Genre.* Philadelphia: University of Pennsylvania Press, 1987.

Hemenway, Robert S. *Zora Neale Hurston: A Literary Biography.* Urbana-Champaign: University of Illinois Press, 1977.

Hicks, Granville. "The New Negro: An Interview with Wallace Thurman." *Churchman* 30 (April 1927): 10.

Hogue, W. Lawrence. *The African American Male, Writing, and Difference: A Polycentric Approach to African American Literature, Criticism, and History.* Albany: State University of New York Press, 2003.

Horowitz, David. *Radical Son: A Generational Odyssey.* New York: Free Press, 1997.

Hoyrd, André. "Of Racialists and Aristocrats: George S. Schuyler's *Black No More* and Nordicism." In *African American Humor, Irony, and Satire: Ishmael Reed, Satirically Speaking,* ed. Dana A. Williams. Newcastle, U.K.: Cambridge Scholars, 2007, 26–35.

Hughes, Langston. *The Big Sea.* 1940. Rpt. New York: Thunder's Mouth Press, 1999.

————. "The Negro Artist and the Racial Mountain." *Nation* 122.3181 (June 23, 1926): 692–94.

Hunter, Tera. "'It's a Man's, Man's, Man's World': Specters of the Old Re-newed in Afro-American Culture and Criticism." *Callaloo* 38 (Winter 1989): 247–49.

Hurston, Zora Neale. "Characteristics of Negro Expression." 1934. Rpt. in *Sweat,* ed. Cheryl Wall. New Brunswick, N.J.: Rutgers University Press, 1997, 59.

———. *Dust Tracks on a Road*. Philadelphia: J. B. Lippincott, 1942.

———. "The Emperor Effaces Himself." N.d. Zora Neale Hurston Collection, James Weldon Johnson, Box 1, folder 15. Rpt. in Henry Louis Gates Jr. and Jennifer Burton, *Call and Response: Key Debates in African American Studies* (New York: W. W. Norton, 2010), 267–71.

———. "How It Feels to Be Colored Me." The *World Tomorrow* 11 (May 1928): 215–16.

———. "Monkey Junk: A Satire on Modern Divorce." *Chronicle of Higher Education* 57.18 (January 2, 2011): B8-B10.

———. *Moses, Man of the Mountain*. 1940. Rpt. New York: Vintage, 1991.

———. "Sweat." *Fire!!* (November 1926): 40–45.

Hutchinson, George. *The Harlem Renaissance in Black and White*. Cambridge, Mass.: Harvard University Press, 1995.

Japtok, Martin. "Pauline Hopkins' *Of One Blood*, Africa, and the 'Darwinist Trap,'" *African American Review* 36.3 (Fall 2002): 403–415.

Johnson, Abby Arthur, and Ronald Maberry Johnson. *Propaganda and Aesthetics: The Literary Politics of African-American Magazines in the Twentieth Century*. Amherst: University of Massachusetts Press, 1979.

Johnson, James Weldon. "About Poetry and Poetry Makers." *New York Age*, December 16, 1915.

———. *Along This Way*. 1933. In *Writings*, ed. William L. Andrews. New York: Library of America, 2004.

———. "Views and Reviews." *New York Age*, February 21, 1918. Quoted in Scruggs, *The Sage in Harlem*, 57–58.

———. "When Is a Race Great?" *New York Age*, March 11, 1918.

Kaplan, Carla. *Miss Ann in Harlem: The White Women of the Black Renaissance*. New York: Harper, 2013.

———, ed. *Zora Neale Hurston: A Life in Letters*. New York: Doubleday, 2001.

King, Martin Luther, Jr. *Why We Can't Wait*. New York: New American Library, 1964.

Knadler, Stephen P. "Sweetback Style: Wallace Thurman and a Queer Harlem Renaissance." *Modern Fiction Studies* 48.4 (Winter 2002): 899–936.

Kornweibel, Theodore. *No Crystal Stair: Black Life and the* Messenger, *1917–1928*. Westport, Conn.: Greenwood Press, 1975.

Lewis, David Levering. Interview with Bruce Nugent, September 11, 1974. Box 1. "Voices from the Renaissance." David Levering Lewis Collection, Manuscripts, Archives, and Rare Books Division, Schomburg Center for Research in Black Culture, New York Public Library.

———. *W. E. B. Du Bois: The Fight for Equality and the American Century, 1919–1963*. New York: Holt, 2000.

———. *When Harlem Was in Vogue*. New York: Oxford University Press, 1979.

Locke, Alain. Foreword. *The New Negro*. xxv–xxvii.

———. "Jingo, Counter-Jingo and Us." *Opportunity* 16.1 (January 1938): 10.

———, ed. *The New Negro*, 1925. Rpt. New York: Atheneum, 1992.

———. "The New Negro." In *The New Negro*, ed. Locke, 3–16.

Lott, Eric. "Response to Trey Ellis's 'New Black Aesthetic.'" *Callaloo* 38 (Winter 1989): 244–46.

Lowe, John. "Hurston, Humor, and the Harlem Renaissance." In *Harlem Renaissance Re-examined: A Revised and Expanded Edition*, ed. Victor A. Kramer and Robert A. Russ. Troy, N.Y.: Whitston, 1997, 305–31.

Malcolm X, "Message to the Grass Roots." In *Malcolm X Speaks*, ed. George Breitman. New York: Grove Weidenfeld, 1965, 3–17.

McKay, Claude. *A Long Way from Home*. 1937. Rpt. New York: Harcourt, Brace, Jovanovich, 1970.

McMurry, Linda O. *To Keep the Waters Troubled: The Life of Ida B. Wells-Barnett*. Oxford, U.K.: Oxford University Press, 1998.

Mencken, H. L. *The Diary of H. L. Mencken*. Ed. Charles A. Fecher. New York: Vintage, 1991.

———. "The Sahara of the Bozart." Rpt. in *A Mencken Chrestomathy*, ed. H. L. Mencken. 1949. Rpt. New York: Vintage, 1982, 184–95.

Morpheus Reloaded. "Pro-Black Thugs, Pimpin' Revolutionaries & Alien Conspiracies: Navigating the Underbelly of the 'Conscious' Community." www.playahata.com/pages/morpheus/blackconscious.htm. Retrieved February 27, 2013.

Neal, Mark Anthony. *Soul Babies: Black Popular Culture and the Post-Soul Aesthetic*. New York: Routledge, 2002.

Nugent, Richard Bruce. *Gentleman Jigger*. Philadelphia: Da Capo, 2008.

———. Interview with Robert E. Hemenway, May 1971. Robert E. Hemenway files. Qtd. in Boyd, *Wrapped in Rainbows*, 136.

Peplow, Michael W. *George S. Schuyler*. Boston: Twayne, 1980.

Randolph, A. Philip. Editorial. *Messenger*. October 1922: 499–500.

———. "Reply to Marcus Garvey." *Messenger* 4.8 (August 1922): 467–71.

Reed, Ishmael. "George S. Schuyler." Introduction to Schuyler, *Black No More: Being an Account of the Strange and Wonderful Workings of Science in the Land of the Free*, A.D. *1933–1940*. New York: Modern Library, 1999. ix-xiii.

———. Introduction. Booker T. Washington, *Up from Slavery*. New York: Signet, 2000.

———. *Mumbo Jumbo*. 1972. Rpt. New York: Atheneum, 1988.

———. *Reckless Eyeballing*. New York: Atheneum, 1986.

———, and Steve Cannon. "George S. Schuyler, Writer." In *Shrovetide in Old New Orleans*, ed. Ishmael Reed. New York: Doubleday, 1978.

Retman, Sonnet. *Real Folks: Race and Genre in the Great Depression*. Durham, N.C.: Duke University Press, 2011.

Rogers, Joel A. *Additional Facts on Marcus Garvey*. Negroes of New York Writers' Program, New York. 1939. Rpt. in Grant, *Negro with a Hat*, 439–40.

Schuyler, George S. *Black and Conservative*. New Rochelle: Arlington House, 1966.

———. *Black No More: Being an Account of the Strange and Wonderful Workings of Science in the Land of the Free*, A.D. *1933–1940*. 1931. Rpt. Boston: Northeastern University Press, 1989.

———. "Black Supremacy in Love." Typescript. Box 8, folder 10, Schuyler Family Papers. Manuscripts, Archives, and Rare Books Division, Schomburg Center for Research in Black Culture, New York Public Library.

———. "Blessed Are the Sons of Ham." *Nation* 124:3220 (March 23, 1927): 313–15.

———. "The First *Real* Witch Hunt." Undated manuscript. Box 8, folder 10, George S. Schuyler Selections, Manuscripts, Archives, and Rare Books Division, Schomburg Center for Research in Black Culture, New York Public Library.

———. "How to be Happy, though Colored." Typescript. Box 11. Schuyler Family Papers, Manuscripts, Archives, and Rare Books Division, Schomburg Center for Research in Black Culture, New York Public Library.

———. "The Negro-Art Hokum." *Nation* 122 (1926): 662–63.

———. "The Reminiscences of George S. Schuyler." New York: Oral History Collection of Columbia University, 1960.

———. "Shafts and Darts." *Messenger* (October 1923): 841.

———. "Shafts and Darts." *Messenger* 8.3 (March 1926): 72.

———. "Shafts and Darts." *Messenger* 8.5 (May 1926): 143.

———. "Shafts and Darts." *Messenger* 8.9 (September 1926): 271.

———. "Shafts and Darts." *Messenger* 9.1 (January 1927): 18.

———. "A Tribute to Caesar." *Messenger* 6.7 (July 1924): 225–27.

———, and Theophilus Lewis, "Shafts and Darts." *Messenger,* April 1924, 108.

———. "Shafts and Darts." *Messenger* 6.8 (August 1924): 238.

Scruggs, Charles. *The Sage in Harlem: H. L. Mencken and the Black Writers of the 1920s.* Baltimore: Johns Hopkins University Press, 1984.

Smethurst, James. *The African American Roots of Modernism: From Reconstruction to the Harlem Renaissance.* Chapel Hill: University of North Carolina Press, 2011.

Talalay, Kathryn. *Composition in Black and White: The Life of Philippa Schuyler.* New York: Oxford University Press, 1997.

Thurman, Wallace. *The Blacker the Berry.* . . . 1929. Rpt. New York: Scribner, 1996.

———. *The Collected Writings of Wallace Thurman.* Ed. Amritjit Singh and Daniel M. Scott III. Rutgers: Rutgers University Press, 2004.

———. "Editorial Essay." *Harlem: A Forum of Negro Life* (November 1928): 1.

———. Foreword. *Fire!!* 1 (November 1926): 1.

———. "High, Low, Past, and Present: Review of *The Walls of Jericho, Quicksand,* and *Adventures of an African Slaver.*" *Harlem: A Forum of Negro Life* (November 1928). In *Collected Writings,* 218–21.

———. *Infants of the Spring.* 1932. Rpt. Boston: Northeastern University Press, 1992.

———. "Negro Artists and the Negro." *The New Republic,* August 31, 1927. Rpt. in *Collected Writings,* 195–200.

———. "Negro Poets and Their Poetry." *Bookman,* July 1928. Rpt. in *Collected Writings,* 205–16.

———. "Nephews of Uncle Remus." *Independent* 119.4034 (September 24, 1927): 296–98. Rpt. in *Collected Writings,* 200–205.

———. "Quoth Brigham Young: This Is the Place." *Messenger* (August 1925): 68.

———. "Review of *Infants of the Spring.*" Unpublished manuscript. In *Collected Writings,* 226–27.

———. "This Negro Literary Renaissance." In *Collected Writings,* 241–51.

Tucker, Jeffrey A. "'Can Science Succeed Where the Civil War Failed?': George S. Schuyler and Race." In *Race Consciousness: African American Studies for the New Century,* ed. Judith Jackson Fossett and Jeffrey A. Tucker. New York: New York University Press, 1997, 136–52.

van Notten, Eleonore. *Wallace Thurman's Harlem Renaissance.* Amsterdam: Editions Rodopi, 1994.

Walker, Alice. "Foreword: Zora Neale Hurston—A Cautionary Tale and a Partisan View." In Hemenway, *Zora Neale Hurston,* xiv–xv.

Wells-Barnett, Ida B. *Selected Writings of Ida B. Wells-Barnett.* Ed. Trudier Harris. New York: Oxford University Press, 1991.

West, Cornel. *The American Evasion of Philosophy.* Madison: University of Wisconsin Press, 1989.

Williams, Oscar R. *George S. Schuyler: Portrait of a Black Conservative.* Knoxville: University of Tennessee Press, 2007.

Wintz, Cary. *Black Culture and the Harlem Renaissance.* Houston: Rice University Press, 1988.

Wirth, Thomas. Introduction. *Gay Rebel of the Harlem Renaissance: Selections from the Work of Richard Bruce Nugent,* ed. Thomas Wirth. Durham, N.C.: Duke University Press, 2002), 1–61.

———. Introduction. Nugent, *Gentleman Jigger.*

Wolseley, Roland E. *The Black Press, U.S.A.* Ames: Iowa State University Press, 1971.

Wright, Richard. "Between Laughter and Tears." *New Masses,* October 5, 1937.

———. "Blueprint for Negro Writing." The *New Challenge: A Literary Quarterly* 2.2 (1937): 53–65.

Index

ABB. *See* African Blood Brotherhood
Adventures of Huckleberry Finn (Twain), 1
"Aframerican Fables," 50–51
Africa, myth of, 82
African American Roots of Modernism, The (Smethurst), 17
African Americans: assimilation of, 41; classism among, 42–43, 90–91, 107; color castes among, 41–43, 66, 67, 107, 109; compared with Klansmen, 46–47; cultural growth of, 72; culture of, significance and meaning of, 11–12; desiring class mobility, 88; disenfranchisement of, 71; diversity of, 49; Du Bois on the collective future of, 62; as educators, 49; generation gap among, 56–57; images of, controlling, 89; leadership class of, 5; leadership crisis of, 105; literature of, as propaganda, 56, 59; patronage of, 74; poetry and fiction writers, politics of, 130n22; problems of, rational approach to, 23, 27, 37, 51; progress for, links to, 86; regional prejudices among, 90–91; shifting to modernity, 21; stereotyping of, 47–48; white audience for, 93; whites' depictions of, 1; working class, 106, 112–13; Wright's influence on literature of, 117
African art, 79, 80
African Blood Brotherhood, 28–29, 40
African Diaspora, 41
African Legion, 99
Agamben, Giorgio, 109
Age (New York), 30

Along This Way (Johnson), 8
America, redefining, 120
American Birth Control League, 106
American Mercury, 27, 51
American Opinion, 24
Amistad, 127
Anderson, Crystal, 122
Anderson, Jervis, 45
angularity: in black expression, 80, 97–98; vulnerability to, 102
Anvil, 116
Armatrading, Joan, 122
art: decoupled from commercial concerns, 74; emerging from the individual, 63
artistic freedom, ideal of, 53–54
arts and letters, indifference toward, 10–11
Ashe, Bertram, 122, 123
Attaway, William, 116
Aunt Hagar's Children (Thurman), 60
authors, goals of, in Harlem Renaissance, 16
Autobiography of an Ex-Colored Man, The (Johnson), 6–7

Bagnall, Robert, 31, 36, 40–41, 42, 45
Baker, Houston A., Jr., 12, 13, 15, 55
Baldwin, James, 14
Baraka, Amiri, 120
Beatty, Paul, 122, 124
Beinecke Library (Yale University), 11
Bennett, Gwendolyn, 77
Bennett, Hal, 120
biblical narratives, adaptations of, 90, 102–4, 112

of, 114; modernity of, 54; as movement, 10; politics of, 12; preservation of, 11; satire as element of, 14–15, 21; Schuyler's association with, 27–28; Schuyler's denunciation of, 26; standards applied to, 12; success of, 13; Thurman's review of, 59–60; Thurman's role in, 55, 56; time frame for, 15; as vehicle for the New Negro, 16; younger generation of, derisive view of, 54

Harlem Renaissance in Black and White, The (Hutchinson), 20, 24

Harlem Shadows (McKay), 84

Harper, Frances E. W., 2

Harper Trophy, 127

Harris, Abram L., 31

Harris, Frank, 84

Harrison, Hubert H., 29, 30

Hegel, G. W. F., 2

hegemonies, forms of, 15–16

Hemenway, Robert S., 91, 98, 104

Herald Tribune (New York), 11

"Here to Yonder" (Hughes), 118

"Her Thirteen Black Soldiers" (Grimké), 31

Hilquit, Morris, 31

Himes, Chester, 116

Hoffman, Frederick L., 2

Hogue, W. Lawrence, 47

homo sacer, 104, 109, 111

homosexuality, depictions of, 55–56

Honolulu, racial tensions in, 33, 34

Hoover, Herbert, 17

Hopkins, Pauline, 3, 94

Horowitz, David, 26

Hotel Messenger, 29–30

House Behind the Cedars, The (Chesnutt), 2–3

Howe, Irving, 14

"How It Feels to Be Colored Me" (Hurston), 101

Huggins, Nathan, 12, 13, 55, 110, 116

Hughes, Langston, 6–7, 8, 10, 15, 16, 72, 75, 76, 94, 110, 116; accepting Mason's patronage, 95; aesthetics of, 55; on African Americans embracing racial identity, 61; arguing for free artistic expression, 53–54; attitude toward Du Bois, 10; collaborating with Hurston, 94, 96–97; defining black artists, 121; drawing on blues and jazz, 93; earning a living wage from writing, 115; fame of, 53; on *Fire!!*, creation of, 58; focus of, 126; on the Harlem Renaissance's demise, 114; on Harlem's entertainment venues, 67; on Hurston, 92; on *Infants of the Spring*, 78; perspective of, 55; portrayal of Thurman, 53; portrayed in *Walls of Jericho*, 66; praise for Thurman, 79; responding to Schuyler's "Negro-Art Hokum," 51; on "Shafts and Darts," 39; as target of satire, 17

human progress, 47

Hunter, Tera, 121–22

Hunting in Harlem (Johnson), 124

Hurston, Zora Neale, 9, 10, 16, 19, 53, 64, 72, 75, 76, 116; acclaim for, 85; aesthetics of, 55; age of, 89, 130n20; antipathy of, for leaders unwilling to share power, 101; anti-Southern bias toward, 93; attitude toward Du Bois, 10; attracted to the folk, 98; autobiography of, 25–26; collaborating with Hughes, 94, 96–97; conflict with Locke, 97, 101; conflict with Wright, 101; criticism of, 91–93, 117; critiquing African American male leadership, 101, 102–3, 105; cynical about government, 104; on Du Bois, 100–101; finding new audience, 91; on Fisher, 108; focus of, 126; forbidden to show her work, 139n24; on Garvey, 98–99, 100, 101; humor in writing of, 93–94; influence of, 115; irony in writings of, 98–99; literary career of, 67, 90, 91, 92; Mason's control of, 94–97; pandering of, 12; peers' respect for, 89–90; political heterodoxy of, 92; portraying the U.S. South, 49–50; satire of, 20, 90; sexist bias toward, 93; standing apart from the Niggeratti, 89; storytelling skills of, 92–93; as target of satire, 17; white patronage of, 92

Hutchinson, George, 12, 13, 20, 24, 62

"If We Must Die" (McKay), 31, 83–84
imperialism, 3
Independent Political Council, 29
individualism, 71
individuality, respect for 74
Infants of the Spring (Thurman), 19, 54, 56, 60, 63, 84, 85–86, 90, 94, 117, 135n8; addressing racial assumptions, 66, 67; addressing U.S. system of racial difference, 68; cynicism of, 67; Lewis's criticism of, 55; overlapping *Gentleman Jigger*, 77–78; publication of, 77; questioning impact of Harlem Renaissance, 68; revealing quarrels among New Negro artists, 58; satire in, 68–74; Thurman's review of, 114
instrumentalism, transcending, 121
intraracial color prejudice, 55. *See also* colorism
Invisible Man (Ellison), 118
irony, 1, 19

Jacobs, Harriet, 1
Jamaica, Garvey as hero in, 100
James, Darius, 122
James, William, 62, 86
Japtok, Martin, 2
jazz, 97
Jefferson, Thomas, 2
Jim Crow, 18, 30
John Birch Society, 22, 24, 25, 120
Johnson, Abby Arthur, 54
Johnson, Charles Spurgeon, 5, 16, 65, 67, 76, 118
Johnson, Helene, 17, 75
Johnson, James Weldon, 6–7, 16, 28, 41, 50, 110; on New York, 8; as target of satire, 17
Johnson, Mat, 124, 127
Johnson, Ronald Maberry, 54
Johnson (James Weldon) Collection, 11
Jonah's Gourd Vine (Hurston), 95
Jones, Edward P., 124
Jones, Gayl, 124
Jones, Kellie, 122
Jones, Lisa, 122

Joyce, James, 12
Juice! (Reed), 125
Jump at the Sun, 127

Kant, Immanuel, 2
Kaplan, Carla, 95
Kelley, William Melvin, 120
Kennedy, Randall, 22
King, Martin Luther, Jr., 22, 23, 24, 26–27, 118–20, 122
Kirchwey, Freda, 135n101
Knadler, Stephen P., 110
Kornweibel, Theodore, 30, 41, 42, 45
Ku Klux Klan, 1, 11, 17, 32, 34, 39, 42, 43, 44

Larsen, Nella, 10, 55, 75
Last Days of Louisiana Red, The (Reed), 120
Lee, Spike, 122
Left Front, 116
leftist radicalism, 116
"Letter from Birmingham Jail" (King), 118–19, 120
Lewis, Cudjo, 95
Lewis, David Levering, 5, 10, 13, 55, 78, 111
Lewis, Theophilus, 4, 16, 28, 31, 36, 38–40, 43–44, 63
Liberator, 83
literature: as measure of a race's greatness, 7; universal types in, 61
Living Is Easy, The (West), 117, 118
Locke, Alain, 10–11, 14, 16, 21, 40, 46, 50, 74, 75, 76, 110; contributing to *Harlem*, 139n23; on the Harlem Renaissance as a movement, 12; Hurston and Mason and, 94, 95–97; political mission of, 72; on racial progress, 67; relationship with Mason, 92; salons with, 72; as target of satire, 17
Loeb, William, 22, 27
Long Way From Home, A (McKay), 83
Looking Glass, The, 63, 132n20
Lott, Eric, 121–22
Lowe, John, 92, 93
lynching, 7, 35

Macaulay Company, 63

Malcolm X, 119–20, 25

March on Washington, 119

Marrow of Tradition, The (Chesnutt), 2–3

Marx, Karl, 29

Marxism, 74–75

Marxist/Black Nationalist African Blood Brotherhood, 17

Mason, Charlotte Osgood, 17, 67, 76, 85, 92, 94–97, 111, 117, 142n2

masses: diversity of, 89; uplift of, 4–5

McCarthy, Joseph, 26, 28

McKay, Claude, 12, 31, 40, 52, 74, 83–84, 115; accepting Mason's patronage, 95; as target of satire, 17

McKinney, Ernest Rice, 31

McMillan, Terry, 122, 124, 126–27

Mencken, H. L., 7, 14; African Americans' respect for, 22; on democracy, 25; influence of, 111, 117–18; intellectual outlook of, 39; as model for Schuyler, 34, 48; opposed to Puritanism, 34; portraying the white South, 48–49; race and, 21, 23; on satire in African American writing, 21; Thurman's admiration for, 58

"Message to the Grass Roots" (Malcolm X), 119–20

Messenger, 5, 23; beginnings of, 29; changing perspective of, 65–66; content of, 31; critical of Garvey, 40–42; editorial staff of, 31–32; iconoclastic rhetoric of, 32; political shift to the center, 39; pro-labor stance of, 39; publishing schedule of, 31–32; reformatting of, 32; satire in, 14–15, 32; Schuyler as editor of, 28–29; Schuyler joining, 32–33, 36–37, 39; serializing Hurston's "Eatonville Anthology," 49; socialist stance of, 31–32; supplanting of, 57; Thurman working at, 62–63

Messenger: A Journal of Scientific Radicalism, 30–31. See also *Messenger, the*

Midland Left, 116

Miller, George Frazier, 31

Miller, Kelly, 17, 28, 34, 40

miscegenation, 34–35

modernism: call to, 57; desire for, 10; Harlem Renaissance and, 12–13

modernist burlesque, 18–19

modernity: American, 18; arrogance and, 18; beholder's definition of, 93; hypocrisy of, 3–4; meaning of, for African Americans, 17–19; of New York, 9; progress toward, hampered by regional and class prejudice, 91; promise of, 89; resistance to, 46–47; Schuyler championing, 46; source of, 47; Thurman and Nugent as exemplars of, 54; UNIA and, 46

modern progress, Hurston's angular approach to, 102

"Monkey Junk: A Satire on Modern Divorce" (Hurston), 90, 101–2

Monthly Award ("Shafts and Darts"), 40, 50

Morpheus Reloaded, 123

Morrison, Toni, 122, 124, 126–27

Mosaic legend, 103–5

Moses, Man of the Mountain (Hurston), 90, 102–5, 113, 117

Moton, Robert Russa, 17, 28, 31, 40

movements, identifying, 19

Muhammad, Elijah, 122

mulattoes, cultural, 121

Mule Bone (play), 96

"Mule Bone" (folk opera), 94

Mules and Men (Hurston), 95, 98

Mumbo Jumbo (Reed), 120, 125

NAACP. *See* National Association for the Advancement of Colored People

Nast, Thomas, 1

Nation, 14, 50, 135n101

National Association for the Advancement of Colored People, 5–6, 17, 26, 28

nationalism, 86

nationalist movements, 46

National Urban League, 5, 17

Nation of Islam, 100

Native Son (Wright), 117

Neal, Larry, 120

Neal, Mark Anthony, 122

Negro art, 80

Perry, Margaret, 107
Pickens, William, 31, 36, 42
Platitudes (Ellis), 124
Play De Blues (Douglas), 80
Plummer, Charles, 50
poetry: conservatism of, in Cullen's work, 83; Johnson's suggestions for, 7; McKay's "racial" sonnets, 83
Post-Soul aesthetic, 123–24, 126, 143n24
Pound, Ezra, 12
pragmatism, 62, 86
Prejudices (Mencken), 49
primitives, Mason's interest in, 93, 111
primitivism, 92–93
Prince Hall Masons, 99
Public Enemy, 122
Pudd'nhead Wilson (Twain), 1
Puritanism, distaste for, 34
Push (Sapphire), 124

Question of the Silver Fleece, The (Du Bois), 7
"Quoth Brigham Young: This Is the Place" (Thurman), 9

Raboteau, Emily, 122
race: greatness of, measured by its literature, 7; overdetermined idea of, 126; whites' beliefs about, 2. *See also* colorism
races, barriers between, 67–68
Race Traits and Tendencies of the American Negro (Hoffman), 2
racial literature, denial of, 59–60
racial revisionism, 32
racism, satire and, 98
Rampersad, Arnold, 62
Rand, Ayn, 47
Randolph, A. (Asa) Philip, 16, 25; as editor of the *Messenger*, 28, 29–32, 36, 37–38, 39; financial support for, 45; on Garvey's organizational ability, 45; opposed to Du Bois, 4; threats against, 42; on the UNIA, 45
Randolph, Jeanette, 64
Randolph, Lucille, 30
Rand School of Social Science, 31

Rapp, William Jourdan, 85
rational, Schuyler's appeal to, 23, 27, 37, 51
Reckless Eyeballing (Reed), 125–26
Reconstruction, 2
Red Summer of 1919, 11, 32, 84
reductio ad absurdum, 19, 72
Reed, Ishmael, 23, 120, 125–26, 127; criticism of Du Bois and Gates, 131n5; on Huggins's assessment of the Harlem Renaissance, 130n25; on Schuyler, 23
Re-forging America: The Story of Our Nation-hood (Stoddard), 106
Regulators, the, 1
Reiss, Winold, 82
Retman, Sonnet, 18–19
reversal, as literary technique, 107–8
revolutionary writings, 83–84, 120
Rising Tide of Color Against White World Supremacy, The (Stoddard), 106
Rodeo Caldonia, 122
Rogers, J. A., 31, 36
romans à clef, 19, 54, 90–91
Roosevelt, Franklin D., 103
Roosevelt, Theodore, 6
Ross, Fran, 124, 125, 127

Sage of Sugar Hill, The: George S. Schuyler and the Harlem Renaissance (Ferguson), 23, 24
"Sahara of the Bozart" (Mencken), 48–49, 117
Sambo stereotype, 47–48
Sanger, Margaret, 106
Sapphire (Ramona Lofton), 124, 126–27
sarcasm, 1
satire: American authors using, with African American characters, 1; conditions for, 3, 15–20; contemporary, 127; demonstrative, 43; effects of, 7–8; genre of, developing, 1; influence of, 14; not expected from women authors, 93–94; objects of, 18; questions about, 14–15; reception of, 93; reversal as technique of, 107–8; role of, 18; self-consciousness and, 126; targets for, 16–17; after World War II, 118–20

Schomburg Center for Research in Black
Culture, 11
Schuyler, George S., 4, 6, 14, 16, 21, 84; as
archconservative, 22, 24–25, 120; arguing
for intellectual elitism, 47; armed services
record of, 33, 35; arrival of, in New York,
33, 45; as the "Black Mencken," 22; on
collectivism, 25, 26; columns of, 23,
26; contributing to *Harlem*, 139n23; on
the civil rights movement, 22, 24, 25;
debt owed to African American leaders
and institutions, 46; demeanor of, 27;
demonstrating meaninglessness of race,
126; discounting inherent differences of
African Americans, 50–51; Du Bois and,
47; on Garvey's demise, 42–43, 45–46; on
the Harlem Renaissance as a movement,
9–10, 12, 26, 29; on the Harlem Renaissance's leaders, 59; on Hurston, 49–50;
iconoclasm of, 10, 23, 27; ideological
descendants of, 22; influence of, 22, 23;
influences on, 34; intellectual outlook
of, 38–39; on interracial sexual liaisons,
34–35; interest in, 22–23, 24; joining the
Messenger, 32–33, 36–37, 39; legacy of,
115–16; on life as an Aframerican, 127;
literary career of, 22, 24, 26, 27, 35, 38;
marriage of, 35; on Martin Luther King,
22, 23, 24, 26; on mass movements, 25,
27; Mencken's influence on, 34, 48; at the
Messenger, 28–29, 32–33, 36–40, 43–44,
46, 47; on Negro art, 50; on New York,
9; portraying the U.S. South, 48–49, 50;
preoccupation of, with miscegenation and
sexuality, 34–35; red-baiting by, 23, 25,
28–29; rejecting racial literature, 59–60;
satire of, as modernist burlesque, 18–19;
socialist interests of, 27, 28, 36–38; on
social progress, 47; Thurman replacing,
at the *Messenger*, 63; and the UNIA, 45;
wit of, 19; work of, access to, 23, 24;
on writing of "The Negro Art Hokum,"
114; writing for the *Courier*, 117; writing
"Shafts and Darts," 38–40; youth of, self-
assessment of, 27

Schuyler, Philippa Duke, 22
Scott, Daniel M., 53, 56
Scruggs, Charles, 7, 21, 23, 24, 39, 48
Senna, Danzy, 122
Service, 35
sexual ambivalence, 110
"Shafts and Darts," 23, 28–29, 38–40,
43–44, 46, 47, 124; "Aframerican
Fables" in, 50–51; Monthly Award in,
40, 50
signifying, 109
Simmons, William J., 48
Singh, Amritjit, 53, 56
slavery: colorism and, 109 ; Exodus narrative and, 103; folklore's roots in, 98; humor used to cope with, 1; miscegenation
and, 39; new forms of, 1, 19; romantic
view of, 2
Smethurst, James, 17
Smith, Ellison DuRant (Cotton Ed),
141n60
"Smoke, Lilies, and Jade" (Nugent), 75
social progress, 47
socialism: as means for fighting American
racism, 37–38; as organizing force for
African Americans, 31; Schuyler's involve-
ment with, 36–38
Socialist Party of the United States, 28, 31,
36
socialist realism, 116
Song of the Towers (Douglas), 80–81
Souls of Black Folk, The (Du Bois), 6, 61
Sowell, Thomas, 22
Spingarn, Arthur, 97
Spingarn Collection (Howard University),
11
Steele, Shelby, 22
Stephansson, Jan Harold, 64
Stoddard, Lothrop, 106
Strivers Row (publishers), 127
Strivers' Row (Harlem neighborhood), 88
Sugar Hill, 88
Survey Graphic, 14, 84
"Sweat" (Hurston), 94, 101
sweetback, 110

CPSIA information can be obtained at www.ICGtesting.com
Printed in the USA
LVOW12*1504220615

443394LV00009B/103/P